D1545905

Real Hallucinations

Philosophical Psychopathology

Jennifer Radden and Jeff Poland, editors

Real Hallucinations: Psychiatric Illness, Intentionality, and the Interpersonal World, Matthew Ratcliffe (2017)

Extraordinary Science: Responding to the Current Crisis in Psychiatric Research, Jeffrey Poland and Şerife Tekin, editors (2017)

Disturbed Consciousness: New Essays on Psychopathology and Theories of Consciousness, Rocco J. Gennaro, editor (2015)

Being Amoral: Psychopathy and Moral Incapacity, Thomas Schramme, editor (2014)

A Metaphysics of Psychopathology, Peter Zachar (2014)

Classifying Psychopathology: Mental Kinds and Natural Kinds, Harold Kincaid and Jacqueline Sullivan, editors (2014)

The Ethical Treatment of Depression: Autonomy through Psychotherapy, Paul Biegler (2011)

Addiction and Responsibility, Jeffrey Poland and George Graham, editors (2011)

Real Hallucinations

Psychiatric Illness, Intentionality, and the Interpersonal World

Matthew Ratcliffe

The MIT Press
Cambridge, Massachusetts
London, England

This book was set in ITC Stone Serif by Jen Jackowitz. Printed and bound in the United States of America.

Library of Congress Cataloging-in-Publication Data
Names: Ratcliffe, Matthew, 1973-, author.
Title: Real hallucinations : psychiatric illness, intentionality, and the interpersonal world / Matthew Ratcliffe.
Other titles: Philosophical psychopathology.
Description: Cambridge, MA : The MIT Press, [2017] | Series: Philosophical psychopathology | Includes bibliographical references and index.
Identifiers: LCCN 2017003353 | ISBN 9780262036719 (hardcover : alk. paper)
Subjects: | MESH: Hallucinations--psychology | Delusions--psychology | Perception | Interpersonal Relations | Philosophy
Classification: LCC RC512 | NLM WM 204 | DDC 616.89--dc23 LC record available at https://lccn.loc.gov/2017003353

10 9 8 7 6 5 4 3 2 1

Contents

Acknowledgments

The argument of this book follows a winding path through various topics and disciplines. Lots of people helped me to navigate it and to arrive at what I hope is a cohesive, persuasive philosophical position. For helpful conversation and correspondence, I am grateful to Anna Bortolan, Matthew Broome, Havi Carel, Jonathan Cole, Charles Fernyhough, Thomas Fuchs, Shaun Gallagher, Philip Gerrans, Emily Hughes, Daniel Hutto, Laurence Kirmayer, Joel Krueger, Martin Kusch, Sophie Loidolt, Graham Parkes, Mark Ruddell, Louis Sass, Tasia Scrutton, Jan Slaby, Benedict Smith, Achim Stephan, Mark Wynn, Dan Zahavi, and many others. Thanks, in particular, to Owen Earnshaw, Jennifer Radden, and Sam Wilkinson. It was through supervising Owen's highly original PhD thesis at Durham University that I began to appreciate the relevance of trust and its fragility to an understanding of psychiatric illness (Earnshaw 2011; available at http://etheses.dur.ac.uk/3225/). Sam and I have had many long conversations about the topics of this book, which led to two coauthored papers. And it was a privilege to be able to share ideas with Jennifer while she was a Visiting Professor at the University of Vienna in 2016. It is also thanks to her earlier advice and encouragement that I sought to publish this book as part of the MIT Press Philosophical Psychopathology series. I am grateful to members of my "phenomenological psychopathology and philosophy of psychiatry" research group at the University of Vienna for all their feedback and support, especially Maike Cram, Marie Dahle, Christoph Durt, Line Ingerslev, Oliver Lukitsch, and Philipp Schmidt. Thanks, as well, to all those students who participated so actively in my Phenomenology and Psychiatry courses at Vienna and offered numerous insightful comments.

Material from the book was presented at events hosted by the Free University of Berlin, King's College London, and the Universities of Aalborg,

Amsterdam, Durham, Edinburgh, Essex, Graz, Guelph, Groningen, Leeds, Memphis, McGill, Ryerson, Vienna, Warwick, and Wesleyan. I thank all these audiences for comments, suggestions, and criticisms. At MIT Press, Philip Laughlin has been an absolute pleasure to work with. I am also grateful to four referees who read my book proposal and two referees who read the entire manuscript, all of whom provided very helpful and encouraging comments.

This book incorporates, in substantially revised form, material from some previously published articles and chapters:

"The Integrity of Intentionality: Sketch for a Phenomenological Study." In *Phenomenology for the Twenty-First Century*, ed. J. A. Simmons and J. E. Hackett, 207–230. Basingstoke: Palgrave Macmillan, 2016.

"Selfhood, Schizophrenia, and the Interpersonal Regulation of Experience." In *Embodiment, Enaction, and Culture: Investigating the Constitution of the Shared World*, ed. C. Durt, T. Fuchs, and C. Tewes, 149–171. Cambridge, MA: MIT Press, 2017.

"How Anxiety Induces Verbal Hallucinations" (coauthored with Sam Wilkinson). *Consciousness and Cognition* 39 (2016): 48–58.*

"Thought Insertion Clarified" (Coauthored with Sam Wilkinson). *Journal of Consciousness Studies* 22, nos. 11–12 (2015): 246–269.*

"Relating to the Dead: Social Cognition and the Phenomenology of Grief." In *The Phenomenology of Sociality: Discovering the "We,"* ed. D. Moran and T. Szanto, 202–215. London: Routledge, 2016.*

"What Is a Sense of Foreshortened Future? A Phenomenological Study of Trauma, Trust, and Time" (coauthored with Mark Ruddell and Benedict Smith). *Frontiers in Psychology* 5, (art. 1026 (2014): 1–11.*

In those cases where permission to reuse material was required, I am grateful to the publishers for granting it. Where material is adapted from coauthored publications, it is taken exclusively from my contributions to those pieces, and with the consent of my coauthors. Four of the above papers (marked with an asterisk) were written as part of the Wellcome Trust–funded project, "Hearing the Voice" (grant no. WT098455), and I am grateful to the trust for its support. At several points in my discussion, I draw on a questionnaire study, which I conducted in collaboration with some project-colleagues: Angela Woods, Ben Alderson-Day, Felicity Callard, Charles Fernyhough, and Nev Jones. This study was closely modeled on earlier work that I had done with another group, for the AHRC- and DFG-funded project "Emotional Experience in Depression" (see Ratcliffe 2015, chap. 1, for details). I thank Benedict Smith, who played a major role in designing the original study, for allowing us to adapt and use material.

I am very grateful to those who completed the voices questionnaire, many of whom described their experiences in considerable detail. I would also like to thank all those people who have approached me informally, in writing or in person, in order to describe and discuss their experiences of psychiatric illness. Without exception, their testimonies have been informative and, indeed, inspiring.

1 Introduction

This book is about the structure of human experience, its fragility, and how it is shaped by relations with other people. It focuses specifically on the nature of auditory verbal hallucinations and thought insertion in psychiatric illness. Thought insertion involves somehow experiencing one's own thoughts as someone else's, while auditory verbal hallucinations are generally taken to consist of hearing a voice or having an experience much like that of hearing a voice, but in the absence of a speaker. In addressing these phenomena, my aims are principally philosophical and also encompass a far wider subject matter. I seek to make explicit something that is essential to all human experience but seldom remarked on, and to offer a detailed account of what it consists of. When we have an experience *of* something, we ordinarily recognize that we are in one or another kind of intentional state, such as remembering, imagining, or perceiving. For instance, if I look at something and have a visual experience of it, I appreciate that I am perceiving it (and, more specifically, perceiving it visually), rather than imagining or remembering it. The same goes for other kinds of intentionality. Put crudely, it is *like something* to remember, which differs from what it is like to perceive. Usually, we do not need to explicitly infer or somehow figure out which intentional state we are in; it is phenomenologically unambiguous and taken for granted. So an experience with intentional content is either intimately associated with a prereflective, unthinking *sense* of the kind of experience one is having or, as I will argue, it incorporates that sense.

In contrast to mundane, unproblematic cases, I will show how thought insertion, and also a substantial proportion of auditory verbal hallucinations, consist of disturbances in the sense of being in one or another kind of intentional state, in what I call the *modal structure of intentionality* (meaning our grasp of the various modalities of intentionality, such as believing, perceiving, remembering, and imagining, as distinct from one another). So, by studying them, we can draw attention to the relevant aspect of experience and come to better understand its nature. I will also make clear how episodic and seemingly localized disturbances such as these arise within the context of less pronounced but wider-ranging alterations in the structure of intentionality. In the process, I will develop an account of how the integrity of human experience, including what we might term the most basic experience of *self*, depends on ways of relating to other people and to the social world as a whole.

The book is phenomenological in emphasis throughout. Where the terms "intentionality" and "intentional state" are used in what follows, they refer to experiences *of* something or other, such as hearing, remembering, or imagining something. I take having an experience of something to be sufficient for *being in an intentional state*, in the phenomenological sense of the term. However, although the relevant experience usually includes a sense of the kind of intentional state one is in, I concede that the phenomenology alone does not always suffice to determine one's actual intentional state. An unambiguous experience of hoping that *p*, fearing that *p*, or feeling guilty about *p* is plausibly sufficient for being in a state of hope, fear, or guilt. In contrast, whether or not you remember that *p* depends not only on whether you have an experience of remembering that *p* but also on whether or not *p* actually happened. While I do not dismiss the possibility of a distinct and wholly nonphenomenological conception of intentionality, it is not my concern here. Furthermore, I maintain that, in those cases that do involve an experience of being directed at something in one or another way, the relevant experience inevitably has some bearing on what kind of intentional state the person is actually in.[1] So my object of inquiry cannot be sidestepped by construing intentionality as something independent of any associated experience, at least not in the human case (and not in any other case where there is an experience of perceiving rather than thinking, believing rather than imagining, and so forth).

We are owed a more detailed analysis of what the sense of being in a given intentional state consists of, but the philosophical task is seldom acknowledged, let alone pursued. Perhaps, for most of us and for most of the time, it is so obvious that we are in one type of intentional state rather than another that the question of how we manage to distinguish between kinds of intentionality does not occur to us. However, the modal structure of intentionality is no mere curiosity, of interest only to those phenomenologists who enjoy analyzing the finer details of experience and to others who study certain psychopathological phenomena. In fact, it is absolutely fundamental to the structure of human experience. As I will show, were it completely absent, there could be no appreciation of occupying a particular spatial and temporal location, and therefore no sense of perspective at all. For this reason, I maintain that the modal structure of intentionality is inextricable from what others have called "minimal self," a primitive form of self-awareness that is integral to all experiences (e.g., Zahavi 2014). Furthermore, once minimal self is construed as principally (but perhaps not solely) a matter of the modal structure of intentionality, it can be characterized more clearly and in much more detail.

Perhaps, one might think, the sense of perceiving something rather than remembering it is wholly constituted by the *content* of an experience, that at least some aspects of experiential content are specific to certain kinds of intentional state and thus serve to identify them.[2] For example, a cat, as perceived visually, differs in certain ways from an imagined or remembered cat. So why bother to raise the question in the laborious way I do here, when the answer is simple and obvious? In fact, the relevant aspect of experience turns out to be multifaceted and complicated. As my consideration of auditory verbal hallucinations and thought insertion will demonstrate, the sense of being in a given type of intentional state is not just a matter of characteristic content. One can have an experiential content more like that of an imagining than that of a perception, and yet have the sense of perceiving something. Furthermore, there can be varying degrees of tension between content and other aspects of sense, resulting in ambiguous experiences that straddle the boundaries between familiar kinds of intentionality. In such cases, I argue, sense is not to be accounted for by appealing to the contribution made by a separate act or attitudinal quality. It is something that cannot be exhaustively characterized in terms of intentional attitude, intentional content, or a combination of the two. Hence my question is not, after all, an easy one to answer.

To account for anomalous experiences of intentionality, the chapters that follow progressively develop the view that different kinds of intentionality incorporate characteristic patterns of anticipation and fulfillment, which are central to the sense of being in a given type of intentional state. For instance, perceptual experiences and episodic memories ordinarily unfold in different ways. A perceived situation might involve feelings of uncertainty or doubt over what is coming next, as well as occasional experiences of anomaly and/or surprise, which are altogether lacking or at least diminished when a sequence of events is remembered. Imagining has an anticipation-fulfilment profile that distinguishes it from both perception and memory, accommodating spatially and temporally unstructured scenarios that can depart wildly from anything that is remembered, currently perceived, or anticipated, but without any sense of potential or actual discrepancy or surprise.

I further show how the various temporal patterns are embedded within an all-enveloping anticipatory structure that is not itself a form of intentionality, at least not in the same meaning of the term, and that they depend on it for their integrity and distinctiveness. Drawing on themes in the work of Edmund Husserl, Karl Jaspers, and Ludwig Wittgenstein, I attempt to clarify a kind of conviction that is integral to this structure, something that is sometimes referred to in terms of "confidence," "certainty," or "trust." It is importantly different from "belief," where belief is construed as taking something to be the case or taking something not to be the case. Something must already be in place for belief to be possible, something that renders intelligible the distinction between taking *p* to be the case and taking *p* not to be the case. By implication, it enables and sustains the modalities of intentionality more generally, given that all other kinds of intentionality are in one way or another dependent on this overarching distinction.

Importantly, in reflecting on the anticipatory structure of experience and the kinds of change it is susceptible to, we also come to appreciate the extent to which and the manner in which experience and thought are embedded in the interpersonal world. I will make clear how the modal structure of intentionality is inseparable from ways of experiencing and relating to specific individuals, other people in general, and the social world as a whole. It is shaped by social development, and it continues to be interpersonally sustained and regulated even during adulthood. Hence it turns out that human experience is intersubjective through and through. The aim is not just to assert or argue *that* this is the case; I seek to show exactly *how* it is the case.

That is an outline of the philosophical position to be developed and defended here. However, this is equally a book about the nature of psychiatric illness, which offers a detailed account of the phenomena of *auditory verbal hallucination* (hereafter, AVH) and *thought insertion* (hereafter, TI). I could have offered a wider-ranging discussion of anomalous experiences or addressed other kinds of experience instead. But, as the overarching aim is to develop an integrated account of (a) the modal structure of intentionality and (b) how interpersonal relations shape experience and thought, AVH and TI are especially effective examples. Throughout the discussion, two very different accounts of AVH remain in the background (both of which are further described in chapter 2). On the one hand, there is the view associated with phenomenological psychopathology that AVH, TI, and other seemingly localized "symptoms" presuppose more fundamental and enveloping disturbances of minimal selfhood, disturbances that are either specific to schizophrenia or at least most pronounced in schizophrenia. This lends itself to a somewhat individualistic approach. In that respect, it is to be contrasted with a position associated with the Hearing Voices Movement. According to this position, AVHs are meaningful symptoms of interpersonally induced trauma. As such, they are essentially relational in nature, and are most effectively "treated" through kinds of interpersonal process that seek to minimize distress caused by voices and empower the subject. In addition, it is maintained that the diagnostic category "schizophrenia" is either misapplied in many instances or altogether misguided. Despite the apparent tension between these two broad approaches, I accept that both contain important insights, and I seek to navigate a path between them. Another reason for focusing specifically on AVH and TI is that these experiences are explicitly relational in structure. One experiences the "voice" or the thoughts *of* someone else, often as addressing oneself. Furthermore, a person's relationship with her voices or inserted thoughts often resembles her relationship with the wider social world. In what follows, I will argue that the interpersonal is central to an understanding of AVH and TI. While this applies equally to many other phenomena that are labeled as "delusions" or "hallucinations," AVH and TI illustrate the point particularly well, given that the relevant disturbance of interpersonal experience is reflected both in their structure and in their content.

Although the discussion of AVH serves as a starting point from which to formulate phenomenological claims with wider applicability, there are also more specific lessons to be learned about the nature of hallucination. Appeals to hallucination are commonplace in philosophy, especially in discussions of perception. In this context, a "hallucination" is usually a kind of hypothetical experience, the possibility of which poses a problem for certain philosophical positions. As Macpherson (2013, 1) writes, "the traditional philosophical conception includes perceptual experiences, identical in nature to experiences that could be had while perceiving the world, save only that they are had while not perceiving." Thus, if I have a visual hallucination of my children standing in front of me, I have an experience that is phenomenologically indistinguishable from one of actually seeing my children standing in front of me. Now, one might insist that philosophers' hallucinations and real hallucinations (such as those that arise in psychiatric illness) comprise two different subject matters. For the philosopher, what matters is the possibility (usually the metaphysical possibility) or otherwise of a certain kind of experience, rather than its actuality. So it does not matter if real hallucinations turn out to be substantially different from those that generate philosophical worries. Then again, it should be noted that, in the scientific and clinical literature, real hallucinations are often defined in much the same way:

> Hallucinations are usually defined as perceptions that occur in the absence of any appropriate stimulus. (Frith 1992, 68)

> Hallucinations are perceptions which occur in the absence of appropriate external stimulation; they can be found in a wide variety of clinical conditions ranging from functional psychosis to focal brain damage. (Halligan and Marshall 1996, 242)

> Voices are defined as a sensory perception that has a compelling sense of reality, but which occurs without external stimulation of the sensory organ. (Hayward, Berry, and Ashton 2011, 1314)

In both cases, hallucinating is said to involve having an experience that resembles a veridical perceptual experience, but in the absence of an appropriate relation between the experience and something external to it. The main difference between real and philosophers' hallucinations is that the latter are cleaner—not just *much like* veridical perceptions but *phenomenologically indistinguishable* from them. A philosophers' hallucination can also be wider ranging and longer lasting; it might envelop one's ongoing experience of the world as a whole, rather than being transient and localized. As indicated by its title, this book is concerned with real hallucinations, rather than with hallucinations cooked up by philosophers. And one of the things I hope to illustrate is that real hallucinations turn out to be much more diverse, complicated, and philosophically interesting than the hypothetical cases. However, insofar as similarity to actual cases might be invoked to make philosophers' hallucinations seem more plausible or intuitive, the discussion is relevant to the latter as well.

In fact, some of those phenomena that are routinely referred to as "hallucinations" in psychiatric contexts are quite unlike veridical perceptual experiences. If you like, "real hallucinations" are not always "orthodox hallucinations." Although I focus principally on supposedly "auditory, verbal" experiences, which are more commonly reported in psychiatric illness than hallucinations in other modalities, much of what I say here applies to hallucinations more generally. One of the first things to note is that the term "AVH" encompasses a range of potentially very different phenomena. There are also hermeneutic difficulties; it is not at all clear how to interpret first-person accounts that might naively be taken to convey orthodox hallucinations. My approach is to distinguish and focus specifically on a substantial subset of AVH experiences, which are singled out both by their phenomenology and by the manner in which they arise. These experiences lack some or all auditory qualities and do not seem to originate in the external environment. They are importantly unlike veridical auditory experiences and instead, I maintain, involve a blurring of the experienced boundaries between intentional state types. What we have is an unfamiliar kind of experience, which is perception-like in some respects but not in others. This interpretation also accommodates TI. In fact, it turns out that certain kinds of AVH are TI under another description. Showing how these two descriptions are compatible serves to further illuminate the nature of the relevant experience and to support the claim that the structure of intentionality is disrupted. Later on, I explain how my approach is able to accommodate other kinds of AVH as well. However, at no point do I claim to offer a comprehensive account of *all* those experiences that might be referred to as such; they are simply too many and too diverse.

As well as being of philosophical interest, the position I develop has potential implications for the understanding and treatment of psychiatric illness. On my account, AVHs are not phenomenologically isolated symptoms, but neither are they reliably associated with established syndromes (clusters of commonly associated symptoms), such as schizophrenia. Much the same kind of AVH experience could be associated with several different diagnostic categories. While this does not directly challenge current classification systems or diagnostic practices, the phenomenological analyses and distinctions offered here could potentially feed into the project of devising more principled classifications for one or another purpose. For instance, I raise some questions concerning the specificity of certain kinds of experience to schizophrenia and the legitimacy of the schizophrenia construct. Most importantly, I emphasize the need to conceive of certain kinds of anomalous experience as inseparable from a wider interpersonal and social environment, rather than as disorders of the individual that subsequently affect interpersonal and social relations.

I have stated that this project is a phenomenological one. For current purposes, phenomenological research is to be construed in a permissive way. My thinking is inspired in many ways by the phenomenological tradition of philosophy. In particular, I draw on some of Husserl's later work at a crucial point in the argument. Nevertheless, this book is not phenomenological in a way that is to be contrasted with work outside of that tradition. There is nothing in what follows to prevent those who are not in any way wedded to phenomenology (in a more restrictive sense of the term) from endorsing both my position and my arguments for that position.[3] Phenomenological research, as conceived of here, is also situated within a wider field of inquiry. Throughout my discussion, it is in dialogue with other areas of philosophy, and with other disciplines. In particular, I seek to illustrate how phenomenology can interact with the cognitive sciences (broadly construed) in ways that are mutually illuminating. My phenomenological analysis takes account of a range of empirical findings. Conversely, it assists in clarifying the subject matter of empirical studies, by calling into question certain prevalent assumptions about AVHs and related phenomena that have served to shape inquiry.[4]

The argument proceeds as follows. Chapter 2 sets up some of the central concepts, themes, and issues in more detail. First of all, I introduce the concept of minimal self and its recent application to schizophrenia and AVH. Then I address the question of whether minimal selfhood includes merely the sense of having some kind of experience or, in addition to this, a more specific sense of the type of intentional state one is in. I propose a refined account of minimal self, according to which it centrally involves the latter: a grasp of the *modalities of intentionality*. I also suggest that some anomalous experiences centrally involve disturbances of modal structure. Following this, I turn to the alternative view that AVHs are diagnostically nonspecific, meaningful symptoms of interpersonal trauma. In so doing, I stress the need to place more emphasis on the interpersonal aspects of psychiatric illness, and show how minimal self, as conceived of here, could turn out to be both developmentally and constitutively dependent on ways of relating to other people. The chapter concludes by considering other recent formulations of the view that delusions and hallucinations originate in a confusion of or blurring between intentional state types, and distinguishing them from my own approach.

Chapter 3 begins by considering the possibility that a number of factors contribute to the sense of being in an intentional state, and that these can come into conflict. The remainder of the chapter argues that TI and certain kinds of AVH are to be understood in this way. There is a difference between experiencing a process of thinking as alien and experiencing thought content as alien. I argue that TI involves the latter. Hence it could just as well be described as experiencing one's own thought contents in a strange, perception-like way. To further support this interpretation, I turn to AVHs and show that a substantial proportion of experiences that are described in AVH terms can equally be conveyed in terms of TI. In fact, people sometimes describe the same experience in both ways. What we have is an anomalous experience that lies somewhere between thinking and perceiving. The content of the experience continues to resemble that of a thought. Even so, a sense of perceiving predominates. More generally, both hallucinations and delusions can involve an altered sense of *what it is to be present or real*. So they are not simply to be thought of in terms of taking something to be the case that is not the case or experiencing something as present that is not present. The chapter concludes by arguing that it is unhelpful to conceive of AVH or TI in terms of a distinction between agency and subjectivity or ownership.

Chapter 4 develops a more specific account of what AVHs consist of and how they arise. It focuses, to begin with, on those that involve a quasi-perceptual experience of "inner speech" or "inner dialogue." Such experiences are often preceded by heightened social anxiety, and I argue that anxious anticipation of one's own thought contents as they arise can constitute an experience of thought content as alien. This approach is then broadened to accommodate not only inner dialogue but also imagination and memory. I further suggest that other kinds of AVH, which are experienced as external in origin and more akin to veridical auditory experiences, can likewise be accounted for in terms of anxious anticipation, but that they come about in a different way. I also make clear how AVHs can fall somewhere in between the internal, nonauditory and external, auditory poles, rather than fitting neatly into one or the other category. The chapter concludes by noting that AVHs tend to be associated with wider-ranging disturbances in a person's relationship with the social world, often involving unpleasant interpersonal circumstances. This sets the scene for an exploration of more enveloping and enduring phenomenological disturbances, in which AVHs are embedded.

In chapter 5, I address the nature of nonlocalized phenomenological changes that can be brought about by traumatic events. The chapter focuses on traumatic events in adulthood. These are often described as *shattering* something that was previously in place. A kind of all-enveloping trust, confidence, or certainty is eroded or lost. To interpret such experiences, I draw on and further develop an analysis offered by Husserl in some of his later work, according to which the modalities of intentionality are embedded in a distinctive kind of anticipation-fulfillment structure, involving a bodily, habitual sense of certainty that pervades experience and gives it structure. First-person accounts of traumatic experience point to global disruption of this structure. Furthermore, although traumatic events inflicted by others might shape how one experiences and relates to people rather than the world as a whole, I make clear why the *style* in which we relate to others is inextricable from the wider integrity of experience.

Chapter 6 brings the various strands of argument together and states the overall position. It addresses several interrelated ways in which other people are implicated in the development, sustenance, and disruption of the modal structure of intentionality. First of all, I consider some of the roles that relations with others play in shaping perceptual experience, focusing on how the cohesive, anticipatory structure of perceptual experience is interpersonally regulated. Then I turn to belief. Drawing on Jaspers and Wittgenstein, I argue that the structure of belief, the intelligibility of the distinction between what is and is not the case, rests on a more primitive sense of certainty, which can be identified with the anticipation-fulfillment dynamic described by Husserl. More generally, the sense of being in a given type of intentional state is largely attributable to its distinctive anticipation-fulfillment profile, and all such profiles depend on an overarching pattern of anticipation and fulfillment, in the guise of habitual confidence or certainty. This pattern is inextricable from a certain way of experiencing and relating to other people in general. When the overall anticipation-fulfillment structure of experience is disrupted, the boundaries between types of intentional states become less clear. This renders a person susceptible to more pronounced and localized disruptions, of the kind implicated in certain delusions and hallucinations. I go on to show how the overall position is consistent with a substantial body of evidence pointing to strong links between traumatic experience during childhood, adulthood, or both, and the subsequent onset of psychosis. Implications for the diagnostic category "schizophrenia" are also considered, followed by some implications for how we go about interpreting first-person accounts. The chapter concludes by exploring some affinities between my phenomenological approach and recent neurobiological work on predictive coding.

In chapter 7, the scope of the discussion is widened to include other kinds of hallucination. While allowing that some of these experiences *may* conform to orthodox definitions of hallucination (according to which a hallucination resembles a veridical perceptual experience but occurs in the absence of the appropriate stimulus), I make clear that many others do not. Drawing on Merleau-Ponty's remarks on hallucination in *Phenomenology of Perception*, I identify a kind of experience that differs both from orthodox hallucinations and from the kinds of experience described in earlier chapters. While it is not modally ambiguous, it is also quite unlike a veridical perceptual experience. It includes a sense of salient and significant possibilities, of the kind that might be associated with encountering a given entity or type of entity. However, other aspects of perceptual experience are lacking. I go on to consider experiences that appear to conflict with my account: AVHs that console and bring comfort. Among other things, I argue that it is unclear how to interpret reports to the effect that a malevolent voice has not disappeared but has instead become supportive and ceased to be a source of distress. In short, exactly the same experience could be described in terms of a voice becoming supportive or, alternatively, in terms of its disappearance. Even so, I concede that some AVHs are quite different from those so far described. In particular, I address hallucinations that occur in grief and bring comfort. The phenomenology of grief further illustrates the extent to which the integrity of experience depends on relations with others, and—in this case—on specific individuals. Furthermore, during profound grief, experiences of the presence and absence of the deceased are multifaceted and often ambiguous. It is wrong to think of these experiences in simple terms, as someone seeming to be there or seeming not to be there.

Again, we see that the sense of presence and reality, which is inseparable from the wider modal structure of intentionality, is not singular or unitary.

Chapter 8 draws the discussion to a close by summarizing and further exploring some philosophical implications of my position. In particular, I address the nature of "belief," and argue that this term, even when it is used in a restrictive and technical way, most likely accommodates a range of subtly different kinds of conviction, different ways of taking something to be the case. This applies not only to psychiatric illness, but also more generally. Issues are therefore raised for the practice of philosophy itself. When one is said to believe a philosophical claim, it is not always clear what kind of conviction is involved or, for that matter, which kinds of conviction are appropriate to which kinds of philosophical position. More generally, the structure of intentionality encompasses a wide range of different intentional state types and does not respect clear-cut, categorical distinctions between them. These subtleties are masked by certain uses of language, in philosophy and elsewhere. Reliance on univocal notions of "belief," "desire," and the like is thus rendered problematic.

2 Schizophrenia and Selfhood

This chapter introduces the concept of minimal self and critically discusses its application to the phenomenology of schizophrenia. I acknowledge that appeals to disturbances of minimal self in schizophrenia are illuminating, insofar as they emphasize how seemingly localized experiences such as AVHs (auditory verbal hallucinations) arise in the context of profound changes in the overall structure of experience. However, I also suggest that a clearer and more specific account of the nature of minimal self is needed. To supply this, I ask whether minimal self incorporates only the sense that one is *having an experience* or whether it further includes a sense of the kind of intentional state one is in, the *kind of experience* one is having. The answer, I argue, has to be the latter. Minimal self centrally involves a grasp of the modal structure of intentionality, a prereflective appreciation of being in one or another kind of intentional state, such as perceiving or remembering. Furthermore, anomalous experiences, of the kind attributed to alterations of minimal self, are plausibly interpreted as disturbances of this modal structure.

I go on to raise the concern that an emphasis on minimal self risks understating the interpersonal and social aspects of psychiatric illness. To do so, I examine an alternative approach, associated with the Hearing Voices Movement. According to this approach, AVHs are meaningful manifestations of distress that usually have interpersonal causes, as opposed to symptoms of an illness called "schizophrenia." Drawing inspiration from both perspectives, I sketch the position to be developed in the remainder of the book, according to which the modal structure of intentionality, and by implication the minimal self, is developmentally and constitutively dependent on interpersonal relations. I do not insist on retaining the term "minimal self," and my analysis of the modal structure of intentionality does not require it. What I do maintain is that, if certain kinds of anomalous experience are to be accounted for in terms of a "minimal self," then it *must* centrally involve the modal structure of intentionality. In addition, it turns out to be relational in nature. Appeals to something more minimal than this lack explanatory power in the context of psychiatric illness. More generally, it is doubtful that they succeed in referring to anything that is not already accommodated by an emphasis on the modal structure of intentionality. The chapter concludes by distinguishing the position laid out here from other versions of the view that delusions and hallucinations originate in some form of confusion between kinds of intentional state.

2.1 Minimal Self

The concept of minimal self is to be understood in exclusively phenomenological terms. Dan Zahavi has provided what is perhaps the most detailed characterization to date. All our experiences, he maintains, have a "first-personal character"; their structure incorporates a sense of mineness, of their originating in a singular locus of experience. Minimal self is not an object of experience or thought, and neither is it an awareness of subjectivity that exists independently of our various other experiences. Instead, it is inextricable from "the distinct manner, or *how*, of experiencing." So it is a condition of possibility for experience, rather than an isolable component of experience. And it is a necessary structural feature of experience, rather than something that is already in place before experiences occur, something *before* or *behind* those experiences.[1] As such, it does not depend on language, narrative, or rational judgment, and is presupposed by such capacities. To conceive of minimal self in isolation from the rest of experience is to perform an abstraction. Nevertheless, while "intertwined" with other aspects of experience, it still has "experiential reality" (Zahavi 2014, 22, 89). It is a real and distinguishable aspect of experience, just as one side of a coin is real and distinguishable from the other, despite the two being inseparable. The claim is not that minimal self is the only kind of self. As Zahavi acknowledges, "self" can legitimately refer to a range of different phenomena (phenomenological or otherwise), all of which need to be carefully distinguished from one another. However, minimal self is at least the most fundamental or primitive notion of self, and is presupposed by any other kind of *self-experience* that might be postulated.

It has been further proposed that this basic sense of self is somehow eroded (although not entirely lost) in schizophrenia. Thus, while the "minimal self" view serves to clarify the phenomenology of schizophrenia, self-disturbance in schizophrenia constitutes evidence for the claim that experience incorporates minimal selfhood.[2] For example, Sass (2014a, 5–6) states that schizophrenia involves a "disturbance of minimal- or core-self experience," of "ipseity," something that concerns the "sense of existing as a vital and self-identical *subject* of experience or *agent* of action." Parnas et al. (2005, 240) similarly describe the erosion of a "first-person perspective" that is more usually "automatic," while Fuchs (2013, 248) refers to disruption of a "first-person perspective" that "inhabits all modes of intentionality and imbues them with a sense of mineness." It is also claimed that a degree or type of self-disturbance distinguishes the phenomenology of schizophrenia from that of other psychiatric conditions.[3] The latter either do not involve changes in minimal-self experience or they involve changes that are less profound than those found in schizophrenia and perhaps qualitatively different as well (Raballo, Sæbye, and Parnas 2009). So this kind of approach has a potential role to play in differential diagnosis. Indeed, Parnas et al. (2005) have devised a detailed interview, the "Examination of Anomalous Self-Experience" or "EASE," with the aim of reliably detecting anomalous experiences that are indicative of schizophrenia-specific self-disorder.

According to the self-disorder approach, seemingly localized symptoms such as delusions and hallucinations develop in the context of global changes in the structure of experience, and are inevitably misunderstood when conceived of in isolation from those changes. AVHs, for instance, are not "atomistic, self-sufficient, thing-like symptoms," but "meaningfully interrelated facets of a more comprehensive and characteristic gestalt change in the patient's experience (field of consciousness) and existence" (Larøi et al. 2010, 235). The overall approach is consistent with there being causal relations between some symptoms and noncausal relations of implication, mutual implication, or even identity between others. For instance, changes in the structure of experience might *cause* anxiety, which then has an effect on other symptoms, perhaps exacerbating or otherwise altering them. Causal relations between symptoms can also include compensatory and defensive reactions. However, a diminished sense of agency might be said to *imply* a perceived world that appears bereft of salient possibilities for meaningful action, and vice versa, while loss of affective response to things and an experience of them as somehow strange, distant, and unfamiliar may add up to different descriptions of a singular phenomenological change (e.g., Sass 2003; Sass and Parnas 2007; Sass and Borda 2015). But regardless of what the finer details might look like, the consistent, underlying theme is that schizophrenia centrally involves a global change in the structure of experience, which encompasses a more usually taken-for-granted and phenomenologically primitive sense of self.

The "minimal self" view is consistent with various first-person accounts of anomalous experience and may also aid in their interpretation. The following passage, from a memoir of schizophrenia by Ely Saks, if often quoted as a first-person description of minimal-self disruption:

> Consciousness gradually loses its coherence. One's center gives way. The center cannot hold. The "me" becomes a haze, and the solid center from which one experiences reality breaks up like a bad radio signal. There is no longer a sturdy vantage point from which to look out, take things in, assess what's happening. No core holds things together, providing the lens through which to see the world, to make judgments and comprehend risk. Random movements of time follow one another. Sights, sounds, thoughts, and feelings don't go together. No organizing principle takes successive moments in time and puts them together in a coherent way from which sense can be made. And it's all taking place in slow motion. (Saks 2007, 12)

Such descriptions, it is suggested, point to a profound loss of phenomenological integrity and unity.[4] This is not simply a matter of having anomalous experiential contents of whatever kind; the very sense of having a singular, unitary perspective, of being a coherent locus of experience, breaks down.

The position to be developed in this book acknowledges that human experience includes something along the lines of the "minimal self," and also that schizophrenia diagnoses are sometimes associated with changes in this aspect of experience. However, it is critical of an associated tendency to downplay or leave unspecified the role of interpersonal experience and relatedness. Of course, significant changes in the structure of self-awareness *imply* changes in the capacity to experience and relate to other people. That much is uncontroversial. But we might also wonder whether social relations play a role in the development or even the constitution of minimal self. According to Zahavi, they do not. Minimal self, he says, is not "a product of social interaction or the result of a higher cognitive accomplishment." Rather, it is "a basic and indispensable experiential feature," one that is not "constitutively dependent upon social interaction" (Zahavi 2014, 63, 95). Hence minimal self is present before the development of social abilities and is also a precondition for their development. It continues to underlie the interpersonal abilities of adults, as an enduring, presocial, phenomenological core.

This way of thinking is consistent with applications of the "minimal self" view to the phenomenology of schizophrenia. While it is widely acknowledged that some of the earliest and most salient symptoms of schizophrenia are interpersonal in nature, it is proposed that these symptoms originate in a "fragmentation from within" (Henriksen, Raballo, and Parnas 2015, 176). A primitive, presocial sense of self is disrupted, and so the primary cause is not to be found in the social world. Instead, the aim should be to identify preexistent "self-disorders" that "antedate the onset of psychosis" and render a person susceptible to it (Raballo and Parnas 2011, 1018). It is further proposed that early intervention, and with it improved outcomes, can be facilitated by the detection of characteristic "experiential anomalies" that often arise well before psychotic symptoms (Cermolacce, Naudin, and Parnas 2007). In addition, it is claimed that more subtle disturbances of self are detectable in nonpsychotic but high-risk subjects, such as first-degree relatives of those with schizophrenia diagnoses (Raballo and Parnas 2011). Some advocates of the view take familial risk factors to indicate genetic causes. For instance, Raballo, Sæbye and Parnas (2009, 348) go so far as to suggest that the "primary relevance" of work on self-disorder in schizophrenia is to "etiological research into the genetic architecture of schizophrenia."

However, it should be noted that, even if minimal self is developmentally and constitutively independent of social interaction, this remains compatible with the view that schizophrenia is, or at least can be, socially caused. More generally, something that does not depend on other people for its development or sustenance can still be disrupted by them. For instance, having a brain does not require a history of social interaction, but brains are not immune to injuries inflicted by other people. So the claim that schizophrenia involves disturbance of a presocial sense of self does not imply a nonsocial account of its origins. The most we can say is that the two are consistent and that talk of "self-disorder" may dispose an inquirer to focus on the individual, rather than on the social environment. Nevertheless, the aim of this book is not to advocate an alternative or complementary emphasis on the social causes of schizophrenia. Instead, I will argue that our most basic sense of self is developmentally dependent on interactions with other people. Furthermore, it is interpersonally sustained, and thus continues to depend on other people even in adulthood. Therefore, minimal self is inseparable from the interpersonal. Although this complements an emphasis on social causes, it is equally compatible with there being non-social causes. To develop the position, I will start by offering a more specific account of what minimal self consists of.

2.2 Modalities of Intentionality

When appealing to the phenomenological reality of "minimal self," "ipseity," "a basic sense of mineness," and so forth, it is unclear what more can be said to someone who professes not to understand these claims or simply refuses to accept them. It will not do to repeat much the same thing again and again, in however many different ways, and eventually concede that there is nothing more to be said. This would leave us with something little or no better than the vague talk of "what-it-is-like-ness" and "how-it-is-ness" that has plagued philosophy of mind for some years. Even if such talk succeeds in *referring* to experience or to some aspect of experience, it provides us with little or nothing by way of *description*. Thankfully, though, it is possible to offer a clearer and more precise account of what minimal self consists of, an account that opens up the possibility of describing its structure in considerable detail, along with the kinds of disruption it is susceptible to. The first step is to ask just how minimal the minimal self can be: does it incorporate only the sense that you are having some kind of experience, or does it also include the sense that you are having an experience of one or another type, such as perceiving, imagining, engaging in inner speech, or remembering?

I maintain that even *minimal* selfhood must include a sense of the kind of intentional state one is in, a sense of the modalities of intentionality. I would even go so far as to suggest that an account of the modal structure of intentionality just *is* an account of minimal self—that nothing else needs to be added. Of course, one might object that the appreciation of a perceptual experience as perceptual and of an imagining as an imagining does not entail the sense of being a singular locus of experience that is responsible for both of them. A weaker claim would be that the modalities of intentionality are necessary but not sufficient for minimal self, and the argument of this book does not require anything more than this. Nevertheless, once it is made clear how the modalities of intentionality are embedded in a unitary anticipation-fulfillment structure, which is itself inextricable from a cohesive set of felt bodily dispositions (a position developed in chapters 5 and 6), I think we have all the unity we need. And, as the modalities of intentionality are bound up with certain kinds of bodily experience, there is no need to appeal to the bodily sense of self as an additional aspect or component. So, if we want to pin down what, exactly, minimal selfhood consists of, I think the most promising approach is to focus on the modalities of intentionality. Unless and until some additional ingredient is clearly described, the task of providing a comprehensive phenomenological account of the structure of intentionality can be identified with that of describing the structure of minimal self.

The question "What constitutes the sense of being in one or another kind of intentional state?" is seldom raised and may strike the reader as unfamiliar. I will therefore start by spelling out, in more detail, what it amounts to. Suppose I am currently looking through a window at what appears to be a bird. I could be mistaken about what I see, and I might well experience some degree of doubt concerning what it is. However, I have no doubt that I am seeing something or other. Even though I am not sure what I see, the status of my experience as one of seeing is never in question. Furthermore, I do not need to explicitly infer that I am seeing; I have a prereflective, immediate, unproblematic appreciation of the experience as one of seeing. To be less specific, I take myself to be perceiving something, rather than, say, remembering it. Among other things, the experience of perceiving something through one or another sensory modality involves a sense of that entity as *here, now*. In cases of externally directed perception, there is also a sense of its being distinct from and usually in close proximity to oneself.[5] Let us focus on this prereflective sense of something or other as both distinct from me and also *here, now*, the sense of its *presence*. This may not be sufficient for the sense of perceiving, and it is certainly not sufficient for the sense of perceiving something through one sensory modality rather than another. Nevertheless, presence is at least necessary for an unproblematic experience of relating to entity *p* in a perceptual way. Of course, we could have an experience of *p* that is somehow ambiguous in this respect and then infer from other sources of evidence that we are perceiving rather than imagining *p*. However, we only resort to such inferences in instances of unusual experience, which lack something that more usually identifies an experience as one of perceiving. It is this *something* that I am concerned with here.

The point applies equally to other kinds of intentional state. In remembering that *p*, we usually have an immediate, unproblematic sense of *p* as past, rather than present, imagined, or anticipated. When imagining, there is a sense of *p* as neither past nor present. In some instances of imagining, *p* is anticipated or at least taken to be possible. In others, *p* is recognized as counterfactual or even impossible.[6] Hence there is a kind of phenomenological achievement to be accounted for here, one that is ordinarily so straightforward and unproblematic that it passes unnoticed.

Broad categories such as "imagination," "memory," and "perception" all accommodate a range of more specific phenomena. So, rather than talking about "imagining" and "remembering" as distinct from "perceiving," we could introduce various subcategories of imagination and memory, as well as different forms of sensory perception. For instance, we might distinguish linguistic or propositional from imagistic imagining (e.g., Currie and Ravenscroft 2002; Goldman 2006). Furthermore, the term "imagination" need not be employed in a contrastive way. We could take the line that perception incorporates imagination and that what we ordinarily refer to as "imagination" is the same thing, but restricted to its nonperceptual applications (Strawson 1974), or at least that some types of imagining are inextricable from how we experience the world and are not simply to be contrasted with veridical perception (Hersch 2003). Even if this is so, it does not prohibit us from using the term in a more restrictive, contrastive way, according to which perceiving something involves experiencing it as present, while imagining something ordinarily involves an appreciation that it is not present and never was present. That is the approach adopted here. For the most part, I also restrict myself to fairly general contrasts. Rather than addressing, for instance, how we might distinguish one type of sensory perception from another or how we might distinguish specifically imagistic imagination from an imagistic form of memory, I am concerned with how wider-ranging intentional state types, such as imagining, remembering, and perceiving, are experienced as distinct. At this level of analysis (which is the level at which the kinds of experience addressed in what follows are to be understood), the prereflective ability to discriminate between types of intentional state can be construed in terms of access to a modal space, which includes a sensitivity to distinctions such as these: is here/is elsewhere; was here/was never here; never existed/has ceased to exist/does exist/will exist; might have existed/might exist now/might come to exist.

Were we wholly unreceptive to such distinctions, we would be unable to distinguish one type of intentional state from another. More specifically, if our *experience* were unreceptive to them, we would be unable to *experience* ourselves as in one intentional state rather than another. Given that our experience is sensitive to these distinctions, it is legitimate to ask what the relevant achievement consists of: in virtue of what do I experience myself as perceiving, remembering, or imagining that *p*, as opposed to encountering *p* in a different or less determinate way?[7]

The sense of being in a given type of intentional state is not simply to be identified with having an experience that is characteristic of being in that state. Furthermore, it is plausible to maintain that neither the sense of being in a given intentional state nor the characteristic experience is sufficient for actually being in a state of that type. Hence the following distinctions need to be drawn:

i. Actually having an intentional state of type *x* with respect to entity *p*
ii. Having an experience that is characteristic of an intentional state of type *x* with respect to *p*
iii. Having the sense that one is in an intentional state of type *x* with respect to *p*

Some phenomena may involve (ii) in the absence of (i). Suppose that, while *p* is absent, person B has an experience much like that of being in the presence of *p*. Given the absence of an appropriate relationship between B and *p*, this would not be a case of actually perceiving *p*, at least not if we grant that the term "perception" applies only to successful or nondeceptive cases. Where B has an experience of *p* and mistakenly takes herself to be in the presence of *p*, we can talk more loosely of "perceptual experience," an experience resembling that which arises when we do perceive something. Where intentionality is construed phenomenologically, as it is here, the relevant experience can be regarded as sufficient for being in an intentional state of one or another kind, given that having an experience *of* something implies being in some kind of intentional state. However, it is not sufficient for being in a state of perception, even if it turns out to be necessary. The point applies equally to certain other types of intentional state. If you have an experience of remembering something that did not really happen, you cannot be said to actually remember it. And, if you have an experience of imagining something that really happened to you, then it is arguable that you are in fact remembering it rather than imagining it. Even whether or not you are thinking that *p* arguably depends on whether your experience relates to your environment in the appropriate way. Anecdotal evidence suggests to me that it is not uncommon, while falling asleep listening to the radio, to confuse the words one hears with one's own train of thought. On one interpretation, this involves an experience that is characteristic of some form of thinking, while one is actually in a different kind of intentional state.

However, at least some phenomena are better construed in terms of the distinction between (ii) and (iii). For instance, the "thinking and listening to the radio" example could instead be interpreted as an experience of hearing, but with a sense of thinking. And take the case of dreaming. Whatever a comprehensive account of dreaming might look like, it is implausible to construe dreaming in terms of having perceptual experiences and beliefs that are no different from those had during wakeful perception. Indeed, it has been suggested that perception- and belief-like experiences that occur while dreaming are actually instances of imagining (Ichikawa 2009). If that is so, it can be added that we do not ordinarily recognize ourselves to be imagining while dreaming. In other words, even if we have experiences that are more like imaginings than like beliefs and perceptions, and even if those experiences *are* in fact imaginings according to some criterion, the dreamer (usually) lacks something of the sense of imagining. So the view that dreaming is a form of imagining is compatible with the view that it incorporates a partial or complete *sense* of believing or perceiving, even if other aspects of the experience are unlike believing or perceiving. To understand experiences like this, it is not enough to distinguish between actually being in an intentional state and having a characteristic experience. We need a further distinction between the kind of experience one is having and the kind of intentional state one takes oneself to be in.

The difference between (ii) and (iii) is also illustrated by certain kinds of emotional experience. Now, emotional intentionality differs from imagining, remembering, and perceiving, given that an unambiguous, straightforward experience of being in an emotional state of type *x* is plausibly sufficient for being in a state of type *x*, at least in some instances. An experience of hope, fear, or guilt can amount to being in an intentional state of hope, fear, or guilt, regardless of the status of its object. For instance, in contrast to remembering that *p*, feeling guilty about *p* does not depend on *p* actually having happened. One can still be in an intentional state of guilt, even when mistaken in thinking that *p* ever happened. However, some emotional experiences are messier than this, and it is perhaps not unusual to take oneself to be in an emotional state of type *x* toward *p* when one is actually in an emotional state of type *y*. I might take myself to be happy about B's achieving *p* when I am in fact resentful, or I might think that I do not feel angry with C and later come to realize that I was angry. People sometimes say "I don't know how I feel about *p*" or "I don't know what I'm feeling right now." Sometimes, the apparent indeterminacy can be explained in terms of uncertainty over what one *should* feel in a given situation, rather than what one *does* feel. In others, it may turn out to be a matter of language: the person struggles to *describe* her feelings. Other cases may involve ambivalence: two or more conflicting emotions are directed at a common object. Nevertheless, I think that at least some instances remain where the person has an emotional experience but is unsure what kind of emotional experience it is, whether she is in state *x* or state *y* with respect to *p*. Have I stopped caring about *p* or am I just very tired? Am I angry about *p* or upset about something else? While the dream case need not involve an experience of indeterminacy, ambiguity, or strangeness, cases of "not knowing how I feel" are often different; the sense of indeterminacy or ambiguity is itself phenomenologically salient.

Mere acknowledgment that there is a *sense of being in one or another kind of intentional state* does not imply anything about what that sense consists of. It need not be construed in terms of something specific, a magic ingredient that is either added to an experience or inserted alongside it, which somehow constitutes the appreciation that it is an experience of one or another type. That in virtue of which an experience is modally unambiguous could involve the absence of something disruptive rather than the presence of something that prevents disruption. Whatever the case, this "something" could turn out to be simple or complicated. The chapters that follow will characterize the sense of being in a type of intentional state in a positive way, thus illustrating that it is not just the absence of something disruptive. It should be added that, although I have distinguished between (i), (ii), and (iii), this is not to imply that the three can be neatly separated. In fact, I take the sense of having a perceptual experience of *p* to be *partly constitutive* of the relevant experience. Perception can be conceived of in dynamic terms, as an exploratory process that involves appearances unfolding in a structured fashion, in accordance with bodily movements and associated expectations (e.g., Husserl 1948/1973, 1952/1989; Noë 2004; Ratcliffe 2008, 2015; Madary 2013). And, in chapters 4 to 6, it will be argued that all forms of intentional experience are essentially dynamic in nature; they incorporate characteristic patterns of anticipation and fulfilment. Insofar as a sense of one's intentional state shapes activities and associated expectations, it cannot be insulated from other aspects of the experience. One would not act in ways characteristic of a perceptual process unless one took oneself to be perceiving. So, if the sense of perceiving were removed from an experience, that experience would not be preserved unscathed. Clean cases, where there is a clear-cut, unambiguous, unproblematic sense of having a type *x* experience but in the complete absence of a type *x* experience (or vice versa), are thus implausible.

The sense of being in a type of intentional state is also relevant to the determination of which intentional state a person is actually in. Now, one could adopt a nonphenomenological account of what it is to actually *be* in an intentional state of one or another type. And I do not dismiss the possibility of a nonphenomenological conception of intentionality, as something wholly distinct from the having of experiences. However, where we are concerned with beings that *do* experience things, it would be a mistake to advocate a complete dissociation between being in an intentional state and having an experience that is characteristic of being in such a state. It is one thing to accept that a perception-like experience might occur in the absence of perception and, conversely, that a perception might occur in the absence of perceptual experience. But a complete divorce between intentional states and associated experiences would be contentious to say the least, raising the skeptical worry that our experiences of perceiving, remembering, or imagining that *p* do not give us grounds for thinking that we really are perceiving, remembering, or imagining that *p* (a concern that would apply equally to experiences of thinking skeptical thoughts). It is more plausible to maintain that, where perception does involve having perceptual experience, the phenomenology contributes to perception but is not in itself *sufficient* for perception. The point applies more specifically to the sense of perceiving. Suppose that types of intentional state are to be identified by their distinctive functional roles, a view that is popular in current philosophy of mind. The sense of being in intentional state *x* (which is part of a wider experience characteristic of intentional state *x*) surely impacts on how it relates to other kinds of intentional state and also to behavior. Where there is a sense of perceiving something that is actually imagined, imaginings will relate to other kinds of intentional state, such as beliefs, and also to behavior, in ways that imaginings would more usually not. This is not to suggest that imagination would take on the functional role of perception in its entirety, just that its functional role would plausibly be disrupted in at least some ways and at least to some extent. So, although a person's sense of being in an intentional state of type *x* or *y* is not sufficient to determine whether she is actually in a state of type *x* or *y*, it is at least a contributing factor. Therefore, it is not something that can be partitioned off and ignored by those philosophers with a more general interest in intentionality.[8]

In insisting that it is like something to perceive that *p*, which differs from what it is like to imagine, remember, believe, or think that *p*, I am committed to the view that there is some kind of "cognitive phenomenology." One might therefore object to my overall approach by drawing on arguments to the effect that there is no distinctively *cognitive* experience. However, I take the line that the nature of cognitive phenomenology can be made clearer by engaging with phenomena such as AVHs and that an account of the modal structure of intentionality, insofar as it is plausible, amounts to a case for cognitive phenomenology and a clarification of what exactly it consists of. Hence it would be a mistake to impose a conception of cognitive phenomenology (or its absence) on our subject matter from the outset.[9]

Another objection that could be raised at this point is that the nature of the relevant phenomenology is in fact fairly obvious, and is such that my question cannot, after all, be distinguished from more familiar ones. Types of experience, it might be argued, are distinguished by their characteristic contents. Granted, some types of experiential content may be common to a number of modalities. For example, visual perception and visual imagination plausibly have certain features in common. However, in order to distinguish one type of intentional experience from another, all we need insist on is that some aspect of content is both consistently present and modality-specific. It could be added that experiences of all types are *transparent*. In other words, when we reflect on the nature of any given experience, we find only its content. For instance, when we see or hear something, there is nothing more to the experience than what is seen or heard: "When we introspect our experiences of hearing, smelling, and tasting, the qualities of which we are directly aware are qualities we experience as being qualities of sounds, odors, and tastes" (Tye 2002, 142). Hence any phenomenological differences between intentional state types have to be attributed to content; there is no other candidate. The sense of perceiving something, and doing so visually, amounts to nothing more than the having of an experience with a content that is specific to visual perception and distinguishes it from, for instance, visual imagination or nonvisual perception. The same applies to all other modalities of intentional experience: broad categories such as imagining, remembering, and thinking are identifiable as such in virtue of their characteristic contents.

If that is right, then there is nothing more to having an experience of type *x* than having an *x*-specific content, and there need be nothing more to the sense of having an experience of type *x* either. So it turns out that a *type of experience* and a *sense of having an experience of that type* are not after all distinguishable. Once we have dealt with the former, there is nothing more to be said. Confusion over which intentional state one is in could thus be attributed to an experiential content that is somehow ambiguous. In addition to or instead of this, it could involve a nonperceptual belief or judgment, in which case the sense of being in an intentional state would again collapse into something more familiar: an intentional state with another intentional state as its object. On such a view, this *sense* might be considered an occasional accompaniment to types of experiences that are more usually unproblematic, rather than something that is ubiquitous and essential to the sense of self.

Perhaps this is the reason why my question is seldom explicitly formulated. But, as I will show in the remainder of this book, it is not a good reason. The sense of being in one or another kind of intentional state is not merely a matter of characteristic phenomenal *content*. It is possible for an experiential content resembling that of intentional state *x* more so than that of intentional state *y* to be associated with a sense of being in intentional state *y*. Faced with this, one could abandon the transparency claim and propose that a separate *attitudinal* phenomenology is necessary and, when combined with content, sufficient for the sense of being in a given type of intentional state. However, the chapters that follow will show that this does not work either. The principal aspects of sense are not to be conceived of in terms of a distinction between attitude and content, and a discrete, *attitudinal* phenomenology has little or no role to play. Sense turns out to be multifaceted, and while experiential content does make a contribution, it can be overridden by other aspects of sense in cases of conflict. Hence perceptual and nonperceptual experiences are considerably more complicated than philosophers often take them to be. Coming to appreciate this is essential if we are to understanding certain forms of anomalous experience. In so doing, we also open the door to a much richer account of the phenomenological structure of intentionality.

How does all of this relate to minimal self? Minimal self is said to involve a sense of first-person perspective that is inseparable from being in an intentional state of one or another type. What is not made so clear is whether it further includes a sense of which type of intentional state one is in. However, it must. If our experience did not respect the distinction between perceiving and remembering, we would have no sense of temporal location. And, if we could not distinguish imagining from perceiving, experienced boundaries between self and environment would break down, to the extent that we would lack any sense of spatial location. My sense of perceiving *a*, *b*, and *c*, while imagining *d*, *e*, and *f*, constrains my potential actions. I cannot make the unseen sides of *a*, *b*, and *c* perceptually available without acting in specific ways, which I may or may not be capable of. This does not apply to *d*, *e*, and *f*. Without the distinction between perceiving and imagining, such constraints would be lacking. Everything would appear experientially and practically accessible in the same ways, thus amounting to a lack of self-location, of having a particular, contingent, changeable standpoint toward the world. Without some sense of spatiotemporal location, it is difficult to see how any experience of being a singular, coherent locus of experience could be sustained. Hence minimal-self experience has to discriminate between types of intentional state. This interpretation is consistent with how the concept is applied in the context of psychopathology. Consider the following:

> Note that in a normal experience, e.g. in a perceptual act, the perceptual act is immediately and prereflectively aware of itself; it is an instance of ipseity. In other words, when I perceive or I think something, I do not become aware of the fact of my perceiving or thinking by some reflective/introspective examination of my current mental activity and comparing it with other possible modalities of intentionality (e.g. fantasizing). Any experience, any intentional act, is normally articulated as ipseity, i.e. it is automatically prereflectively aware of itself. The difficulties in this domain point to a profound disorder of ipseity. (Parnas et al. 2005, 242)

This passage does not explicitly endorse the less minimal conception of minimal self. Nevertheless, it is stated that we do *not* take ourselves to perceive rather than fantasize by reflectively comparing two kinds of experience. Hence, although the subsequent claim that an intentional act is "prereflectively aware of itself" need not be interpreted as its being prereflectively aware of the type of intentional act that it is, the stronger interpretation is implied by preceding context. Further support for this interpretation is offered by the EASE, which addresses, among other things, an "inability to discriminate modalities of intentionality" that is indicative of anomalous self-experience (Parnas et al. 2005, 242). For Sass (2014a, 6), minimal self is likewise associated with the modal structure of intentionality: "Disturbances of spatiotemporal structuring of the world, and of such crucial experiential distinctions as perceived-vs-remembered-vs-imagined, are grounded in abnormalities of the embodied, vital, experiencing self." His view, as I understand it, is not that disturbance of selfhood *causes* erosion of these distinctions, or that disturbances of selfhood imply other kinds of phenomenological disturbance but not vice versa. The relationship is instead one of mutual implication: minimal selfhood, the coherence of world experience, and a sense of relating to the world are all aspects of a unitary phenomenological structure, one that includes the modalities of intentionality.

This is not to suggest that there is no tension between my account and other conceptions of minimal self. In fact, Zahavi (2017) rejects my view that the modalities of intentionality are integral to minimal self and insists on a more primitive "what-it-is-like-for-me-ness." But I do not see sufficient grounds for postulating a more primitive level of self, and the detailed account of the modal structure of intentionality developed in what follows is intended as an analysis of the same aspect of experience that he refers to. Furthermore, an emphasis on the modalities of intentionality facilitates a clearer, more detailed, and more specific account of self-disturbances in psychiatric illness. It is not simply a matter of perspectival disintegration, but of wide-ranging disturbances in the sense of intentional modalities as distinct from each other, something that can take a number of subtly different forms. As we will see, these disturbances can be described in detail. Appealing to an additional, separate disruption of what-it-is-like-for-meness lacks explanatory power: it seeks to explain something that has already been satisfactorily accounted for in terms of modal structure, by invoking something that does little to illuminate the relevant phenomena.

2.3 Other People

A breakdown of the modal structure of intentionality would inevitably involve changes in the structure of interpersonal experience. If one could not distinguish self from nonself in the usual way, one could not, by implication, distinguish self from other either. More specific distinctions, such as that between one's own thoughts or experiences and those of others, would be similarly affected. We could take the view that disruption of interpersonal experience is secondary: it is implied by the erosion of a more fundamental, pre-intersubjective sense of self. Even those who emphasize the interpersonal, relational phenomenology of psychiatric illness sometimes write as though this were so. For example, Fuchs (2015, 199) states that a "disturbance of the pre-reflective, embodied self must necessarily impair the patient's social relationships." He adds that self-disturbance can be exacerbated by subsequent social problems. Nevertheless, self-disturbance retains priority over relational disturbance, given that the former implies the latter but not vice versa. Proponents of the "minimal self" approach have also acknowledged that "hallucinations are expressive of a disturbance of the relation between the individual and her (interpersonal) world" (Larøi et al. 2010, 233). Again, however, this is compatible with the view that changes in interpersonal experience, and with them the onset of AVHs, are ultimately symptomatic of minimal-self disruption (Henriksen, Raballo, and Parnas 2015).

I propose instead that the integrity of intentionality, the sense of being in one kind of intentional state rather than another, depends on a certain *way* of experiencing and relating to other people, both developmentally and constitutively. Hence the most minimal or primitive sense of self possessed by a socialized, adult human is also an interpersonal self. It follows from this that certain events, of a kind that disrupt intersubjective development and/or interpersonal experience in adulthood, can also impact on the structure of intentionality and thus on the most basic sense of self.

This emphasis on the interpersonal helps to bridge an explanatory gap between global changes in the structure of experience and symptoms that are seemingly localized and episodic. Not all cases of schizophrenia involve AVHs, and estimates of their prevalence range from 50 percent to 80 percent (e.g., Hoffman and Rapaport 1994, 256; Delespaul, de Vries, and van Os 2002, 97). If schizophrenia without AVHs can also involve self-disorder, we need an explanation of why self-disorder only sometimes generates AVHs. Perhaps, one might suggest, AVHs occur only with a certain degree or kind of self-disorder, while the threshold for schizophrenia is lower or the diagnosis is broader in scope. However, what still needs explaining is why AVHs are usually experienced sporadically rather than constantly, and why their contents tend to be thematically consistent and often unpleasant in nature. The self-disorder approach offers at least a partial account of how AVHs arise, according to which thought and, more specifically, *inner speech* becomes conspicuous, object-like, and thus more akin to certain contents of perceptual experience: "Inner speech becomes transformed from a *medium of thinking* into an object-like entity with quasi-perceptual characteristics" (Parnas and Sass 2001, 107). However, the story is importantly incomplete. It is not at all clear how to account for the content-specificity of AVHs in terms of nonspecific changes in the structure of experience and thought.[10] It can be added that AVHs with unpleasant contents are diagnostically nonspecific. They are associated with several categories of psychiatric disorder, and seemingly similar phenomena are also reported in the nonclinical population (e.g., Watkins 2008; Johns et al. 2014). If AVHs in some or all of these contexts turn out to be phenomenologically indistinguishable from those associated with schizophrenia, then either (a) self-disorder of the relevant kind is not specific to schizophrenia or (b) self-disorder is not necessary for AVHs, even if it turns out to be sufficient for them.

To begin addressing the content-specificity problem, let us consider a very different approach to AVHs, one that places much more emphasis on their content and also on their interpersonal context. The approach in question was pioneered by Marius Romme and Sandra Escher (e.g., Romme et al. 2009; Romme and Escher 2012). It is credited with giving rise to the Hearing Voices Movement, and has been adopted by organizations including Intervoice and the Hearing Voices Network.[11] As the term "movement" suggests, it would be wrong to think of this merely as a theory or a looser set of empirical claims. There is also a salient normative dimension to it; the movement is principally concerned with how those who hear voices *should* be regarded and treated, by the medical profession and more generally. It aims to combat social injustice, empower people, and challenge prevalent attitudes in psychiatry and elsewhere. However, the stance that it adopts also includes a number of descriptive claims concerning the nature of what others refer to as "AVHs," and it is these that I focus on here.[12]

According to Romme and Escher, anomalous experiences such as *voices* with distressing contents owe much to the voice-hearer's current and historical relations with other people. Childhood trauma, neglect, and abuse are frequently implicated, as are social anxiety and social isolation in adulthood. Voices are not meaningless symptoms of illness but meaningful phenomena to be interpreted in the light of past events. A voice might express past events metaphorically; what it "says" might be similar or identical to remembered utterances; and it might even be recognized as the voice of an abuser. In addition, the emotional content of a voice-hearing experience and the person's emotional reaction to that experience both mirror past and/or current relationships with specific individuals or people in general.

The content of the experience is central to this approach, as are interpersonal relationships and the emotional dynamics they involve. Given that voices somehow reflect interpersonally induced emotional distress, there is an emphasis on trying to make sense of what they say and on helping the person come to terms with historical events. The intention is not so much to get rid of the voices as to change how the voice-hearer relates to them and to the social world, to help her take back control.[13] For instance, an approach called Voice Dialogue involves addressing the voice rather than the person who hears it, with the aim of altering how the person understands and relates to her voice, such that it may eventually become benign or supportive (e.g., Corstens, Longden, and May 2012).[14] An associated theme is that psychiatric diagnoses and treatments can themselves be disempowering, exacerbating a person's sense of helplessness in the face of a hostile social world. A voice-hearing experience does not have to be distressing and is not intrinsically pathological. To label voices per se as symptoms of illness is to stigmatize and alienate people, as well as increase the distress caused by their voices (Romme et al. 2009).

The hearing voices literature consistently emphasizes the extent to which voices are socially embedded: "Hearing voices must not be seen as an isolated, individual experience. There is always an interaction between voice hearer and society, voice hearer and family, voice hearer and mental health professional" (Romme et al. 2009, 4). The relationship between traumatic events involving other people and the onset of voices is not made fully clear. However, emotional disturbance is said to play a central role. For instance, it is suggested that those who have suffered childhood trauma in the form of neglect are less able to regulate emotions and are consequently more prone to stress, which can somehow trigger voice-hearing (Romme et al. 2009, 41). More generally, it is proposed that what disposes a person toward having these experiences is emotional and relational in nature:

> It is very important to explore the links between the voices, the trauma and the involved emotions that lie at the roots of the voice-hearing experience. To learn to cope with these emotions is more relevant for the recovery process than learning to cope with the voices alone. To get more control over the voices, however, opens the gateway to getting at the social-emotional problems that are at the roots. Voices serve as a defence mechanism avoiding confrontation with the problems and the emotions involved. (Romme et al. 2009, 47)

As this passage suggests, the approach maintains that the relationship between traumatic experience and voices is not always transparent to the voice-hearer. Distressing voices often involve a form of dissociation, whereby the person detaches himself from painful emotions, which then manifest themselves as alien voices. So he may lack an explicit, reflective appreciation of the causes of his voices, as well as their relationship to painful life events. The task is to make sense of them with him, to grasp their emotional meanings and their relationships to his life-history. Hence "psychosis" is to be reconceived of as an "emotional crisis" (Romme and Escher 2012).[15]

One concern I have about this approach is its lack of clarity concerning the implications for diagnostic categories and, more specifically, the schizophrenia construct. It is not clear whether the position is that (a) the diagnosis "schizophrenia" has been overextended or (b) the diagnostic category "schizophrenia" is misguided and should be abandoned altogether. For instance, Longden, Madill, and Waterman (2012) argue that phenomena such as AVHs should be construed as dissociative rather than psychotic, and cite numerous studies pointing to a link with trauma, especially childhood trauma. Voices, they say, are "dissociated or disowned components of the self (or self-other relationships) that result from trauma, loss, or other interpersonal stressors" (2012, 28). So it would seem that the issue concerns whether something should be categorized as psychosis (and, more specifically, schizophrenia) or as dissociation. But, at the same time, they question the legitimacy of a distinction between the two, in suggesting that "trauma-induced dissociation" and "psychosis" are different ways of interpreting a common phenomenon, the latter inappropriately. Lack of clarity over the status of diagnostic categories is accompanied by a lack of clarity over the nature of "voices." It could be that we are dealing with a singular, unitary phenomenon. Alternatively, "voices" might encompass a range of importantly different phenomena, embedded in different phenomenological and interpersonal contexts. Consequently, the scope of the hearing voices approach is also unclear.

What is clear, however, is that there are tensions between the stance of the Hearing Voices Movement and the minimal-self account of schizophrenia and AVHs. The latter is much more accepting of the schizophrenia construct and places far less emphasis on the interpersonal. There is also a tension between an emphasis on *dissociative* emotional disturbances and the claim that disruptions of minimal selfhood fuel *psychotic* phenomena. Nevertheless, I think the two positions can be integrated, to a considerable degree, through the acknowledgment that minimal self is developmentally and constitutively dependent on a way of relating to other people. For now, I seek only to set out the position. I will defend it in later chapters.

It might seem that there is an obvious objection to the view that minimal self somehow depends on relations with other people: if the modalities of intentionality arise during social development, young infants and all nonsocial organisms are implausibly denied the status of "minimal self." Infants may well be born with various rudimentary intersubjective abilities, but, to the extent that the structure of intentionality is contingent on social-developmental processes, that structure is lacking at the outset. However, what I am suggesting does not entail such a position. One alternative would be to maintain that infants are born with the capacity for intentional states of type *x* and *y*, and that, as they develop, they come to distinguish other types of intentional state as well. So a richer sense of minimal self is formed, and disturbances of intersubjectivity involve regression to something more primitive. There is the worry, though, that this would descend into a purely verbal dispute over whether minimal self should be taken to involve the capacity to experience *x* as distinct from *y*, or whether it should, in some instances at least, include further discriminative capacities. In any case, such an approach would be wrongheaded. Self-development should instead be conceived of as a transformative process. Suppose infants are born with a capacity for intentional states of type *y*, which do not correspond exactly to *any* of the types of experience that typical adults discriminate between. It is not that one first experiences *y* and later comes to experience *z* as well; *y* is a developmental precursor to a modal structure that does not retain *y* in unadulterated form. Furthermore, the development of *y* into *z* does not revert back to *y* when it goes awry; one is left with neither.

More generally, development does not have a rewind button. Instead, capacities that enter into developmental processes become hostages to fortune; there is no going back. All sorts of mundane examples serve to illustrate the point: starved of light from birth, one is not left with the capacities of infant eyes; deprived of the opportunity to walk, one is not left with the musculature of infant legs. In the case of minimal self, it is equally coherent to suppose that infants possess a minimal self of type A, a capacity for certain types of distinguishable and coherently integrated intentional experience, but that adults possess a minimal self of type B, involving a repertoire of intentional states that is qualitatively different from A. When development is derailed, the resulting lack of phenomenological coherence is quite unlike both the typical infant case and the typical adult case. So there is a need to distinguish *possible* kinds of minimal-self experience from the *actual* kind(s) found in adult humans. Even if it is accepted that selfhood is possible in the absence of interpersonal relations, there are no grounds for insisting that this same kind of selfhood is preserved in unadulterated form throughout social development, as an underlying core. I admit that nonsocial and presocial forms of minimal self are at least conceivable and may well be actual. However, the distinctive modal structure of human experience is the outcome of a social developmental process. Once that process begins, there is no going back, and the sense of self that unfolds is susceptible to kinds of disruption that could not arise in the asocial case. Furthermore, even in adulthood, the integrity of intentionality continues to depend on a certain distinctive way of relating to the social world, one that is vulnerable to disruption.

Although studies of child development have not explicitly addressed the modal structure of intentional experience, many authors emphasize how interpersonal interaction is not simply an outcome of cognitive developmental processes but something integral to them. Relations with other people, principally caregivers, shape developmental outcomes. As Hobson (2002, 75) puts it, "being affected by others is a design feature of human beings—a design feature that transforms what a human being is." He describes, in detail, how parent–child interactions involve affective, dialogical processes of growing sophistication, and maintains that it is out of relatedness that "children develop what are called 'perceptual,' 'cognitive,' 'conative,' and 'affective' psychological functions" (1993, 105). Hobson (2002, xiv) goes so far as to state that the eventual capacity to *think* depends on certain ways of relating to and interacting with other people during development. Patterned affective interaction is thus integral to the developmental process. It serves as a kind of scaffolding for development, enabling the formation of species-typical capacities that could not arise in its absence.

Various others have made complementary claims. For instance, Trevarthen (e.g., 1993) maintains that the interpersonal self is developmentally prior to thought, and that the capacity to think is founded on forms of affective communication. Stern (e.g., 1993) similarly proposes that the ability to elicit, share, and regulate each other's feelings has an important role to play in cognitive development. While these accounts do not explicitly set out a position concerning the structure of intentionality and its development, they are compatible with what I am proposing. Tronick et al. (1998) come closer to endorsing such a position, in suggesting that interaction with a caregiver during childhood, or with a therapist during adulthood, can serve to "expand" consciousness into "more coherent and complex states" (290). Others state that the most basic sense of self, even consciousness itself, is dependent on interpersonal relations. Zeedyk (2006, 326) makes the strong claim that capacities including "self-awareness, representation, language, and even consciousness" originate in distinctive kinds of relation with caregivers, involving what she calls "emotional intimacy." Reddy (2008, 27) likewise suggests that certain kinds of second-person engagement or "I-you" relation are partly constitutive of the development of mind.[16] Such claims are plausibly construed as encompassing, among other things, the changing modal structure of intentionality. That structure depends on interpersonal processes for its development and is therefore rendered vulnerable to them. What we have is an interpersonally regulated, self-transformative process. There are no grounds for insisting on a core self that remains insulated from the process as other capacities are laid down on top of it. The view that minimal self is developmentally, and later constitutively, bound up with interpersonal experience does not imply that minimal-self disturbance sometimes or always has social causes. Disruption of the modal structure of intentionality, and with it the capacity for interpersonal experience and relatedness, could have any number of different causes. Nevertheless, in chapters 4, 5, and 6, I will suggest that the emphasis placed by the Hearing Voices Movement on interpersonal trauma is plausible in many cases (although we should be careful not to overgeneralize).

Is this *interpersonal minimal self* still a *minimal self*? For my purposes, it does not really matter whether the term "minimal self" is ultimately retained. My position is that, if we do want to talk in terms of a basic sense of selfhood of a kind that is altered in severe psychiatric illness, then we should be talking about what I address here. In the case of a socialized human being, there is nothing more primitive to be found, no underlying presocial self. There is nothing *beneath* or *before* the modal structure of intentionality, a structure that is inextricable from a way of being immersed in the interpersonal world and consequently vulnerable to certain kinds of disruption.

2.4 The Appearance of Hallucination

The approach sketched in this chapter parts company with most philosophical discussions of hallucination. A hallucination is generally taken to be a perceptual experience that is much like or identical to perceiving *p*, but had in the absence of *p*. No distinction is drawn between the having of an experience and the sense of having it. However, there is at least some affinity between what I have said so far and the conception of hallucination associated with a type of "disjunctive" theory of perception. There is also common ground between the position I seek to develop and a philosophical account of "real hallucinations" that takes them to be "mistaken imaginings" rather than nonveridical perceptual experiences. To conclude the chapter, I will further clarify my position by comparing and contrasting it with both.

The disjunctive theory of perception, or the version of it that I have in mind, involves a commitment to *naive realism*. Central to this is a *strong transparency claim*. A weak transparency claim would be that the content of perceptual experience *seems* to consist of features of our surrounding environment that perception reveals to us. The strong transparency claim takes this at face value; the properties we experience are not constituents of an experience but exactly what they seem to be: properties of entities in our environment. When I look at a tree, my experience somehow incorporates the tree's actual properties, rather than an experiential content that could equally arise in the absence of sensory contact with the actual tree (e.g., Martin 2002, 2004). So I could not have an experience with those same properties in isolation from the tree. It follows from this that a *hallucination* of the tree, whatever it might consist of, cannot be phenomenologically indistinguishable from a veridical experience of the tree. If this is correct, then hallucinations turn out to be doubly deceptive. We take ourselves to be having an experience of *p*, in a case where *p* is absent and where the experience does not in fact resemble an experience of *p*:

> As paradoxical as it may sound, the explanation of how illusions or hallucinations can fix beliefs requires that we think of such situations as not only being misleading as to how the subject's environment is, but also as being misleading about themselves. (Martin 2002, 401)

The theory has little or nothing to say about what hallucinations *do* consist of. It offers only a negative characterization, according to which they involve the absence of experience, but in a way that somehow eludes first-person detection. So a "perfect hallucination" is not a perfect replica of a veridical experience. Instead, it involves a complete inability to detect the difference via "reflection alone" (Martin 2004, 76).[17] If the strong transparency claim is accepted, this must apply to both hypothetical and real hallucinations. If the properties of perceptual experience are identical to the properties of perceived objects, then hallucinations cannot incorporate those properties. But this is compatible with maintaining that it seems to us as though they do. As Martin (2002, 421) remarks, "it can hardly be denied that it is possible for one to have an illusion or hallucination which is indistinguishable for one from a veridical perception."[18] To put it in my terms, what we have here is a wholly intact sense of perceiving, but in the absence of any perceptual experience.

Martin is right to distinguish taking oneself to undergo a given type of experience from actually undergoing it, and to acknowledge the possibility that hallucinations involve the former rather than the latter. However, insistence on a wholly negative account of hallucination (as an absence of something, combined with lack of reflective insight into this absence) is unhelpful. In cases of real hallucination, as I will show, the sense of being in an intentional state cannot be cleanly extricated from a wider experience that is characteristic of being in that state. Furthermore, the various aspects of this *sense* can be described in considerable detail, as can other aspects of perceptual and nonperceptual experience. So, in the case of perception, there are no grounds for maintaining that the relevant phenomenology is exhausted by properties of the environment (even if one is willing to grant that perceptual experience somehow incorporates such properties). Furthermore, in cases of real hallucination, it would be wrong to say that there is an absence of perceptual experience, coupled with a lack of insight. There is often an experience of strangeness, ambiguity, and tension. The person's sense that she is having a type-*x* experience is lacking in one or another respect, and she may be well aware that there is a conflict between a predominantly type-*x* sense and other aspects of the experience that are indicative of a type-*y* rather than type-*x* intentional state. Of course, Martin could respond that he is concerned with philosophers' hallucinations, which are merely possible, rather than with actual forms of experience. However, if certain real hallucinations involve taking oneself to have a perceptual experience when one does not, and we have a detailed analysis of what the relevant *sense of having a perceptual experience* consists of, it is not clear why this account should be withheld for cleaner, hypothetical cases that are similarly said to involve taking oneself to have a perceptual experience when one does not. The alternative would be to adopt a rather peculiar position, where we know what the sense of perceiving actually consists of, but we disregard it and postulate a different, hypothetical sense of perceiving, which we refuse to say anything more about. Given the approach to be developed here, the door is left open for the disjunctivist to argue that at least some properties of perceptual experience are specific to the veridical case and consistent with the strong transparency claim. However, that is not my project. Instead, I am concerned with something that the disjunctivist only touches on, in raising the possibility of taking oneself to have a perception-like experience when one does not: the wider-ranging modal structure of intentionality.

An emphasis on the modalities of intentionality also complements, in certain respects, the suggestion that some hallucinations and delusions are misplaced imaginings rather than perceptions or beliefs (Currie 2000; Currie and Jureidini 2001; Currie and Ravenscroft 2002).[19] One motivation for this view is that much of what seems odd about delusional "belief" is quite mundane in the context of our imaginings. So delusions would be a lot less puzzling if they turned out to be imaginings rather than beliefs: "Much of what exemplifies the strange and disordered thought of people with schizophrenia would not be remarkable if it were treated by the subject as belonging to the flow of her own imaginings" (Currie 2000, 173). For instance, imaginings are insulated from requirements such as consistency with a person's various beliefs. The view that delusions are imaginings is thus complemented by the observation that delusions are recalcitrant to revision in the light of glaring inconsistencies. Hallucinations, it is suggested, can be explained in the same way, but in terms of a confusion between imagination and perception, rather than imagination and belief. So what we have in both cases is a disorder of "attitude identification," where a person takes himself to be in intentional state *x*, when he is actually in intentional state *y* (Currie 2000, 173). This approach allies itself with a self-monitoring account of the relevant experiences, according to which they arise owing to the breakdown of mechanisms that more usually serve to identify them as self-generated (e.g., Frith 1992). There is a failure to monitor imaginings that arise in response to perceptual experiences. These are then experienced as non-self-generated or not "willed by us" (Currie 2000, 179). Depending on the kind of imagining involved and whether or not it includes sensory qualities, it is mistaken either for a perception (as in the case of an AVH) or for a belief (as in the case of delusion).

Imagining that *p* while taking oneself to either believe that *p* or perceive that *p* could be construed in terms of being in intentional state *x*, while having the sense that one is in intentional state *y*. In this respect, the account I will develop here complements a mistaken imaginings approach. However, there are also some important differences. First of all, there is a difference in emphasis: my approach is principally phenomenological, while that of Currie and his coauthors is not. Second, while they account for delusions and hallucinations in epistemological terms (a person is in one type of intentional state but mistakes it for another), I maintain that things are seldom, if ever, so tidy. A partial sense that one is in intentional state *x*, accompanied by an experiential content resembling that of *y* more so than *x*, is experienced *as* strange, ambiguous, or indeterminate. What we have is not simply one intentional state that is mistaken for another but an unfamiliar kind of intentionality, something that is experienced as somehow different from both. One thus faces the task of conveying to others a type of experience that does not fit into familiar categories. It is plausibly the interpreter, more so than the patient, who is responsible for mistaking an unusual experience for a simple perception or belief. Sarbin (1967), for instance, suggests that clinicians are often too hasty in taking what are actually reported imaginings to be phenomenologically indistinguishable from everyday perceptions or beliefs. As we will see in chapter 3, first-person reports tend to be more hesitant and equivocal.

Another point of departure is that I seek to account for various seemingly localized phenomena in terms of more general disturbances in the modal structure of experience and to describe what that structure consists of. It is not just a matter of misidentifying some of one's imaginings as perceptions and/or beliefs. There is more to it than that: shifts in the modal structure of intentionality also alter the repertoire of intentional state types that one is capable of. One is more prone to a blurring of the boundaries between belief/perception and imagination because none of one's "beliefs," "perceptions," or "imaginings" involve quite the same kind of intentionality that they previously did.

Nevertheless, it should be acknowledged that the mistaken imaginings account proposed by Currie and colleagues is not exclusively epistemological. They also recognize that the subject may have an "ambiguous relationship with the thought content," such that it can play a psychological role somewhere in between that of a belief and an imagining (Currie 2000, 174). Furthermore, believing that you believe something can eventually lead you to believe it. So there is the possibility of a transition from mistaken imaginings to full-blown beliefs. Elsewhere, Currie and Jureidini (2004, 423) explicitly reject a categorical distinction between imagination and belief. They conceive of imagination and belief as a space, with two main clusters and various outliers. The criteria that determine whether a psychological state is closer to one or the other cluster include "truth-tracking, coherence with other elements of the system, potential to motivate, emotional power, subjection to the will, and ... narrative valence: the capacity to play a role in a more or less elaborate and engaging narrative." There is, they state, "little use left for a sharp belief/imagination distinction." Egan (2009) also proposes a blurring of the boundaries between imagination and belief. He distinguishes types of intentional state in terms of their functional roles. For instance, beliefs have a characteristic relationship to evidence, to other kinds of intentional state, and to behavior. On that basis, he argues that delusions cannot be classified as "straightforward, paradigmatic cases" of belief or imagination (2009, 268). They are insulated from evidence to an extent that beliefs are usually not, but they are not as insulated as imaginings, and the same applies to their relationship with behavior. Egan thus introduces the term "bimagination" to refer to an intermediate form of intentionality that resembles belief in some respects and imagination in others.

The claim that there is no categorical distinction between belief and imagination is consistent with my own position. But again the emphasis is different, given that I want to focus on the phenomenology. Furthermore, the postulation of states that lie somewhere in between belief and imagination risks losing a distinction that an epistemological approach continues to recognize, between the intentional state one takes oneself to be in and the intentional state one is actually in. That a person has an intentional state with features of *y* and *z* does not tell us anything about what the more specific sense of being in an intentional state of type *y* or *z* consists of. Hence, in appealing merely to a blurring between intentional state types, there is the risk of missing something important: the tensions that can arise between a sense of one's intentional state and other aspects of experience. With this, we also lose sight of the role played by the wider modal structure of experience, a more enveloping sense of the various kinds of intentional state as distinct from one another.[20]

So, in summary, there are distinctions to be drawn between (a) epistemic and constitutive formulations of the view that delusions and hallucinations can involve confusing different kinds of intentional state; (b) phenomenological and nonphenomenological formulations of both kinds of view; and (c) accounts that emphasize circumscribed, episodic confusions between intentional states types, and a wider-ranging approach that also seeks to understand these phenomena in terms of changes in the overall structure of intentionality. The remainder of this book develops a phenomenological, constitutive, and wide-ranging approach toward anomalous experiences, and toward the structure of intentionality more generally.

3 Thought Insertion Clarified

This chapter makes a case for the view that certain kinds of anomalous experience, often but not always associated with schizophrenia diagnoses, consist of disturbances in the modal structure of intentionality. Here, and in chapter 4, the emphasis is on episodic, localized disturbances. Chapters 5 and 6 then address wider-ranging and longer-term changes in the structure of intentionality that render one vulnerable to these disturbances. The principal aim of the current chapter is to show that the sense of being in a given type of intentional state cannot be accounted for solely in terms of characteristic experiential content. An experience can have a content that continues to resemble that of intentional state *x* more so than that of intentional state *y*, while the sense of being in intentional state *y* predominates. In such cases, the sense of being in one type of intentional state rather than the other is not clear-cut and unproblematic. The different factors that contribute to sense come into conflict with each other. With this, there is an awareness of undergoing a peculiar kind of experience.

My approach provides a way of interpreting experiences that are otherwise puzzling and difficult to pin down. The chapter begins with a consideration of TI (thought insertion), the experience of one's own thoughts as somehow alien and emanating from elsewhere, usually from another person. What is experienced as alien, I suggest, is a thought content rather than an act of thinking. TI involves a perception-like experience of something that still resembles, in certain respects, the content of a thought. To support this interpretation, I compare the phenomenology of TI to that of AVH (auditory verbal hallucination). After making clear that the category "AVH" accommodates a range of quite different experiences, I identify a distinctive subset of AVHs and argue that they are indistinguishable from TI. What we have here is a common experience, which might be described in terms of

AVH, TI, or both. It involves an unfamiliar kind of intentionality that lies somewhere between thinking and perceiving, a quasi-perceptual experience of thought content. This can coexist with more familiar kinds of intentional state. Hence a person might say that she *hears* various worldly events, and *hears*—in a different way—her voices. The chapter concludes by arguing that the distinction between agency and ownership/subjectivity, which is often used to make sense of TI, does little to illuminate the relevant phenomenon.

3.1 The Sense of Perceiving

Experiencing what is "here, now" as different from what is "not here, not now" is essential to our ordinarily effortless appreciation that we are perceiving rather than remembering or imagining. In chapter 2, I referred to this in terms of a sense of *presence*. It can be added that intentional states also presuppose a sense of *reality*, meaning a wider-ranging grasp of the distinction between what is and what is not the case. Without any sense of that distinction, we would be insensitive to the differences between intentional states such as imagining and believing. Although such extreme changes in the structure of intentionality are unusual, more subtle alterations in the sense of undergoing one or another type of experience are commonplace. For instance, illness or jet lag can involve an all-enveloping and lingering sense of one's perceptual experience as somehow lacking, not quite right. On other occasions, one might have the fleeting and more localized experience of something as oddly unreal, not quite there. Here is a first-person account of certain kinds of *unreality* experience, offered by a psychologist some years ago:

> In my own experience the feeling of reality rises and falls. ... Lack of sleep reduces the feeling of reality; so too, in even greater degree, does muscular fatigue of the eyes. ... At such times the external world seems to lack solidity: it awakens no interest; people appear as trees walking; thought moves sluggishly; indifference to the consequences of actions ensues; consciousness of self ebbs. ... The haze of an autumn day that makes objects seem far-off, immense, veiled, has the same effect upon mental experience. ... The roar of a big city, the presence of a crowd of people reduces the sense of reality. ...
>
> Not only do sense stimulations bring on a feeling of unreality that extends from the sense world to the world of thought and emotion, but the reverse may happen. Prolonged reading or thinking on philosophical topics has the same results. (Quoted in Landis 1964, 352)

Similar descriptions can be obtained from a wide range of sources. For instance, they are commonplace in literary fiction (Ratcliffe 2015, chap. 2). It is hard to pin down exactly what the relevant phenomenological changes consist of, especially when the world as a whole seems somehow distant, unreal, strange, or unfamiliar. Elsewhere I have referred to the many variants of the sense of reality and belonging as "existential feelings." I have analyzed these feelings in terms of the kinds of salient possibility that are phenomenologically accessible to us, possibilities that are inextricable from a range of felt bodily dispositions (Ratcliffe 2005, 2008, 2015). I do not adopt the term "existential feeling" in this book, partly because my account equally concerns the structure of episodic, content-specific experiences, and partly because my discussion of the interpersonal and social backdrop against which these experiences occur is much broader in scope than my earlier analysis of existential feeling. Even so, the position developed here complements, and can be regarded as an elaboration of, that analysis. It serves to situate existential feeling within a dynamic account of interpersonal and social experience, as well as placing more emphasis on how global changes in the anticipatory structure of experience (in other words, changes in existential feeling) relate to localized intentional experiences. The phenomena addressed here are more extreme than the subtle shifts in the sense of presence and reality we all experience from time to time. In the more usual case, a sense of presence might be somehow lacking from perceptual experience, or one's imaginings might be somehow perception-like. Even so, the nature and extent of that change is not such as to compromise an appreciation of the differences between types of intentional state. While a perceptual experience might be imagination- or memory-like in certain respects, it remains an unambiguously perceptual experience, albeit an unusual one.

Let us start by focusing specifically on the sense of presence in perceptual experience—the sense of something as here, now, and as existing independently of my experience of it. To understand experiences where that sense is to some degree disrupted, we first need to acknowledge that "presence" is not a singular, unitary achievement. Hence alterations in the sense of presence cannot be adequately conceptualized solely in terms of varying degrees, like turning the volume of a radio up or down. In addition, there are qualitative differences to be discerned. The question of what our experiences of presence consist of is seldom addressed.[1] The most detailed, nuanced account I know of is that of Aggernaes (1972, 222–227), who identifies seven pairs of opposing factors that together constitute an experience of something as present or otherwise. There are, he says, "qualities" of sensation/ideation, behavioral relevance/irrelevance, publicness/privateness, objectivity/subjectivity, existence/nonexistence, involuntariness/voluntariness, and, finally, independence/dependence from "a quite unusual mental state in oneself."[2] This list is problematic for several reasons. Without further refinement, it is unclear whether or how certain criteria are to be distinguished from others or how the various criteria relate to each other, a concern that applies to "public," "objective," and "existent" versus "private," "subjective," and "nonexistent." Aggernaes states that the quality of existence involves taking something to persist even when nobody is experiencing it. But is the claim that taking an entity to exist involves taking it to be there when nobody is currently perceiving it, or does existence further involve the appreciation that an entity would endure even if there were no people at all? Depending on which, we might get quite different answers to the questions of whether books, $10 bills, companies, share prices, and currency exchange rates "exist" in the relevant sense. One might also object that this "quality" is merely a combination of two other qualities: objectivity (accessibility to different sense modalities) and publicness (perceptual accessibility to anyone with a typical human perceptual system). A further concern is that the meanings of such terms can shift subtly, depending on their context of use. We might say that something exists only if it does not depend wholly on a person's thought contents, but there is equally a sense in which thought contents exist. Other contrasts are easier to pin down, but too much is left unsaid. For instance, what exactly are qualities of "sensation" and "ideation"? And a quality of dependence/independence from one's own unusual mental state tells us nothing about what the alleged "quality" consists of. It just redescribes the appreciation of presence or reality that we are seeking to account for in appealing to the various other qualities. The contrast between voluntary and involuntary is problematic for other reasons. We might actively imagine something while perceiving something in a more passive way, but an imagining could just as well be passive while a perception involves effortful, exploratory movement. So, even if the distinction can be drawn in a clear-cut way, it remains unclear whether or how it applies to the sense of presence.

The account also suffers from a more general lack of clarity, as it is not stated which combinations of qualities are necessary and sufficient for a sense of presence. To complicate matters, it could be that different combinations of qualities are sufficient for presence, thus implying that there are qualitatively different senses of presence. And perhaps combinations that are sufficient for some entities in some situations are not sufficient for other entities in other situations. Take behavioral relevance, for instance. Not everything that we experience as present is actually or even potentially behaviorally relevant. In many instances, it seems plausible to suggest that a lack of behavioral relevance will impact on the sense of presence. Suppose you suddenly notice what appears to be a train heading toward you at high speed, but you feel no inclination to get out of the way, no behavioral or affective responsiveness at all. This might well contribute to a strange experience of the train as not really there or not fully there. Yet, when you look up at a cloud, at least when there is no threat of rain or of its obscuring the sun, the cloud is surely experienced as "there" in an unproblematic way but at the same time as behaviorally irrelevant.

Despite such concerns, Aggernaes's account remains informative for current purposes, given that it explicitly acknowledges the nonunitary, multifaceted structure of presence and indicates that this structure is amenable to further analysis. It also points to the possibility that some of the contributing factors can come apart and even compete with each other, perhaps generating a sense of presence that is incomplete, ambiguous, or conflicted. We can add that there may be a dimensional aspect to this. Rather than being *either* fully operative *or* fully absent, the various factors might be heightened or diminished, and some might be heightened while others are diminished. Where conflict arises, we can further ask why it is that one factor overrides another, and not vice versa.

These points apply equally to the other modalities of intentionality. Although Aggernaes does not consider intentional states more widely, he could equally have asked questions such as "How do we distinguish remembering from imagining?" and "What constitutes the sense of something as past, the sense that it really happened?" The experiences considered in this chapter do not involve losing the sense of perceiving. Rather, they involve having a sense of perceiving something when one is not perceiving it. However, it will be argued in later chapters that this is partly attributable to a much wider-ranging diminishment in the sense of perceptual presence, which reduces the phenomenological gap between perceiving and imagining, rendering the person more vulnerable to experiences that fall between the two. With that in mind, it is worth noting what Aggernaes has to say about AVHs and the sense of presence. When asked about the qualities of their AVH experiences, not all of his subjects offered the same responses. This would not be surprising, even if their experiences were actually very similar, given potential difficulties involved in interpreting some of the eight criteria. But, in fact, responses were fairly consistent: for all criteria but one, the majority were "positive," rather than "negative" or "doubtful" (or, in the case of the behavioral relevance criterion, "relevant" rather than "irrelevant"). Interestingly, the exception was "publicness," where thirteen responses were positive, two doubtful, and thirty negative. In light of this, we might wonder how to interpret subjects' responses to the other criteria. How could something be experienced as existent, objective, independent of one's own mental states, and yet not public?

There is no straightforward contradiction here, as it is possible in principle for something to be part of the mind-independent world and at the same time perceptually inaccessible to the majority of people or even to all but one of them. There is a distinction between epistemic and ontological privacy: one can have exclusive epistemic access to something the existence of which does not depend on one's own mental states. On one interpretation, then, there is no tension. However, this may not be the right interpretation. Consider an alternative scenario. Suppose subjects recognize that these phenomena are not part of a shared world and do not even experience them as part of that world. Perhaps, in other circumstances, this recognition would suffice to override competing factors that contribute to a sense of presence. What, though, if the relevant experiences arise against the backdrop of a wider sense of isolation and estrangement from others; what if the person's more general appreciation of being embedded in a public world is diminished, such that the experienced contrast between "public" and "private" is lessened? In such a scenario, experiencing something as wholly disconnected from a public world would seem less strange, less out of kilter with other perceptual experiences. With a lessening of the public/private contrast, other aspects of the experience might make a more pronounced contribution than they otherwise would to the sense of perceiving something, rather than, say, imagining it. Of course, these suggestions are highly speculative, but chapters 4 through 6 will further develop and defend a position along such lines. The first step in the argument, which occupies the remainder of this chapter, is to show that the characteristic content of perception and other aspects of the sense of perceiving can come apart. To do so, I turn first to TI and then to AVH.

3.2 Two Interpretations of Thought Insertion

In recent years, TI has received considerable attention from philosophers, but their descriptions of the experience are often ambiguous. Graham (2004, 90) describes it as a matter of "undergoing conscious thoughts and directly knowing what they are about (their content) but failing, in some sense, to experience them as one's own. One fails to self-ascribe." The person experiences the production of thoughts, but somehow experiences them as emanating from somewhere else, usually from a personal source. This is clearly of philosophical interest, as it poses a potential challenge to what Graham (2004, 92) calls the "principle of present-tense ascription immunity," the assumption that having a thought implies having an associated awareness of it as one's own. As Campbell (1999, 609) puts it, TI calls into question the intuition that "you can get it wrong about which psychological state you are in, but you cannot get it right about the psychological state but wrong about whose psychological state it is." Nevertheless, the current consensus seems to be that TI is not, after all, such a threat to entrenched philosophical and everyday assumptions. To diffuse the tension, we can appeal to a distinction between subjectivity and agency (Stephens and Graham 2000) or ownership and agency (Gallagher 2005). In brief, an inserted thought remains "mine" insofar as I experience myself as the subject of that thought, but it is experienced as alien insofar as I am not the agent of it. So long as immunity to error concerns subjectivity/ownership and not agency, it is compatible with the existence of TI.

However, matters are not so simple. There is a distinction to be drawn between experiencing thought contents as alien and experiencing a process of thinking as alien (where the latter experience may or may not encompass thought contents as well). Of course, the phenomenology of thinking—assuming there even is such a thing—is heterogeneous; there is no single *experience of thinking*. Effortful thinking can be contrasted with daydreaming, and coherent trains of thought with incongruous and unanticipated interruptions. But, although thinking is active, effortful, and thematically coherent to varying degrees, an overarching distinction remains between the (admittedly variable) experience of thinking and what is thought, comparable to the distinction between seeing and what is seen, or hearing and what is heard. Which of these does TI involve? The philosophical literature on TI is overly reliant on a few choice examples, which serve in almost every case as the principal or sole basis for discussion. Here are the two most popular ones:

> I look out of the window and I think that the garden looks nice and the grass looks cool, but the thoughts of Eamonn Andrews come into my mind. There are no other thoughts there, only his. ... He treats my mind like a screen and flashes his thoughts into it like you flash a picture. (Mellor 1970, 17)

> Thoughts are put into my mind like "Kill God." It's just like my mind working, but it isn't. They come from this chap, Chris. They are his thoughts. (Frith 1992, 66)

Both descriptions are ambiguous in the relevant respect. Is Chris's *thinking* experienced as occurring in one's own "mind," or, alternatively, the *thought contents* that his thinking produces? Is Eamonn Andrews "flashing" his *thought processes* onto a screen, or just the contents of his thoughts? This lack of clarity persists in many philosophical accounts of TI. For example, Stephens and Graham (2000, 4) state that "[in TI] the experience of thinking is not 'I think' but 'Someone else is putting their thoughts in my head.'" Does one experience the thoughts as having been put in one's head, and thus as having originated elsewhere? Alternatively, does one experience the act of their *being put there*, which would be more akin to experiencing someone else's thinking?[3]

I propose that TI involves experiencing thought contents as alien, rather than thinking. Person B is not mistaken about whether she is the owner and/or agent of her thinking. What happens, rather, is that she experiences *p* as the content of an unfamiliar, quasi-perceptual experience, rather than the content of a thought. The experience is perception-like, insofar as B experiences something as present (rather than as remembered, anticipated, or imagined) and as emanating from elsewhere. However, it remains thought-like, to the extent that the content of the experience continues to resemble that of an act of thinking. To be more specific, it resembles the content of a certain kind of thinking, usually referred to as "inner speech" or, less frequently but perhaps more accurately, "inner dialogue" (Fernyhough 2004; Fernyhough and McCarthy-Jones 2013). So the experience is strange because it involves a thought content but *no* experience of thinking, something that is quite different from experiencing an act of thinking as alien. This interpretation has the advantage of rendering the phenomenon more tractable, given that such confusions are perhaps not so unfamiliar. As noted in chapter 2, we sometimes lack insight into the nature of our emotions: we might take ourselves to be happy for someone when we resent their achievements, or fail to recognize how upset we are about something. Occasionally, we might take ourselves to remember something when we actually imagine it, or feel uncertain about whether we are remembering or imagining it. The point applies equally to dreaming, if it is taken to involve an intentional state of imagining or even a *sui generis* intentional state of dreaming, one that is not recognized as such. So, what we have here is an extreme instance of something familiar, rather than something that is utterly unfamiliar to most of us and difficult to even make sense of—someone else using your experience as a medium in which to think.[4] Nevertheless, as we will see, this interpretation does not render TI mundane or detract from its philosophical interest. My proposal is that TI involves disruption of the modal structure of intentionality, something that is indispensable to the integrity of experience, the sense of self, and the ability to distinguish self from nonself.

What grounds are there for adopting the content-interpretation? There is no evidence in the TI literature for the view that it concerns thinking rather than thought content; stock examples are compatible with both interpretations. However, there is also a positive case to be made for the content view. To make that case, I compare TI to AVH, a comparison that turns out to be mutually illuminating.

3.3 Verbal Hallucinations and Inserted Thoughts

If one accepts (a) that hallucinations are perceptual experiences that arise in the absence of appropriate external stimuli, and (b) that TI involves an alienated *act* of thinking, then AVH and TI turn out to be very different. While AVH involves experiencing p in the absence of p, TI involves thinking that p but experiencing one's thinking as someone else's. So, while AVH consists in a familiar kind of experience (albeit a nonveridical one), TI involves an experience that is intrinsically anomalous and strange: having a thought process that one does not think. Even if we set aside (a) and instead emphasize the widespread view that AVHs involve confusing one's own inner state—usually, one's own "inner speech"—with externally directed perception, the two phenomena remain distinct. An inner speech approach is compatible with (a), if it is accepted that the resulting experience is much like or even indistinguishable from an auditory verbal perception, but not if an experience of misplaced inner speech is taken to be very different from veridical auditory perception. Either way, though, TI differs from AVH, as it involves correctly identifying a type of intentional state (an act of thinking) but wrongly attributing a state of that type to a person other than oneself, rather than mistaking one type of intentional state (thinking in inner speech) for another (perceiving).

Given this difference, it is puzzling that various authors have sought to account for both experiences in the same way, often by appealing to an agency–ownership distinction. Some have further suggested that AVH and TI are actually different descriptions of the same phenomenon, at least in some instances of AVH (e.g., Langland-Hassan 2008, 373). A content-interpretation of TI makes clear how this could indeed be so. If TI involves experiencing thought contents as (a) present, and (b) emanating from elsewhere, then it shares these characteristics with perceptual experiences. So it could equally be described in terms of a perception with an unfamiliar kind of content. Conversely, if AVH content is not perceived to originate in a localized external source and does not have the full range of auditory properties, it could equally be described in terms of experiencing an alien thought.

Nevertheless, it would be a mistake to simply identify AVH with TI, as AVHs are phenomenologically diverse. That they are heterogeneous is hardly controversial and has long been recognized. Consider the following remarks from Jaspers' *General Psychopathology*:

> We often find "voices" as well, the "invisible" people who shout all kinds of things at the patient, ask him questions and abuse him or order him about. As to content, this may consist of single words or whole sentences; there may be a single voice or a whole jumble of voices; it may be an orderly conversation between the voices themselves or between them and the patient. They may be women's, children's or men's voices, the voices of acquaintances or unknown people, or quite undefinable human voices. Curses may be uttered, actions of the patient may be commented on or there may be meaningless words, empty repetitions. Sometimes the patient hears his own thoughts spoken aloud. (1963, 73)

More recent accounts have provided specific inventories of variables. These include volume, auditory qualities (such as accent), number of voices, degree of personification, emotional tone, thematic content, mode of address (second- or third-person), level of control over voices, level of distress associated with them, and the presence or absence of hallucinations in other modalities. Distinctions can also be drawn between AVHs that consist of commands, advice, comments, and/or abuse. The various differences and commonalities between these experiences do not seem to track established diagnostic categories in a reliable way (e.g., Nayani and David 1996; Larøi 2006; McCarthy-Jones et al. 2014). Hence some have suggested that subcategories of AVH should be identified in order to acknowledge differences between types of experience that syndrome-based diagnostic categories are insensitive to, differences that reflect the involvement of different causal mechanisms (e.g., Jones 2010).

It might be objected that any attempt to identify TI with AVH is at odds with the fact that AVHs have auditory properties, which are experienced as originating in specific locations that are physically external to the subject (e.g., Wu 2012). In contrast, TI is experienced as neither auditory nor as emanating from the external environment; it is *alien* in a quite different and less straightforward way. However, there are significant difficulties involved in interpreting statements along the lines of "I hear a voice," as well as more specific descriptions of the relevant experiences. A detailed and insightful discussion of these difficulties (which are seldom acknowledged in the clinical literature) is offered by Sarbin (1967). He takes it as given that AVHs are "imaginings" of one or another kind. But, rather than asking why there might be a first-person confusion between imagining and perceiving, he places the emphasis on why an interpreter might construe an imagining, reported in whatever way, as a nonveridical perceptual experience:

> What are the antecedent and concurrent conditions that lead a person publicly to report his imaginings in such a way as to lead a psychologist, psychiatrist, or other professional to designate the described imagining as an hallucination? (1967, 363)

Sarbin is critical of a tendency to assume that first-person reports are straightforward, easy-to-interpret descriptions of experience, and notes that various nonphenomenological factors influence the linguistic content of first-person reports. For instance, whether or not a person qualifies his testimony with "as if" depends not just on his ability to recognize an experience as distinct from a veridical perception but also on his linguistic abilities, which vary considerably depending on whether he is well educated, a native or nonnative speaker, an adult, or a child. Sarbin adds that, in certain contexts, such as that of reading a poem, the interpreter is expected to supply the "as-if." Furthermore, words such as "real" and "unreal" are used in a range of ways and therefore pose interpretive challenges: the "nonidentity of meaning of 'real' for the diagnoser and the patient reflects some of the problems in the employment of the words real and reality" (Sarbin 1967, 377).[5] For instance, "unreal" could mean "not a genuine instance of something" or "nonexistent," and it can be added that the meaning of "nonexistent" is itself far from transparent. Sarbin also raises concerns about the term "hallucination," which he takes to be "pejorative" and "generally applied to the reported imaginings of people already considered degraded" (1967, 379). If that is right, then we run the risk of adopting an uncharitable interpretive stance from the outset, of assuming a lack of first-person insight and descriptive ability, rather than being sensitive to the subtleties and nuances of first-person descriptions that often point to something far less straightforward than orthodox hallucination.

There is a particular linguistic challenge involved in attempting to convey kinds of intentionality that may be wholly unfamiliar to an interlocutor, experiences that lie somewhere between perceiving and thinking, or between imagining and believing.[6] Such experiences can involve a range of subtle tensions between various factors that more usually contribute, in a cohesive, unproblematic way, to the sense of being in a given intentional state. Wide-ranging disturbances of interpersonal experience also need to be taken into consideration by the interpreter. If someone experiences everyone else as potentially hostile, distant, or inconsequential, then her ability and willingness to communicate will no doubt be affected. Furthermore, if her sense of the distinction between what is and is not the case has been eroded, she cannot be interpreted as making straightforward claims concerning what is and is not the case, of a kind that we would more usually take for granted. So, what appears to be a straightforward communicative utterance might turn out not to be. When it comes to interpreting first-person reports, one implication of this is that a clear line cannot be drawn between metaphor and literal utterance. Consider the following:

> Once more my playmate became strangely transformed and, with an excited laugh, once more I cried out, "Stop, Alice, I'm afraid of you; you're a lion!" But actually, I didn't see a lion at all: it was only an attempt to describe the enlarging image of my friend and the fact that I didn't recognize her. (Sechehaye 1970, 23)

The utterance "you're a lion" could be taken to express an orthodox hallucination, a false belief, or both. But it is actually an attempt to express or convey an unusual experience in terms of something more specific that is, in some respects, isomorphic with it. In both cases, there is the sense that something large, predatory, powerful, and frightening is fast approaching. As noted earlier, the sense of presence and reality is multifaceted. Hence experiences such as this should not be assumed to involve something appearing as straightforwardly present. In this case, it may be more accurate to say that there is a vague, ambivalent sense of the presence of a lion or something like a lion, rather than a straightforward—albeit unpleasant—perceptual experience of another person.

Despite these concerns, I concede that some AVHs resemble (to varying degrees) veridical auditory perceptual experiences. Many accounts of AVHs emphasize such experiences. For example, Garrett and Silva (2003, 445) endorse the view that "the subjective quality of sensation" is a "near-universal feature of auditory hallucinations," while Wu (2012, 90) premises his model of AVHs on the fact that they "*sound* like voices." Nevertheless, it is generally conceded that there are differences in perceived origin. Some AVHs are experienced as originating in specific, external locations, while others seem to come from within the head, within one's bodily boundaries, or from nowhere in particular. For example, David (1994, 285) observes that most but not all subjects experience voices as arising "inside the head," while Nayani and David (1996) report that 49 percent of their subjects heard voices through their ears, 38 percent internally, and 12 percent in both ways. The auditory element seems to vary considerably in the internal cases. Leudar et al. (1997, 888–889) state that 71 percent of their subjects heard only internal voices, 18 percent heard voices "through their ears," and 11 percent heard both. In all cases, though, the voice was "verbal" and had "phenomenal properties like hearing another person speaking." Hence they suggest that, regardless of their perceived origins, AVHs are "very much like hearing other people speak." However, others describe AVHs as predominantly internal and as *lacking* in auditory properties. Stephens and Graham (2000) argue at length that most "voice-hearers" do not actually hear voices at all; Frith (1992, 73) maintains that an AVH can involve something more abstract than hearing a voice, "an experience of receiving a communication without any sensory component"; and Moritz and Larøi

(2008, 98, 104) suggest that the term "voice-hearing" may well be a misnomer, an "inaccurate term to express that their cognitions are *not their own*."

Of course, we should proceed with caution here, as different first-person descriptions do not imply different experiences, while similar descriptions may eclipse important phenomenological differences. But let us accept that at least some of those experiences categorized as AVHs, perhaps the majority, are experienced as internal in origin and lacking in some or even all auditory qualities. As Stephens and Graham (2000, 35) remark, "voices are not, in general, experienced as audition-like. Even when voices involve auditory hallucination, one may plausibly question whether their auditory or audition-like character explains their alien quality." The question thus arises of why internal, nonauditory AVHs are experienced as alien at all, as emanating from elsewhere. In the external case, the "hallucinatory" character of the experience can plausibly be accounted for in terms of something seeming to be both physically external and auditory in nature. However, as internal AVHs differ in both location and sensory perceptual character, they cannot be alien or external in the same way.

For current purposes, a broad distinction between external, audition-like AVHs and internal, nonauditory experiences will prove informative, serving to contrast quite different kinds of experience that also arise in different ways. As we will see in the next chapter, this is not to be identified with a distinction between *hallucinations* and *pseudo-hallucinations*. And it is not to be conceived of as a clear-cut distinction, as it allows for in-between cases. I further acknowledge that the category of unambiguously *internal* AVHs accommodates different kinds of experience, kinds that vary in their auditory qualities. But what unites the "internal" cases is that they consist of disturbances of the modal structure of intentionality and fall somewhere between familiar intentional state categories. External, audition-like AVHs do not.

The remainder of this chapter focuses on internal AVHs, with the aims of showing that (a) the same experience can be described in terms of either AVH or TI, and (b) the fact that it can be described in both these ways aids us in interpreting it: what must it be, such that TI and AVH descriptions both apply to it? My discussion focuses on some first-person accounts, which were obtained via an Internet questionnaire study I conducted in cooperation with colleagues. Participants were invited to provide open-ended, free-text responses to questions that included "Please try to describe your voice(s) and/or voice-like experiences," "How, if at all, are these experiences different from hearing the voice of someone who is present in the room?" and "What kinds of moods or emotions are associated with your voices?" All respondents quoted here had psychiatric diagnoses. All numbered quotations that appear in this and later chapters were obtained via the study.[7]

Before considering some of these testimonies, I should make clear *how* they are to be used here. I rely on them primarily for the purpose of illustration, in much the same way that a philosopher might quote from published autobiographies or from first-person descriptions found in the clinical literature. So I do not treat the questionnaire as a scientific study in its own right. And I do not rely on it as my primary source of evidence for the existence of certain kinds of experience. The first-person accounts considered here are consistent with what numerous published studies classify as AVHs (which is not, of course, to suggest that all published studies categorize exactly the same range of phenomena as AVHs). Some of these testimonies also help to exemplify the interpretive issues raised earlier. For example, one respondent writes, "the voices were intrusive and alien to me, and I was certain they were coming from outside of me, even though I did not hear them aurally but experienced them in my head" (9). The way the word "outside" is used here suggests that we should not be too hasty in classifying a given experience as "internal" or "external." Here, the "voices" are not experienced as external to the subject but as internal to the head. However, they are also experienced as having originated from elsewhere. So there is an ambiguity in talk of externality; an experience of *something as outside* is to be distinguished from an experience of *something inside that seems to have come from elsewhere*. More generally, these testimonies tend not to consist of straightforward pronouncements about the nature of experience; they are hesitant and ambivalent, sometimes conceding that some or all of the words used to describe an experience are inadequate to the task: "It sounds mundane but it's impossible to understand what it was like from the words alone" (4). Hence the phenomenology cannot simply be read off first-person reports. Rather, testimonies such as these offer important clues, pointing to new directions we might follow in seeking to better understand them. They draw attention to possibilities that more cursory references to the various qualities of voices cannot. More specifically, they serve to illustrate how an emphasis on the modalities of intentionality can shed light on the nature of otherwise puzzling experiences that people struggle to describe.[8]

Although communicating and interpreting AVH experiences is no simple matter, the existence of a substantial difference between internal and external AVHs can be conveyed in a fairly straightforward way by those who experience both types. Even if a person struggles to describe her internal and her external AVHs, what she can still do is explicitly contrast them: whatever experiences *x* and *y* might consist of, *x* is not the same as *y*. And, although internal AVHs are not always said to be wholly bereft of auditory properties, first-person accounts indicate that they are quite different from audition-like AVHs that seem to originate in the external environment:

"They are inside my head. I do sometimes hear voices that are indistinguishable, but it's shorter and much less frequent." (15)

"There are two kinds—one indistinguishable from actual voices or noises (I hear them like physical noises, and only the point of origin (for voices) or checking with other people who are present (for sounds) lets me know when they aren't actually real. The second is like hearing someone else's voice in my head, generally saying something that doesn't 'sound' like my own thoughts or interior monologue." (17)

"The voice is inside my head at times, appears to come from within my brain. But at other times, specifically when my name is called, it seems that it comes from outside, almost like someone is trying to catch my attention." (27)

Now, suppose the sensory qualities of internal AVHs do not differ from those of certain thought contents. What we would have is a perception-like experience of thought content, an unfamiliar kind of experience that could be communicated in either of two ways:

I experience content *p* as a thought content that I did not think.

I experience content *p* as a perceptual content, but one that is anomalous in lacking certain perceptual properties.

And this is exactly what we find. Internal AVHs are not experiences of a familiar kind that are regarded as strange only because they turn out to be nonveridical. Like TI, they are intrinsically strange. They involve an unfamiliar kind of *perception-like* intentional state, a view that is consistent with the observation that people frequently struggle to convey them. These experiences are sometimes said to be "almost like" something else; it is "as though" something were the case. For instance, they might be described as akin to telepathy:

"The commentary and the violent voices I heard as though someone was talking to me inside my brain, but not my own thoughts. Almost like how telepathy would sound if it were real. I don't know how else to explain it." (4)

"…There are things I 'hear' that aren't as much like truly hearing a voice or voices. … Instead, these are more like telepathy or hearing without hearing exactly, but knowing that content has been exchanged and feeling that happen." (7)

"Telepathic conversations between me and most other people." (8)

"The best way to describe it is telepathy, in different grades of vividness, from bearable to intrusive." (33)

It might be objected that this conflicts with the observation that even internal AVHs are usually reported in terms of audition, rather than other kinds of perceptual experience. However, for most people, information of the relevant kind is usually received via auditory channels, at least in the absence of visual stimuli such as reading materials. So, even when bereft of the usual sensory qualities, it lends itself to description in those terms. Furthermore, talk of hearing and sounds is often qualified, and auditory terms may appear in scare quotes (as in 7 above). How, we might ask, should "sound" be interpreted when someone says that the "voices don't sound like my thoughts" (3)? Could the same experience just as well be described in terms of "voices" not *feeling* like one's thoughts, or their being incongruous in some other way? As for talk of "loudness," this seems in some cases to convey a kind of affective intrusiveness: "My thoughts aren't as loud, nor do they usually intrude and affect how I feel" (21). In distracting from other things and demanding attention, it is perhaps more like the intensity of a pain than the volume of a noise.

Furthermore, these experiences are not invariably described in auditory terms. An internal AVH that lacks auditory properties might also be compared to an experience of reading, but in the absence of any perceived text:

"When you read a book, you hear it in the voice of the author or the narrator, but you know that voice isn't yours. It's a lot like that." (5)

"Other times, I have 'seen voices' in the sense that the message or phrase or voice came across my mind's eye in literal typographic form." (7)

"… The voice seems partly real, but at the same time distorted. It can also appear as a face or a text. I cannot really describe the sound." (Patient quoted by Henriksen, Raballo, and Parnas 2015, 167)

So it would seem that "hearing a voice" is sometimes a synonym for the sense of receiving a meaningful, linguistic content, but without the kinds of sensory experience that this more usually involves. Karlsson (2008, 368–369) observes that some people do not or cannot "distinguish between their voices, sights, visions, touches and smells," and that "voice" serves as a "generic term" for all of them. The common theme is not that something is "heard" in a literal way, but that it seems to have originated elsewhere. This is consistent with Hoffman et al. (2008), who maintain that, when people distinguish their voices from ordinary linguistic thoughts, the sense of non-self-origin has a more central role to play than any associated auditory properties. In other words, the content is experienced in a perception-like way; there is a sense, the nature of which remains to be clarified, of receiving something from elsewhere, a sense that does not depend on a specific type of sensory-perceptual content.[9]

The view that some internal AVHs do not have specifically auditory qualities is complemented by reports of voices in congenitally deaf subjects. Atkinson (2006) observes that, when deaf "voice-hearers" are questioned about auditory properties such as pitch or volume, questions are often met with a "disdainful response." She suggests that talk of "voices" in this context instead conveys the experience of receiving a message or communication and recognizing its linguistic content. However, she also acknowledges the potential involvement of visual imagery and/or motor perception, pointing to a degree of heterogeneity.[10]

Given all of this, the term "AVH," although frequently used to refer to the kinds of experience addressed here, is quite clearly misleading. Some of these experiences are not "auditory" in any informative sense of the term. Hence, at this point, and for the remainder of the book, I will withdraw the "A" and refer instead to *verbal hallucinations* (hereafter, VHs). However, my doing so should not be taken to imply that the "V" and the "H" are themselves unproblematic.

Having seen that some internal or nonlocalized VHs are not auditory and instead involve a sense of receiving some kind of meaningful content from elsewhere, we can also see how VH and TI can be descriptions of a common experience. A perception-like experience with a thought-like content could be described in either way. That this is indeed the case is best illustrated by first-person accounts that describe the same experiences in terms of both voices and inserted thoughts, or blur the boundary between the two types of description:

"The voice inside my head sounds nothing like a real person talking to me, but rather like another person's thoughts in my head." (1)

"The voices inside my head are like thoughts, only they are not my own." (2)

"... It definitely sounds like it is from inside my head. It's at some kind of border between thinking and hearing." (18)

"The voice is not strictly audible, does not turn my head toward a speaker, there is no real speaker, just a thinker who can make their thought known to me. I hear but I don't hear with my ears." (30)

"A voice-hearing experience is more like hearing thoughts." (37)

Although one might quarrel over the precise nature of the experiences that people are trying to describe here, what such accounts do make clear is that a singular experience of whatever kind *is* sometimes described in both ways, as an audition-like, perceptual experience with an unfamiliar content and as a thought content that is experienced in an odd, perception-like way. Having got that far, we can go on to ask what the relevant experience could be like, such that it is amenable to both descriptions. And the most plausible answer is that it involves a perception-like experience of something that continues to resemble, in some respects, the content of a thought or of a certain kind of thought. The interchangeability of TI and VH descriptions thus constitutes evidence in support of the content-interpretation of TI. People *do* describe the same experience in terms of perceiving that *p* and experiencing the thought that *p* as alien. By postulating an unfamiliar kind of experience that falls somewhere in between thinking and perceiving, we can make sense of such reports. Hence, in the absence of conflicting evidence that supports the "alienated thinking" view of TI, the content-interpretation is to be preferred.

I concede that some internal VHs are likely to have certain auditory or audition-like properties, and thus further lend themselves to description in terms of hearing voices. Even so, this need not conflict with the claim that they are TI under another description. The view that thought is sometimes or always *wholly* bereft of auditory properties is far from uncontroversial. Most approaches to VHs take them to involve misattributed "inner speech" rather than simply "thought," where inner speech is only one form that our thoughts can take. And Hoffman (1986), among others, suggests that inner speech includes "auditory imagery." Furthermore, as will become clearer in later chapters, internal VHs are most likely not restricted to perception-like experiences of inner speech. They can instead involve the erosion of phenomenological boundaries between perception and imagination (of one or another kind) or perception and memory, and auditory properties may be more pronounced in some of these cases. There is also plausibly a degree of variation in how inner speech or inner dialogue is more usually experienced; some may experience it in a more audition-like way than others. A further complication is that, in taking internal VHs to be perception-like, we should not assume an exclusive resemblance to sensory perceptions of the external environment. They are experienced as falling within one's bodily boundaries and, in this respect, they more closely resemble interoception or proprioception. But, given that meaningful communications are ordinarily received from sources external to the body, they differ from bodily experiences as well. This further emphasizes the point that VH/TI involves an unusual kind of experience, something that is not quite like thinking, externally directed perception, or perception of bodily states.[11]

3.4 An Unfamiliar Kind of Intentionality

What we have here is a way of experiencing, a kind of intentionality, that does not fit into established categories. It is not a matter of having an experience that is indistinguishable from or much like one of perceiving, believing, remembering, or imagining. But neither should it be regarded simply as an "in-between" state, which blurs the boundaries between two kinds of intentionality and can be placed somewhere on a spectrum. Rather, aspects of one kind of experience are paired with the sense of having another kind of experience. And neither sense nor content is left wholly intact and unambiguous, experienced exactly as it would be in the context of an unproblematic pairing. The experience is intrinsically strange. Even if a sense of its being a perceptual experience predominates, it is also recognized as a peculiar kind of perception, different from the more familiar kinds of sensory experience that occur alongside it.

My discussion is thus consistent with observations of "double-bookkeeping" in people with hallucinations and/or delusions, a phenomenon described by Bleuler (1950) in terms of conflicting attitudes that are simultaneously adopted in relation to some content. For instance, a patient might laugh at something that she claims at the same time to firmly believe. This tension also applies to the relationship between belief content and action: "Kings and Emperors, Popes, and Redeemers engage, for the most part, in quite banal work, provided they still have any energy at all for activity" (129). Bleuler construes this in terms of two things running in parallel but without “interfering with each other”; there is a “double registration” or “double orientation” (378). More recently, this kind of experience has been addressed in the context of phenomenological psychopathology. For instance, Sass (1994, 3) describes double-bookkeeping as follows:

> Many schizophrenic patients seem to experience their delusions and hallucinations as having a special quality or feel that sets these apart from their “real” beliefs and perceptions. ... Indeed, such patients often seem to have a surprising, and rather disconcerting, kind of insight into their own condition.[12]

Similarly, van den Berg (1982, 105) observes that psychiatric patients usually know “full well the difference in nature between their hallucinations and their perceptions.” Voices, he writes, are often given a “special name,” in virtue of their having a “recognizable character of their own which distinguishes them from *perception* and also from *imagination*.” What we have is something that resembles, in certain respects, two different kinds of intentional state, while remaining phenomenologically distinguishable from both of them. As Straus (1958, 166) writes, “the voices are heard, they are acoustic phenomena, but they are also different enough to contrast with all else that is audible. The mode of their reception is rather a being-affected, similar to hearing.” They are, as he puts it, “quasi-acoustic.” It is this *being-affected* that I seek to address. The content of an experience may continue to resemble that of a thought, but it somehow *affects* one in a way more like that of a perception. In other words, one has something of the *sense of perceiving* and perhaps even the sense of perceiving through one or another sensory modality. Consider the following description:

> I did not hear them as I heard real cries uttered by real people. The noises, localized on the right side, drove me to stop up my ears. But I readily distinguished them from the noises of reality. I heard them without hearing them, and recognized that they arose within me. (Sechehaye 1970, 59)

Reference to “hearing without hearing” serves to emphasize the seemingly paradoxical nature of the experience. There is a sense of hearing, but with little or nothing of the associated content. However, “readily distinguishing” such experiences from the “noises of reality” also indicates that they arise against the backdrop of a modal structure that remains to some degree intact. One can still hear and think in more familiar ways, distinguish thinking from hearing, and distinguish both from anomalous experiences that might be described in terms of thought or audition. This is consistent with the finding that the majority of clinical and nonclinical voice-hearers are able to distinguish their "voices" from veridical auditory perceptions and also from thoughts (Moritz and Larøi 2008; Hoffman et al. 2008). Indeed, Leudar et al. (1997, 889) report that none of their subjects "systematically confused the voices with other people speaking—they know when they are 'hallucinating.'"

VH/TI experiences can take the form of *occasional* interruptions, occurring against the backdrop of a more generally unproblematic sense of the modalities of intentionality. However, they can also be more enduring, a near constant accompaniment to more typical experiences of thinking and perceiving. In both scenarios, the fact that VH/TI is distinguishable from more familiar forms of experience does not imply that a wider-ranging sense of the modalities of intentionality remains wholly intact. It could be that VH/TI involves a particularly pronounced manifestation of a much more encompassing disturbance in the modal structure of experience. In other words, none of the person's beliefs, memories, thoughts, and imaginings involve quite the same kind of intentional experience that they previously did. This phenomenological change renders her vulnerable to more pronounced disruptions that are temporally localized and/or limited to certain thematic contents. Chapters 5 and 6 will develop an account along these lines.

One might wonder how all of this relates to the widespread view that TI is a *delusion*. It cannot simply be that VH is a hallucination and TI a delusion, as they can amount to different descriptions of a common phenomenon. On one account, the difference is just a matter of whether or not the person comes to regard her experience as veridical. It feels *as if* the content comes from elsewhere, but whether or not this either constitutes or gives rise to a delusion depends on whether or not she accepts that it comes from elsewhere, whether she *endorses* the content. It is debatable whether a sense of the content's coming from a personal source, sometimes a specific individual, is intrinsic to the experience or whether it involves the embellishment of a core experience. However, the latter is plausible, given that VHs are personified to varying degrees (Bell 2013). And, as noted by Hoerl (2001, 189), patients "seem much more unequivocal that the thoughts in question do not belong to them than they are about possible ways in which others might be implicated in their occurrence." A high degree of personification is plausibly linked to delusion formation, given that it involves an increasingly elaborate attempt to *make sense of* the experience in terms of another agent, who may have specific characteristics and intentions.

In seeking to understand the personification process, we should again consider the modal structure of intentionality. Suppose a person starts to imagine personalities behind his VH experiences, and gradually integrates these experiences into a coherent narrative, involving one or more characters. If the wider modal structure of intentionality is disrupted, he might not experience the result as an unambiguous work of imagination. So an underlying disturbance of intentionality that led to the "voice" in the first place could also contribute to an increasing sense of its specificity and reality. We can thus see how a "hallucination" might evolve into a "delusion." Nevertheless, neither term is really adequate to the experience. It is not that one first takes something to be "here, now," in an unproblematic way, given that the relevant experience is unlike ordinary sensory experiences. Furthermore, where a more encompassing sense of reality has been altered, one does not simply accept or reject the deliverances of experience in the form of beliefs, given that one no longer distinguishes what is the case from what is not the case, or what is "here, now" from what is "not here, now," in the way one once did. Hallucination and delusion therefore involve kinds of intentionality that differ from perception and belief.

Despite this complication, it is easy enough to maintain a rough distinction, along conventional lines, between a hallucination and a delusion of VH/TI. Both may be ambivalent in certain respects, different from everyday perceptions and beliefs, but the delusional case at least involves *some kind of acceptance* that the experiential content emanates from elsewhere, from a personal source that can be variably specific in nature. This acceptance is also oddly recalcitrant to revision, in a way that *taking something to be the case* is more usually not. If that much is accepted, then it also seems plausible to suggest that a TI description of the experience lends itself to a delusional interpretation more so than a VH description. Saying that one "hears a voice" serves to express an anomalous experience but does not operate as an explanation of it (unless one further insists that the experience is a veridical one). However, TI includes more specific reference to causes. So it is less likely to be used as a noncommittal description of an experience, and more likely to operate as an explanation or interpretation: "I have the anómalous experience *because* B is inserting thoughts in my head." That said, the same phenomenon could equally be construed in terms of "other people really speaking in my head," and a TI description does not *imply* endorsement of a TI explanation. So it would be wrong to insist that TI descriptions invariably involve a greater degree of acceptance than VH descriptions. Chapter 6 will further problematize the delusion–hallucination distinction, through a consideration of wider-ranging disturbances in the modal structure of experience. In so doing, it will also address the kind of *certainty* that attaches to delusional beliefs, and show how it is inextricable from the way in which a person experiences and relates to others in general.

3.5 Agency and Ownership

As noted earlier in this chapter, one way to make sense of TI without accepting that it involves a radical error of identification or a weakening of the self–world boundary is to distinguish between experiences of *subjectivity* and *agency* (Stephens and Graham 2000) or *ownership* and *agency* (Gallagher 2005). The claim is that we experience ourselves as the owners of our thoughts; they arise *within* the boundaries of our subjectivity. We also experience ourselves as the agents of our thoughts; we *think them*. An inserted thought is experienced as produced by another agency, one that uses one's own mind as a medium in which to think. So one owns the thought but is not the agent behind it. I will conclude the chapter by suggesting that this distinction does not illuminate the nature of TI (although I do not seek to reject the distinction outright; it may well be informative in other contexts), and showing how my approach dispenses with the need for talk of retaining ownership and losing agency.

The agency–ownership distinction could be applied to an intentional state, its content, or both: I am the agent and/or owner of intentional state *x* and/or its content *p*. In one sense, experienced ownership of an intentional state implies ownership of its content. In short, if I experience myself as perceiving, then I experience myself as having a perception of something. And, if I experience myself as thinking, then I experience myself as having a thought about something. Even in the case of TI, one takes oneself to be having an experience with some content. What is anomalous is not that the experiential content is disowned but that it is taken to be non-self-generated, when contents of that kind are more usually self-generated. However, there is another sense in which one does *not* take oneself to own what is experienced. Bortolotti and Broome (2009, 208) ask whether you can really be said to own something that you feel so "radically alienated" from.[13] And the answer is that you do not experience yourself as owning the inserted *thought* any more than you experience yourself as owning a chair in virtue of looking at it (where "ownership" is understood in terms of something's falling within one's psychological boundaries). What you *do* own, however, is an experience of that thought content, an experience of its originating from elsewhere. By analogy, when you hear someone say "I hate you," you have an experience that includes the content "I hate you," a content that you might be said to "own." But, just as the experience of a chair can be distinguished from the actual chair, experience of the utterance can be distinguished from the actual utterance. In both cases, there is a sense that what one experiences is non-self-produced. This is all that talk of continued ownership conveys: one has an experience of *p*, but it is an experience of *p*'s originating in an external source. "I own *p*" is just another way of saying "I am not the agent that produced *p*; I merely experience *p*." It therefore adds nothing to the view that TI involves a lack of experienced agency.[14]

Should we just say, then, that TI involves experiencing content *p* with no associated sense of agency, the result being a perception-like experience? That's not very helpful either. Perception, like thought, can involve a sense of agency; it is not a wholly passive process. We actively look, we listen, we interact with our surroundings, and we physically manipulate objects in order to reveal their hidden features. As various enactivist approaches to perception have emphasized, perception is a matter of exploratory activity (e.g., Noë 2004). And we need not endorse one or another enactivist position in order to accept the less committal view that perceptual experience involves varying degree of agency, rather than passive receipt of sensory information. Of course, it should be added that we do not experience ourselves as wholly responsible for the *contents* of our perceptions. Whatever theory of perception might be adopted, it seems fair to say that we experience the contents of our perceptions as largely determined by things external to ourselves. So perceptual experience might involve some sense of agency, but we do not attribute our perceptual contents to our own agency. Whether or not you see a table depends on where you turn your head, but it is the presence of a table that ensures you see a table and not a rose bush when you do turn your head in a given direction. Perceptual contents are experienced as environmentally dependent in this way whereas thought contents are not. Hence the claim needs to be more specific: although perceiving and thinking can both involve a sense of agency, thought *contents* are experienced as dependent on our agency to a degree or in a way that perceptual contents are not.

However, it is not at all clear what the relevant *experience of agency* is supposed to consist of or when it is present. The experience of "having the thought that *p*" is not a singular one, and encompasses various cases that seem to involve little or no awareness of agency. One might struggle to think through a philosophical problem and, in the process, experience a coherent stream of thought as self-generated and effortful. But the song that suddenly, unexpectedly, and effortlessly pops into one's head is quite different, as are occasional and uncomfortable thoughts that do not cohere with one's own values, such as "Why not punch him on the nose to see how he reacts?" Such thoughts can arise unannounced and even be surprising, but this need not interfere their being experienced as unambiguous instances of thought. More generally, intentional states are experienced with varying degrees of agency. You might try to remember something or actively think through the details of a past situation, piecing the various events together in a coherent way. Alternatively, you might remember something in a much more passive, spontaneous way, the content of which has little bearing on your current concerns. The point similarly applies to imagining. Ordinarily at least, the degree of activity or passivity associated with the arrival of an experiential content has little or no bearing on your prereflective appreciation of it as a content of perception, imagination, memory, or current inner speech. So it is not clear why the *phenomenological* difference between having the thought that *p* and having an experience of *p* as emanating from elsewhere should be attributable to the presence or absence of a sense of agency. All we have so far is this: when you experience an intentional state of type *x*, the content of *x* is experienced as self-produced, and when you experience an intentional state of type *y*, the content of *y* is experienced as non-self-produced.

Of course, matters hinge on what we take a sense of agency to consist of. Given that the kinds of intentional state I am concerned with here can all involve varying degrees of effort, intention, and conscious anticipation, "agency" could be taken to refer to something else instead. But the most plausible candidate is just the sense that an experiential content is self- rather than non-self-produced, whatever that sense might consist of. And this just amounts to a redescription of the phenomenon we are seeking to account for. In TI, a thought content is experienced in a perception-like way. In other words, it is experienced as having arisen from elsewhere, as non-self-produced. To understand the nature of this experience, we need to address what the senses of perceiving and thinking actually consist of, and show how a sense of perceiving might come to be associated with a thought content. Couching this in terms of agency involves either restating the problem in such a way as to leave the relevant phenomenology wholly unclear, or appealing to a kind of agency-experience that is intramodally variable, shared by different modalities of intentionality, and does not distinguish the sense of thinking something from the sense of perceiving something.[15]

Where nonlocalized changes in the modal structure of intentionality are concerned, I am more sympathetic to the view that something along the lines of a diminished sense of agency is implicated. As chapters 4, 5, and 6 will argue, an all-enveloping experience of passivity and disengagement from the social world can diminish a person's general grasp of the distinction between things being or not being present or the case. This then renders her vulnerable to more localized anomalous experiences, including VH/TI. Even so, it remains unhelpful to claim that these experiences arise due to the loss of an episodic awareness of agency that more usually contributes to an experience of thinking and serves to identify it as such.

I allow that experiences of agency do at least contribute to the *attitudinal* phenomenology of intentional states. Nevertheless, they are not responsible for the sense of being in one or another type of intentional state. The prereflective, wholly unproblematic appreciation of being in an intentional state of whatever type is compatible with varying degrees of experienced agency. Furthermore, it is not clear that there is anything more to the specifically *attitudinal* phenomenology of an intentional state. Perhaps there is but, even if so, it is not responsible for the sense of being in one kind of intentional state rather than another. As will become clear in chapter 5, the principal constituents of sense do not conform to a distinction between attitude and content. Experiential content is also a contributing factor. In cases of anomalous experience, content can come into conflict with these other constituents and is sometimes overridden by them (as in the case of VH/TI). But this gives us all we need to account for the sense of being in a given type of intentional state. There is no role left for an additional, exclusively attitudinal ingredient to play.

To summarize, chapter 2 raised the possibility that the sense of being in a given type of intentional state can be accounted for in a simple way, by appealing to type-specific experiential content. However, in this chapter, we have seen that an appeal to characteristic experiential content is inadequate, and cannot account for the phenomenology of VH/TI. The difference between thinking that *p* and perceiving that *p* cannot be wholly attributable to different contents, as VH/TI involves something that resembles thought content but at the same time seems to come from elsewhere. Furthermore, appealing to the presence or absence of a sense of agency does not serve to illuminate the phenomenon.

Chapter 4 will develop an account of how such experiences come about and what they consist of, an account that does not appeal to the sense of agency. Being in a perception-like relationship to thought contents is sometimes described in terms of a *feeling* of their coming from elsewhere: "They do not feel as if I thought them the way normal thoughts do. They came from elsewhere, be it some other mind or some other force. ... In general the main identifier of voice-hearing, or other things that aren't my own thoughts, is simply that they do not feel as if they came from me" (7). It is this feeling that I seek to clarify. I will argue that it centrally involves a change in the *anticipatory* structure of experience, and that this structure makes a substantial contribution to the sense of being in one or another type of intentional state.

4 Voices of Anxiety

In the previous chapter, I argued that VHs (verbal hallucinations), of the kind that can also be described in terms of TI (thought insertion), are disturbances in the structure of intentionality rather than nonveridical but unambiguously perceptual experiences. The content of these experiences is unlike that of an auditory perception or a perception in any other sense modality, and yet they still incorporate a *sense of perceiving*. In this chapter, I develop an account of what that sense consists of. My account challenges orthodox approaches to VHs, in suggesting that they do not arise out of a lack of conscious or nonconscious anticipation, but are instead constituted by a certain *way* of anticipating one's own thought contents as they coalesce. I focus principally on internal VHs with unpleasant contents, such as abuse, threats, and disturbing commands. These are frequently associated with heightened anxiety, and it has been hypothesized that anxiety is not only caused by VHs but somehow implicated in their production as well. The main task of the chapter is to show *how* anxiety induces VHs. Anxiety, I propose, is most centrally a type of *affective anticipation*, and affective anticipation contributes to the sense of being in one or another kind of intentional state. Ordinarily, we do not anxiously anticipate the arrival of our own thoughts. When we do, the result can be a quasi-perceptual experience of thought content. Hence a dynamic perspective is required, according to which anxiety precedes a full-blown VH experience and is partly *constitutive* of the ensuing experience. My phenomenological analysis implies that anxiety also has a *causal* role to play in the production of VHs, and thus has implications for nonphenomenological, mechanistic accounts as well.

I go on to argue that anxiety is equally implicated in the generation of many external VHs (which more closely resemble veridical perceptions), but that these arise via a different process. Other VH experiences, which fall somewhere in between the categories of "external, auditory" and "internal, nonauditory," involve combinations of the two processes. Further diversity is accommodated by acknowledging that the category "internal VH" encompasses different kinds of modal confusion: the sense of perceiving could attach to a memory, to an imagining, or to inner speech. The chapter concludes by observing that VHs of these kinds generally occur against a backdrop of wider-ranging social anxiety and estrangement from other people, something that amounts to a shift in the person's overarching *style of anticipation*. So my position is not simply that anxious anticipation of thought contents results in quasi-perceptual experiences, but that it can do so in the context of wider-ranging phenomenological changes, which are themselves to be understood in terms of anxiety and social isolation.

4.1 Anxiety

VHs are often accompanied by social anxiety, along with a pervasive sense of estrangement from other people. It is unsurprising that social anxiety tends to be associated with some degree of social withdrawal: someone who anticipates social situations with feelings of dread, or experiences most or even all other people as threatening, will be likely to retreat from social situations and feel disconnected from others even when in their presence (Hoffman 2007). This chapter emphasizes the role of social anxiety; the sense of isolation will become a more prominent theme in chapters 5 and 6.

In addressing how social anxiety contributes to VHs, I should first make clear how "anxiety" is to be understood here. In clinical contexts, anxiety is conceived of in a number of different ways, both currently and historically.[1] More generally, the term can refer to various kinds of experience, some of which have specific thematic contents, while others are more diffuse and wide-ranging. For current purposes, a rough characterization will suffice, and I do not wish to insist on clear-cut distinctions between anxiety, fear, dread, and the like. Anxiety is, most centrally, a form of affective anticipation, something that is inextricable from how one's current surroundings appear salient. How one experiences the present is shaped by a sense of what is to come; one anticipates the arrival of something that is somehow dangerous and threatening to oneself. Associated with this is an experience of passivity before it; one cannot avoid it, resist it, or shield oneself from its effects. This kind of anticipation might be associated with the arrival of a specific event, but it can also be much wider-ranging, a pervasive way of experiencing the interpersonal and/or impersonal world.[2]

Anxiety, I further maintain, consists primarily in a kind of bodily feeling. Elsewhere, I have argued at length that most or even all bodily feelings are not just experiences *of* the body. It is *through* our feeling bodies that we experience the significance and salience of our surroundings. Various felt bodily dispositions, such as feeling drawn to explore something, pick it up, or retreat from it, are inextricable from an experience of that entity as significant in one way or another—as immediately relevant in the context of a project, offering the possibility of pleasure, obstructing what one is doing, posing a threat, and so forth (see, e.g., Ratcliffe 2008, 2015). This chapter is concerned principally with experiences of anxious anticipation that are directed toward something specific. However, I also acknowledge that such experiences are generally embedded in and shaped by a background of nonlocalized anxiety. Chapter 5 will explore that background in more detail and, in the process, further clarify the relationship between anxious anticipation and bodily experience.

To begin with, I address the relationship between anxiety and those VH experiences that involve disturbances in the structure of intentionality. Later in the chapter, I show how an emphasis on anxiety can also account for at least some external, audition-like VHs. Until chapter 7, the discussion is limited to VHs with distressing thematic contents, such as repeated insults, threats, terms of abuse, and distressing commands. As Aleman and Larøi (2008, 33) observe, voices "may insult and criticize the patient, tell the patient to do something unacceptable ... or threaten the patient." According to numerous studies, the majority of "voice-hearers" have this kind of VH experience, often only this kind. For example, Nayani and David (1996, 182–186) found that "the most commonly encountered hallucinated utterances," experienced by 60 percent of their subjects, were "simple terms of abuse," and that "vulgar expletives" were most common, while Leudar et al. (1997) report that 53 percent of their subjects heard abusive voices, and that abusive voices were especially prevalent among those diagnosed with schizophrenia.

Although VHs with distressing contents are often associated with schizophrenia, they also arise in several other psychiatric conditions, including post-traumatic stress disorder, psychotic depression, bipolar disorder, and borderline personality disorder, as well as in nonclinical subjects (Johns et al. 2014; Upthegrove et al. 2016). First-person reports of abusive, insulting, or threatening voices in these populations have much in common (Aleman and Larøi 2008, p.78).[3] In what follows, I offer an account of VHs that is consistent with their diagnostic nonspecificity. The proposal is that they arise due to pronounced and pervasive social anxiety, of a kind that is common to several psychiatric conditions. However, this is not to imply that the VHs associated with different psychiatric diagnoses are all exactly alike or that diagnostic categories have no discriminatory power at all. It may be possible to tease out subtle differences between these experiences that track, at least to some degree, different diagnoses. Nevertheless, my aim here is to describe something that they share: a disturbance in the anticipatory structure of experience. This disturbance, I argue, constitutes the experience of thought as perception-like.

It is easy to see why VHs, especially those with unpleasant contents, might be accompanied by anxiety and also depression, given that such experiences can be very distressing. However, anxiety and depression frequently arise before the onset of VHs, and anxiety is particularly prevalent among voice-hearers in both clinical and nonclinical populations (Allen et al. 2005; Kuipers et al. 2006; Paulik, Badcock and Maybery 2006). It is important to distinguish two observations: (a) generalized anxiety is present before the onset of VHs; and (b) there is heightened anxiety immediately before and during VH experiences. Social anxiety is predictive of schizophrenia diagnoses, and it has been proposed that the frequent presence of depression and anxiety before the onset of psychotic symptoms points to a causal role for affective disturbances (Broome et al. 2005). Moreover, there is evidence to suggest that anxiety, more so than depression, is specifically associated with "positive symptoms" such as VHs (Freeman and Garety 2003). Anxiety may also be more directly implicated in the generation of VHs. According to Delespaul, de Vries, and van Os (2002, 97, 101), it is the "most prominent emotion during hallucinations," and level of anxiety is the "strongest predictor of hallucination intensity." Others have hypothesized that heightened anxiety both triggers VHs and shapes their contents, although the mechanism remains unclear (Freeman and Garety 2003).[4] That view is consistent with first-person descriptions of the emotions that immediately precede VHs. For example:

> "Usually when I hear auditory hallucinations I am upset about something, my body is in a heightened state of alertness and sometimes even in fight or flight mode." (2)

"It's worse when I'm stressed, anxious or scared." (3)

"When I am feeling anxious they grow stronger. When I am alone as the day goes on they get stronger." (6)

"Fear, unsafety ... not knowing." (19)

"Loneliness, depression, anxiety, feeling unloved, deserted, uncared for." (28)

"Anxiety, usually when overly tired or stressed." (34)

Of course, the fact that VHs often arise in a context of social anxiety and are immediately preceded by heightened anxiety does not, in itself, imply a causal relationship. It can be added that treating the anxiety often leads to a reduction in VH frequency and severity, thus lending further support to the view that anxiety plays a causal role (Kuipers et al. 2006, 28). Nevertheless, the question of *how* anxiety might cause VHs remains open. In the remainder of this chapter, I develop a specifically phenomenological or personal-level account, according to which a sense of alienation from one's own thought contents is constituted by anxiety, in a way that equally implies a causal relationship. This account also has significant implications for subpersonal, mechanistic theories of how VHs come about.

4.2 Anticipation

Most attempts to explain the occurrence of VH and/or TI focus on nonconscious or "subpersonal" processes, rather than exploring the associated phenomenology in any depth. However, to provide a subpersonal account that is relevant to a given phenomenon, we need at least some appreciation of what that phenomenon actually consists of and thus what needs explaining. A problem for any account of VH-generating mechanisms is that the phenomena in question are diverse, something that is not always sufficiently acknowledged. Indeed, the broad categories of "internal and nonauditory" and "external and auditory" VHs are so different from each other that there are no grounds for supposing that the same mechanism underlies both, and section 4.4 of this chapter will argue that it does not. Nevertheless, my interpretation of internal VHs in chapter 3 (to be further developed in what follows) is at least consistent with the predominant view that VHs occur owing to a failure of "source monitoring." This view, which operates as a premise for more specific mechanistic accounts of VHs, maintains that they involve a failure to discriminate between "self-generated and external sources of information" (Bentall 1990, 82). It is supported by several sources of evidence, all of which indicate that those who experience VHs have a more general tendency to misattribute self-generated experiential contents to external sources. For instance, they are more likely than others to misattribute self-generated words in certain memory tasks, to ascribe their own speech to others when it is played back to them, and to report false positives when asked to detect signals in noisy environments (Bentall and Varese 2013).

This is compatible with the proposal that VHs involve both localized and more general disturbances of intentionality. A quasi-perceptual experience of thought content could also be described in terms of a failure to clearly distinguish something internally produced from something externally produced. However, an emphasis on the modal structure of intentionality gives us a more specific account of what the relevant experience consists of, and thus of what it is that requires explanation. In the case of an internal VH, misattribution of source occurs when an ordinarily unproblematic sense of perceiving as distinct from thinking, imagining, and/or remembering, is disrupted. So the "misattribution" is integral to the experience, and does not require the subject to adopt a complementary belief about the origin of experiential content. Neither does it imply a subjective inability to distinguish anomalous experiences involving source confusion from mundane perceptual experiences. A subpersonal account of the neurobiological mechanisms involved in generating the experience should be consistent not only with the phenomenologically noncommittal observation that source is misattributed but also with the more specific phenomenology. In this way, phenomenological research can serve to guide and also constrain mechanistic accounts, a point I will return to in chapter 6.

Although the position I will develop here is compatible with the claim that VHs involve a failure of source monitoring, it conflicts with a more specific and highly influential account of *how* the failure arises. This account maintains that VHs occur because of a breakdown of predictive processes that ordinarily accompany the generation of thought and, more specifically, inner speech. The idea is that mechanisms involved in thought production resemble, in relevant respects, those at work in bodily action and motor control. When we act (where "acting" is construed permissively, to include purposive actions, facial expressions, fidgeting, eye movements, and anything else that we might be said to do "voluntarily"), we ordinarily experience our actions as self-produced, and we readily distinguish them from bodily movements caused by external stimuli. For instance, a self-produced eye movement and its visual effects are experienced as quite different from an external force on the eye and associated disturbances of the visual field. Differences like this are plausibly explained in terms of subpersonal mechanisms that predict the generation of self-produced movement and then match anticipated consequences with what actually happens. In a mundane instance of self-initiated movement, both the movement and its sensory effects are predicted, and the actual effects match the predicted effects. However, when a movement is not anticipated or when its consequences depart substantially from what was anticipated, it is attributed wholly or partly to an external source.[5] Frith (1992) suggests that such a mechanism is also involved in the production of thought and speech. As a thought is generated, a signal is produced that predicts its occurrence. A comparator then matches the actual output with what was anticipated, registering any discrepancies.[6] Where (a) the initial "a thought is about to occur" signal is not produced or (b) there is a mismatch between what was anticipated and what actually happens, there is no experienced "intention" to think that thought. So the thought appears to be non-self-generated, as though it originated from elsewhere. In other words, it is experienced as VH or TI.

Frith's original statement of the view faces several familiar objections. For instance, in cases of audition-like VH, the appeal to misplaced inner speech does not account for why voices have auditory qualities, why they are sometimes attributed to a particular person, or why they seem to emanate from a specific external location (e.g., Wu 2012). In addition, Frith's account of the experience of thinking is phenomenologically implausible. He states that thinking, like other actions, "is normally accompanied by a sense of effort and deliberate choice as we move from one thought to the next," and the hypothesized mechanism is supposed to underlie this experience of intention (Frith 1992, 81). However, it is far from clear that thought is ordinarily effortful or that thoughts are experienced as *deliberate choices*. Another objection is that the episodic and content-specific nature of VHs remains unaccounted for. Why is it not the case that all thoughts are experienced as voices or as inserted? It could be that the mechanism is sporadically disrupted, but this would not account for the thematic consistency of VHs (Gallagher 2005, chap. 8). There is also a lack of clarity over what, exactly, is anticipated. It cannot be the full content of the thought, as anticipating a thought with the content *p* would itself involve having a thought with the same content, which would itself need to be anticipated, leading to an infinite regress.[7] Another concern is that the mechanism appears redundant. While we need to distinguish our own actions from other bodily movements, we do not need to distinguish self-generated thoughts from non-self-generated thoughts, as all of our thoughts are self-generated.

More recent versions of the prediction-failure view address some of these concerns. For instance, Cahill and Frith (1996, 289) concede that the absence of an "I did it" tag is not sufficient to generate VHs. There must also be a prior vulnerability, in the form of a disposition to misattribute events of indeterminate origin to external sources:

> We would like to suggest that in some schizophrenic patients who experience auditory hallucinations the (internal?) speech generation system is compromised in terms of a dysfunction in a "corollary discharge" system, which at a preconscious level leaves internally generated events unlabelled as such. This, coupled with a coexisting proclivity or propensity for (mis)attributing events to external agents results in the experience of auditory hallucinations.

With this modification, there is no longer the pressure to account for *all* properties of VHs in terms of prediction failure. A further concession is that the relevant processes are wholly nonconscious and need not be associated with an explicit *intention* to think. And it has been added that these processes have potential functions, such as keeping thoughts on track (Campbell 1999). In recent writings, Frith also states that his earlier appeal to both an anticipatory process *and* a subsequent comparison process (which matches expected outputs with actual outputs) was misplaced. Instead, he suggests, delusions and hallucinations are specifically associated with failure of the "predictive component," while "the retrospective component remains intact" (2012, 53). So the position we are left with is that failure of a subpersonal prediction mechanism is necessary but perhaps not sufficient for the generation of VH/TI.

One might think that, as the mechanism is nonconscious, a consideration of the associated phenomenology has little to contribute. However, such mechanisms are invoked to explain a type of experience, and they should at least be consistent with the nature of the experience in question. Otherwise, there is a risk not just of falsehood but of irrelevance. By analogy, an account of color perception that appealed to the mechanisms involved in smell would be beside the point. With that in mind, the widespread emphasis on prediction failure is problematic. Its phenomenological correlate is supposed to be a thought that is experienced as unanticipated, as coming out of nowhere, and the sense of alienation is attributed to this unpredictability. As Fletcher and Frith (2009, 56) put it, "an inner voice is unpredictable and therefore feels alien." So, even without the claim that we *intend* our thoughts, a continuing assumption is that we more usually anticipate their arrival in some way.

While I agree that anticipation is central to an understanding how anxiety induces VHs, I propose that VHs are not attributable to a *lack* of anticipation but instead to *how* one anticipates. There are two objections to the orthodox emphasis on a lack of anticipation. The less problematic of these is that absence of conscious anticipation is not sufficient for VHs. Many thoughts arrive unannounced, such as a song that suddenly starts "playing in one's head" or a seemingly random thought that does not cohere with the gist of one's thinking and may also disrupt one's train of thought. In response, perhaps even these thoughts are anticipated to at least some degree and therefore differ from VHs. It is difficult to arbitrate between conflicting phenomenological claims here. And, even if a complete lack of conscious anticipation is conceded for some thoughts, one could still insist that these thoughts are accompanied by nonconscious predictive processes, the absence of which makes a thought seem strange in some other way. But a more serious problem for the prediction-failure view is that lack of conscious anticipation is not necessary for VHs. In short, many voice-hearers *do* anticipate their voices, to the extent that they may be able to solicit a voice, dialogue with it, and predict the thematic content of what it will "say" next. In fact, it has been reported that a majority of voice-hearers are able to converse with their voices (e.g., Garrett and Silva 2003, 449). In one influential study, 51 percent of subjects stated that they had at least some control over their voices, 38 percent that they could initiate a voice, and 21 percent that they could stop a voice (Nayani and David 1996, 183). First-person reports vary considerably. Some say that they can anticipate their voices, some that they cannot, and some that they can do so on occasion. For example:

"Although I can and sometimes do call them up by focusing my mind in a certain way … that only works in a very quiet environment where I am alone or won't be disturbed by people." (7)

"Sometimes I know it's more likely to happen because I start to feel a bit anxious but other times it comes from nowhere." (3)

"Sometimes, it's like a wave and then I hear them." (22)

Nevertheless, it is at least safe to assume that some voice-hearers anticipate some of their voices. Furthermore, VHs often involve prolonged, thematically consistent communications. So, even if they are not anticipated to begin with, anticipatory processes are at work while they occur. If a VH experience is generated by lack of anticipation, we might wonder why the whole episode is misattributed, rather than just an unanticipated, initial part of it. Sometimes, lengthier VH experiences also include structured dialogue: "I have won arguments (with them) before" (22). This similarly involves some sense of when a voice will respond and what it is likely to say. Thus, when we turn to the relevant phenomenology, a simple contrast between anticipating and failing to anticipate is unhelpful. Of course, prediction-failure accounts are concerned only with nonconscious processes. However, it is not clear how a conscious process involving some form of anticipation is to be accounted for by appealing to an associated nonconscious process that does not. It also seems reasonable to assume that any phenomenological or "personal-level" ability to predict the onset and content of a VH implies the existence of subpersonal prediction mechanisms, unless one wishes to concede that the phenomenology is wholly autonomous of the neurobiology, thus rendering the latter explanatorily redundant. I do not want to dismiss the prediction-failure view outright; that would be too hasty. But I do maintain that it needs to be refined and elaborated, so as to distinguish the kinds of anticipation still at play (both conscious and nonconscious) from those that are allegedly disrupted. A further account is then needed of why some kinds of anticipatory process contribute to the recognition of a thought as self-generated while others do not.

One could respond to this line of criticism by insisting that prediction failure is specific to very short-term anticipatory processes that accompany the generation of thoughts, something that is compatible with the retention of longer-term anticipatory processes. However, my emphasis in what follows is also on short-term anticipation, on how thought content is anticipated as it arises, with specific reference to VHs that are experienced as internal in origin and lacking in auditory qualities. Although references to anticipating and even having control over voices do not usually distinguish between external and internal VHs, it would be implausible to insist that only external VHs can involve anticipation. Internal, nonauditory VHs are at least sometimes anticipated as well. Indeed, it is more likely that reports of soliciting, dialoguing with, and arguing with one's voices concern these internal, inner-speech-like voices. As one questionnaire respondent remarks, "My voices are thoughts, not auditory voices. ... We talk. They respond" (12).

My proposal is that internal VHs are constituted by a distinctive *kind* of anticipatory structure. To develop this position, I will start by considering an account of VH/TI proposed by Gallagher (2005). This account is problematic, insofar it accepts the usual assumption that VHs can be accounted for by appealing to an absence of anticipation. Nevertheless, it remains informative for two main reasons. First of all, it not only places an emphasis on anxiety but also seeks to show exactly how anxiety induces VHs. Second, it recognizes how an emphasis on anxiety can account for the content-specificity of VHs, something that other kinds of prediction-failure account have failed to accommodate. Gallagher's discussion encompasses both VH and TI. He does not say whether or how the two differ, but I want to show how a substantially modified version of his approach can be applied specifically to the kind of internal VH/TI experience described in chapter 3.

Gallagher maintains that acts of thinking ordinarily incorporate an experience of anticipation. It is not that you anticipate thinking something before you think it. That, he acknowledges, would fall foul of the infinite regress objection: anticipating the thought that *p* would involve a thought with the content "the thought that *p*," which would itself be anticipated by a further thought, and so on. What is anticipated is less determinate in content. He offers the analogy of listening to a melody, where you might not anticipate hearing a specific note, but you do have at least some appreciation of what will come next, as illustrated by the surprise that is felt when a note is out of tune.[8] By analogy, you might anticipate the general theme of a thought, the full content of which is more specific (see also Hoffman 1986). Gallagher (2005, 190) suggests that the sense of having produced a thought depends on such "anticipatory" processes, rather than on "sensory feedback." In this respect at least, his account remains consistent with Frith's more recent view (Frith 2012). Gallagher's idea is that, if a thought were not anticipated at all, it would arrive fully formed, rather than crystallizing out of something that is congruent with it but less determinate in content. This would amount to a sense of its emanating from elsewhere, like the unanticipated and fully formed communications we receive from other people. He further suggests that such experiences could be brought about by "unruly emotions such as anxiety." In brief, anxiety disrupts anticipation and, were it to immediately precede a particular thought, that thought might "appear as if from nowhere"; it would be "sudden and unexpected" (2005, 194–200). This enables him to account for the content-specificity of VH/TI. Heightened anxiety is likely to be specific to certain perceived, remembered, and anticipated situations:

> This may happen in the presence of certain individuals, or in a certain kind of situation, or confronted with a certain object, or in rehearsing certain thoughts. In those cases or similar circumstances, and in line with the episodic and selective nature of positive symptoms, a subject would then (but not always) experience thought insertion or similar loss in the sense of agency. (Gallagher 2005, 200)

Situations that elicit heightened anxiety will also be situations in which thoughts with certain contents are likely to arise. For instance, whenever one sees or remembers a particular person, one's thoughts may gravitate around certain themes. If the perception or memory of that person elicits anxiety, the anticipation of those thoughts is likely to be disrupted, more so than thoughts in general.

There is something importantly right about this, but the emphasis on a lack of anticipation is mistaken. In fact, I suspect that having unanticipated thoughts is a fairly mundane experience, one that need not involve any sense of alienation. Instead, I propose that VHs arise when thought contents are themselves anticipated in a distinctive *way* as they take shape: one anxiously anticipates one's own thought contents. All instances where one anticipates *p* can be qualified in terms of the following:

1. Determinacy of content: *p* can be more or less specific.
2. Mode of anticipation: *p* can be anticipated as certain, uncertain, probable, improbable, doubtful, and so forth.
3. Affective style of anticipation: anticipating *p* can involve a range of emotions, such as excitement, curiosity, hope, or fear.

By appealing to a combination of (1) and (3), I will argue that VHs arise due to a distinctive affective style, that of anxiously anticipating an increasingly determinate thought content. I will assume that the mode of anticipation, (2), is usually that of certainty or high probability. The notion of a *style of anticipation* will be central to my discussion throughout the remainder of the book.

4.3 Alienated Content

A first step in understanding how VH/TI can occur due to anxious anticipation is the appreciation that (a) certain types of affective anticipation are ordinarily associated with certain types of intentional state, and (b) affective anticipation contributes to the sense of being in one or another type of intentional state. The point can be illustrated with reference to emotional experiences more generally. I take it as uncontroversial that many emotions either are intentional states or at least incorporate intentional states: A is afraid of *p*; B feels guilty about *q*. This is not to imply that the intentionality of emotion is a matter of cognitive "judgment" or "appraisal" rather than "affect" or "feeling." There are various ways of arguing that some or all emotional feelings are themselves intentional, and that their objects are not restricted to one's own bodily states (see, e.g., Goldie 2000; Prinz 2004; Ratcliffe 2008). That is the position endorsed here, although I also allow that there is more to many emotional experiences than just feelings or combinations of feelings.

A given type of emotion, directed at a particular object, is compatible with certain other types of intentional state being contemporaneously directed at that same object, but not all types. For instance, feeling guilty about something is associated with remembering it but not with imagining it or anticipating its occurrence. And fearing something is associated with anticipating its occurrence but not with remembering that it has already occurred. Granted, there are apparent exceptions. For instance, one might quite rightly feel guilty about something that has not yet happened, in a situation where one has already set the wheels in motion such that it probably *will* happen. However, the guilt remains past-directed: one feels guilty about *p* in virtue of the fact that one remembers doing *q*, where *q* is likely to cause *p*.

We might say that certain emotions are *properly associated* only with certain other kinds of intentional state. This could be understood in various ways: an "improper" association might be regarded as epistemically or behaviorally misleading, irrational, biologically dysfunctional, socially inappropriate, or inappropriate in some other respect, and some of these criteria will most likely converge in any given case. My emphasis here is on the fact that it *makes sense* to feel guilty about something that one has done or at least something that has happened, but not about something that has not happened and may never happen. Similarly, it makes sense to fear the arrival of a potential threat, but not to fear the arrival of something that has already happened (where the object of fear is the past event, rather than its anticipated effects or the possibility of something like it happening again). The content of the relevant emotions can be expressed in terms of propositions such as "Something will or might happen that could harm me or someone I care about"; "I did something I should not have done"; and so forth. And they make sense when they are temporally consistent with their objects. We can also add spatial consistency as a requirement. For fear of *p* to make sense, the proximal and distal effects of *p* must be such as to potentially affect one, or something one cares about, in some way.

When remembering is associated with feeling guilty, it is debatable how the two relate. Perhaps there is a singular kind of intentional state, that of *guiltily remembering*. Alternatively, a distinction might be drawn between two intentional states with the same object. Or it could be that one first remembers something and then feels guilty about it; so guilt borrows its content from a preceding intentional state. However, even if the two experiences are—according to some criterion—distinct, it is plausible to suggest that they affect each other. It is not psychologically impossible to fear what has already happened or to feel guilty about a merely imagined state of affairs. Even so, the experience would be a strange one. In the case of guilt, one might then think "I am wrong to feel guilty about this" or, alternatively, "Perhaps I am not just imagining it; maybe I actually did it." Indeed, were one to feel persistent, intense, recalcitrant guilt about something merely imagined, the sense of imagining having done it rather than remembering having done it might well become less secure; it would start to *feel* like something one had actually done. More generally, I propose the following: where an emotion or feeling *x* is properly associated with the content of intentional state *y* but not with the content of intentional state *z*, its association with *z* can result in *z*'s taking on some of the phenomenological characteristics of *y*. In extreme cases, the result is a novel kind of experience, one that is neither *y* nor *z*. It follows from this that the two are in fact inextricable, rather than being wholly separable experiences of a common object. To be more specific, a sense of one's intentional state is partly constituted by certain feelings that share the same object. And, as argued in chapter 2, the sense of being in an intentional state cannot be cleanly separated from the wider experience that a state of that kind typically involves.

Where there is recalcitrant guilt over *p*, it contributes to the sense that *p* actually happened and that one was somehow implicated. This is not to suggest that feeling guilty is necessary for a sense of something as past. Rather, the claim is that, when one does feel guilt, it contributes to the sense of something as past rather than merely imagined. A similar point applies to fear: fear of something that is taken to be past could disrupt the sense of that event as firmly anchored in the past. I suggest that anxious anticipation induces VHs in the same way, by shaping the sense of which intentional state one is in. Anxious anticipation of *p* is not necessary for the sense of encountering *p* perceptually. However, when one does anxiously anticipate *p*, anxiety can contribute to the experience of relating to it in a perceptual or perception-like way. Anxiety is not ordinarily associated with our own thought contents and, when it is associated with them, they are experienced as the contents of a perception-like intentional state that also retains some of the features of thought.

This proposal requires further clarification. It is commonplace to think something and also feel anxious about it. So there is the objection that first-person thoughts clearly are proper objects of anxiety. However, what we are ordinarily anxious about is the state of affairs we are thinking about, not the having of a thought about that state of affairs. For example, where the thought content is "I might lose my job," I am anxious about actually losing my job, not about having the thought that I might. Feeling anxious about "the thought that *p*" is a more unusual experience. How could this account for VHs, though? There is a sense in which anxiety is intrinsically alienating or externalizing. It presents its object—however determinate—as something unpleasant that one has to confront. The object of anxiety is something that threatens, something one feels helpless in the face of. So it is important to distinguish different experiences of "externality" here. To say that an object of anxiety is essentially external to oneself is not to insist that it be experienced as physically external to one's bodily boundaries. Our own bodily experiences can also be objects of anxiety. A person who fears she has a serious medical condition may become increasingly anxious about certain persistent bodily sensations. And chronic illness can involve more widespread feelings of bodily alienation. The body is encountered in a way that is strange and previously unfamiliar, as an actual or potential impediment to one's activities and an object of anxiety, rather than something in which one has implicit trust (van den Berg 1966; Carel 2013). Where an object of anxiety is physically external to oneself, one can feel alienated from it in a comparable way. Feeling comfortably immersed in the interpersonal world can be contrasted with feeling uncomfortably separate from it. When suffering from pronounced social anxiety, one does not simply feel physically separate from others. There is a different kind of separation; one is estranged from them, threatened by them, vulnerable and helpless before them.

In this respect, anxiety is comparable to at least some experiences of pain. Consider an intense, lingering pain in the hand that persists independently of any external stimulus. The pain is not experienced as external to the body but as located within one's bodily boundaries, in the hand. All the same, there is a feeling of alienation from it, in the sense that one is faced with something unpleasant, something one seeks to avoid, to push away, but can do nothing about. The recognition of being inseparable from the pain and unable to detach oneself from it, the recognition that it is *not* physically external, exacerbates the kind of alienation I am interested in here. The pain is something that opposes one's engagement with the world, something that one is forced to confront and cannot escape or deny. Hence something can be experienced as external and alien or, alternatively, as internal and alien. The sense of alienation that I am attributing to anxiety has nothing to do with perceived physical location.[9] And neither does that which many voice-hearers describe, since the voices are internally located and yet alien.

The view that internal VHs occur when thought contents become objects of anxiety is consistent with the observation that many voice-hearers dread their voices and, more specifically, what it is that the voices "say." The distressing content is something the person is confronted with, something she might try unsuccessfully to resist or avoid. Of course, it could be that the person experiences *p* and is subsequently anxious about it because of its strangeness and unpleasantness. Although that is no doubt so, anxious anticipation also contributes to the relevant experience. To appreciate what internal VHs consist of and how they arise, we need a dynamic account of the relationship between anxiety and thought content. To illustrate what happens, consider more familiar experiences that involve an indeterminate, affectively charged thought content coalescing into something more determinate. Take the realization that you have left your bag on the train. As you walk out of the station, this might begin as a surge of anxiety, the content of which can be roughly characterized as "something is wrong"; "I've not done something," or "something important is missing." This becomes "I've left something on the train" and then "I've left my bag on the train," after which the repercussions of what has happened start to sink in. Indeterminate content *p* arises, eliciting anxiety, and one anxiously anticipates the dawning of *q*, where *q* is a more determinate form of *p*. (The initial experience can also occur when nothing is wrong, in which case the content sometimes remains indeterminate, and the feeling fades upon recognition that all is well.)

The view that thought contents can increase in determinacy as they form is consistent with various proposed explanations of VHs. For instance, Fernyhough (2004) suggests that inner speech is more usually condensed and fragmented, and that an experience of alienation is attributable to its anomalous re-expansion. Gerrans (2014 198) distinguishes inner speech from thought, noting that inner speech can be construed as a linguistic "outcome" of thought processes that are not themselves inherently linguistic. And, according to the influential theory proposed by Hoffman (1986, 503), VHs are generated by disruption of a discourse planning process, which involves "abstract planning representations that are linked to goals and beliefs." These provide a broad sense of what is coming next and precede more determinate contents. More generally, the received view is that VHs involve experiencing one's own inner speech as non-self-produced, rather than one's thoughts per se. And this emphasis on inner speech suggests a process via which thoughts are converted into inner speech (Stephens and Graham 2000, 81).[10] Hence it could be that a thought content of some other kind provokes anxiety, the object of which is the subsequent content of inner speech. For current purposes, I do not need to endorse a specific theory of what happens or how it happens. All I am committed to is the claim that thought content *p* precedes thought content *q*, where *q* is a more determinate form of *p*.

It might be objected that the content of the thought remains the same throughout this process—that it is simply translated into inner speech. However, whatever else the process might involve, it is plausible to insist on increasing degrees of content determinacy. This becomes more readily apparent when the predominantly emotional content of many VHs is emphasized. As already stated, I accept that many emotions are intentional states with contents that can be conveyed in linguistic form. However, even if one wishes to insist that they also include some kind of propositional content prior to their linguistic expression, this is not the same as their incorporating inner speech. It has been argued that spoken language serves not just to convey preformed emotional states but also to individuate or even partly constitute them, at least in some instances. Among other things, language can shape the content of an emotion (e.g., Campbell 1997; Colombetti 2009). Similar points are made by the phenomenologist Maurice Merleau-Ponty (1945/2012), for whom speech increases the determinacy of thought (and emotion): "the most familiar thing appears indeterminate as long as we have not remembered its name" (182); "the clarity of language is in fact established against an obscure background" (194). He refers specifically to emotional content and to how words can somehow "extract" from objects and "express" their "emotional essence" (193). Something like this can also be found in the writings of some psychotherapists. For example, Gendlin (1978/2003, 38) discusses the way in which we can have an inarticulate "felt sense" of a problem or situation. He remarks on the inchoate feeling that you have forgotten something or failed to do something and how, on some occasions, "suddenly, from this felt sense, it bursts to the surface." Although he distinguishes the "felt sense" from emotions such as anxiety, his account is more generally consistent with the view that determinate linguistic contents can arise out of less determinate emotional contents that have an anticipatory structure.

Keeping in mind the view that spoken language can render the content of an emotional state more determinate, let us consider the emotional content of many VHs and its congruence with the wider emotional state or mood the person is in at the time. Take the following remarks:

> "They constantly bombard me with thoughts of self-harm and suicide. … It's like they want me to be dead. They want me to be a failure. They want me to cease to exist." (6)

> "It's all my fears and hopes coming down, irrational and amplified." (10)

> "Very mood congruent. When I am experiencing an extreme mood state the more I experience these things. When I am stable I almost never experience these things." (20)

Associated moods here include "mania, severe depression, agitation, high anxiety" (20), and "sadness, despair, frustration, panic" (6). It is informative to revisit Hoffman (1986) in the light of such observations. His approach has a cognitive emphasis throughout. The abstract plans and goals that he claims enable discourse planning have, it seems, a propositional structure, although their content is less specific than that of inner speech. But consider an example Hoffman uses to illustrate his point. When asked to describe where she lives, a patient says the following:

> Yes, I live in Connecticut. We live in a 50-year-old Tudor house. It's a house that's very much a home ... ah ... I live there with my husband and son. It's a home where people are drawn to feel comfortable, walk in, let's see ... a home that is furnished comfortably—not expensive—a home that shows very much my personality. (Hoffman 1986, 506)

The overall theme that constitutes a sense of "where things are heading" is a consistently emotional one.[11] And utterances are not merely mood-congruent; what we have here is also the articulation or expression of an emotion or mood, something that renders its content increasingly specific. Now, let us assume that inner speech (and perhaps also the imagined speech of others) can play a similar role to spoken language. Thus, in the case of an abusive "voice," there is an unpleasant emotional content *p*, which provokes anxious anticipation of a more determinate linguistic content *q*, one that is elicited by *p* and also consistent with *p*. Anxiety is intrinsically alienating and so its object, the thought that *q*, is experienced as alien, as something unpleasant that one faces and is unable to avoid. Whatever forms of anticipation our thinking more usually involves, anxious anticipation of thought content is not one of them. That style of anticipation is more typical of certain affectively charged perceptual experiences. So an unfamiliar, perception-like experience of thought content arises.[12]

It might be objected that the thought content "I've left my bag on the train" is not experienced as alien and that the process sketched here therefore fails to account for the "alien quality" of VHs. But there is a crucial difference between the two cases. In the train example, one is anxious about the *fact* that one has left one's bag on the train, not about the *thought* content "I've left my bag on the train." In the case of a VH with the content "You're a worthless piece of filth," the thought content is itself an object of anxiety. The way it is anticipated as it coalesces thus renders it alien, something unpleasant that one feels helpless in the face of.

Hence the more usual emphasis on a lack of anticipation is misleading.[13] To revisit the melody analogy, consider listening to a piece of music that involves a buildup of tension (an opera by Wagner, perhaps). We feel that something intrusive is about to blast in; it is on its way. And yet, when it arrives and conforms to the indeterminate expectation we had of it, it is still experienced as disruptive, as having arisen from elsewhere, as set apart from the music that preceded it. The same applies to moments of suspense in films. We might experience a growing tension, appreciate that something horrible is about to happen, and even have a fairly good idea of what actually will happen—perhaps somebody is about to be eaten by a shark. Even so, when it does happen, it is still shocking, still experienced as a disruption of what came before. To further analyze such experiences, a more refined account is needed of what exactly is anticipated, the extent to which it corresponds to what actually occurs, and the extent to which anticipated and actual times of occurrence match. It could be that the event is expected to occur within a given timeframe, but not at a particular moment. As it is not expected "right then," it is still surprising. Nevertheless, I suggest that affective style of anticipation is more important. Whether and how something appears surprising or shocking is not just a matter of how likely its occurrence was taken to be and when exactly it was expected to occur. I do not expect to find a ten-cent coin on the floor as I walk out of my office. But, if I do, I will not feel especially surprised, and its being there will not be experienced as in any way incongruous with what came before. What matters is the kind of significance something has. Even if we know that something horrible is about to happen and even if we know roughly when it will happen, it is still experienced as interrupting what came before. Similarly, the kind of "surprise" associated with VHs can be thought of principally in terms of the disturbance of something, rather than in terms of the arrival of something that was largely unanticipated. Experiencing something as incongruous in one or another way involves a distinctive kind of anticipation, rather than a lack.

What I have proposed is consistent with empirical findings concerning (a) the thematic content of many VHs, (b) the prevalence of anxiety, and (c) the occurrence of similar kinds of VH experience in several psychiatric conditions and in at least some of those nonclinical subjects who report "hearing voices." Importantly, it is also consistent with first-person accounts and can aid us in interpreting them. Hayward, Berry, and Ashton (2011, 1313) observe that "the relationships that hearers develop with their hallucinations share many properties with interpersonal relationships within the social world." Both tend to be characterized by a sense of isolation, vulnerability, and powerlessness in the face of something menacing (Birchwood et al. 2000).[14] In fact, VH contents are sometimes explicitly described as linguistic manifestations of negative, self-directed emotional appraisals, which reflect troubling interpersonal relationships and are themselves a source of distress. For example:

> "I heard the voices of demons screaming at me, telling that I was damned, that God hated me, and that I was going to hell. ... It's hard to describe how I could 'hear' a voice that wasn't auditory; but the words used and the emotions they contained (hatred and disgust) were completely clear, distinct and unmistakable, maybe even more so that if I had heard them aurally. ... The voices I heard reflected all the judgmental attitudes I had heard from my family and church." (9)

Like the judgments of other people, the judgments that form the content of the VHs are themselves feared; they are associated with "anxiety/panic and incapacitating depression" (9).

It is also interesting to note how such experiences are sometimes described not only as *unlike* hearing something but also as somehow *clearer* than hearing, or as involving a sense of reality that is, in some way, more pronounced than that of an ordinary perception. As Karlsson (2008, 365) observes, voices can seem "more real than reality," in a way that is "overwhelming," even when they are experienced as emanating from within. We can make sense of this by returning to a point made in chapter 2: different factors contribute to a sense of presence or reality, factors that can conflict with each other and sometimes override one another. While some factors may become more pronounced, others may be diminished. In fact, the experience of a voice as *more real* than an object of auditory perception is partly attributable to its *not* coming from outside. Given this, its content is importantly unlike that of an auditory experience. When you hear a self-directed utterance, there is the possibility of error: perhaps it wasn't directed at me after all; perhaps I misheard what was said; perhaps it was not intended in the way I initially thought. Even where there is no doubt concerning the content and intended recipient of a communication, the possibility remains of challenging or rejecting what has been said. However, when faced with a linguistic manifestation of one's own self-directed emotional appraisal, these possibilities do not apply. Its content cannot be reinterpreted or rejected, at least not in the same way. What we have here is a peculiar kind of intentionality. In one sense, the voice is experienced as less real, given that it is removed from the public world. Yet it is also more real, as one cannot distance oneself from it in order to reinterpret or repudiate its pronouncements. This is consistent with the observation that voices are generally "perceived as being extraordinarily powerful" (Chadwick and Birchwood 1994, 191). The *judgment* of the voice comes with a heightened sense of authority; it knows you to an extent and in a way that makes its content irresistible:

"It's not just like hearing a person's voice who is in the room with you—in a way it is much more intimate, but can also be much more remote." (7)

"I did not hear the voices aurally. They were much more intimate than that, and inescapable." (9)

"It's more ghostly [than a real person's voice], it knows everything about you because it's a part of you." (10)

"They know me more intimately than others usually do." (36)

But why should this *intimacy* override the recognition that the voice does not originate in a public world, in a realm that is physically external to oneself and accessible to others? As will become clearer in chapters 5 and 6, the answer is that the sense of being immersed in a shared world is already altered and diminished. None of the person's perceptions and thoughts are embedded in a public world in the way they once were, and so the ordinarily taken-for-granted distinction between a consensus reality and his own experience of it is eroded. VH contents are consistent with a wider sense of alienation, passivity, helplessness, and interpersonal threat. To be more specific, they are crystallizations of negative, self-directed emotions that reflect his estrangement from the social world. Consider the following: "I hate everything about myself. ... I hear a voice that confirms everything I think about myself and sometimes it feels as if it is the only one that will tell me the real truth about myself. ... I can never concentrate on anything but how I am feeling and the voice I hear." Here, there is a combination of distressing, self-directed emotions and heightened attentiveness toward them.[15] The content of the voice is intimately associated with the content of these emotions: "I took an anti-psychotic to stop the voice and it helped a bit as I don't have something that seems so real confirming my feelings so outrightly."[16] Reference to a voice "confirming" feelings indicates that it not only expresses preformed feelings but also adds to them in some way. This, I suggest, is to be understood in terms of its giving them a more determinate content, one that is an object of anxious anticipation. Feelings of inadequacy and the like are initially indeterminate, but can take on a more determinate linguistic guise that *confirms* the emotional appraisal it is congruent with and out of which it arises.

My position is consistent to some extent with endorsement accounts of VH/TI, according to which a thought is experienced as alien because its content is in tension with other aspects of the person's self-conception and is therefore not endorsed by her:

> A person denies that she is the agent of a given thought because she finds that she cannot explain its occurrence in terms of her theory or conception of her intentional psychology. ... Whether a person regards a thought (subjectively) in him as something that he *thinks*, rather than as a mere episode in his psychological history, depends upon whether he finds it explicable in terms of his conception of what he believes and desires. (Stephens and Graham 2000, 162, 165)[17]

However, lack of endorsement does not *follow* formation of thought content. Instead, the person dreads the content *as it arises*, feels helpless before it, and is unable to repudiate it when it comes to fruition. The experience is one of ineffectively resisting the arrival of a negative emotional judgment regarding oneself:

> "It's mocking me, I hate that one. ... I am left in a state of fear. ... They don't sound like me. They are angry most of the time. I don't like to think of mean things, I try hard not to, but the more I try not to think the more the voices get nasty." (22)

Some first-person accounts further indicate a process of exactly the kind I have described, where an experience induces anxious anticipation, which itself proceeds to shape the experience in question:

> "It's very difficult to describe the experience. Words seem to come into my mind from another source than through my own conscious effort. I find myself straining sometimes to make out the word or words, and my own anxiety about what I hear or may have heard makes it a fearful experience. I seem pulled into the experience and fear itself may shape some of the words I hear." (32)

> "I have come to recognise the voices as expressions of anxiety, perhaps even a recognition of a fear I have about myself that I am not prepared to entertain as being part of my personality." (34)

In the case of (32), there is anxious anticipation of what is coming next, rather than lack of conscious anticipation, and this influences what is subsequently experienced. And, as further indicated by (34), anxiety about one's own thought contents is inextricable from a sense of their being alien;

the anxiety is constitutive of *disowning* something distressing. Consider also the following:

"There is a certain temporal weirdness to my voices often, which sort of alerts me to the fact that they aren't just someone else in the room. It's hard to describe, but in a certain way it feels as if they are 'echoey,' not in the normal auditory sense of echoey, but in the temporal sense—that they were somehow heard before they were said, or maybe understood or 'felt' before they were heard. The discrepancy is tiny, but it is noticeable and I have learned to notice that." (7)

Again, the view that VHs involve linguistic crystallizations of more diffuse emotional experiences serves to illuminate. Here, the VH experience is preceded by an emotional experience with a consistent, albeit less determinate, content. The person therefore senses its coming, and does so on the basis of something that has already happened. The VH is the *echo* of the emotion out of which it coagulates, something that was *felt* before it took on a more specific linguistic form.[18]

We can also understand the experience of "command hallucinations" in these terms. McCarthy-Jones et al. (2014) report that 67 percent of their subjects experienced commands, while 80 percent experienced voices addressing them in the second person. It is commonplace for people to voice their emotional self-evaluations in the second person, an observation that plausibly applies to inner dialogue as well: "Why on earth did you do that?"; "You just made a fool of yourself"; "Come on, you can do it!" So it is to be expected that VHs, if they are linguistic manifestations of negative, self-directed emotional states, will often take a second-person form. As for commands, many emotions are motivational and either incorporate or are at least very closely associated with action tendencies. An emotion can thus involve a disposition, or even an urge, to do something. So it is natural to suppose that some disturbing emotions will manifest themselves in the form of instructions or commands. As for "voices" that mention the subject in the third person, some or all of these may be better accounted for in terms of external VHs of a kind addressed in the next section, where there is a more audition-like experience of "them talking about me."

So far, I have construed VHs in terms of thought contents of whatever sophistication and duration. However, as noted in chapter 3, these can also be personified to varying degrees:

"The voice I hear in my head sounds different from my own inner voice, speaks differently and it is a person with a completely different personality that I have no control over." (1)

"The voices inside my head definitely have their own personalities, their own belief systems, their own values and morals." (2)

Personification can be partly accounted for in terms of thematic consistency. Insofar as VH contents are consistent, one might come to think of them as emanating from a singular personal source, while different thematic clusters might be attributed to different sources. Imaginative elaboration also has a role to play, and an increasingly detailed picture of the personality in question could feed into the anticipatory process, shaping VH experiences as they occur. Furthermore, general disturbances in the modal structure of intentionality would increase the likelihood of confusion between imagining and perceiving (as also mentioned in chapter 3). So the voice-hearer might anxiously anticipate imaginative episodes where someone gives linguistic form to an emotional judgment, thus alienating her not only from the voice but from its owner as well. The process could also involve memories of a particular individual, which might themselves be imaginatively embellished. We would therefore expect to see cycles of increasing personification, rather than the sudden arrival of a personality behind a voice. Along with this, the content of communications might become more specific and elaborate, as the contents of self-directed emotions are imaginatively enriched. Further thematic complexity could be added through the construction of an accompanying, contextualizing narrative, involving the activities of however many agents, which itself takes on some of the "qualities" of reality, something of the *sense of believing*. All of this is consistent with the observation that VHs often become more elaborate over time:

Those with longer histories described more hallucinated words and tended to produce more instances of hallucinated utterances. Furthermore, the non-recent group described a greater number of voices and a greater range of emotional expression and grammatical style of address including commenting on thoughts. A delusional construction of the significance of the voices (e.g. CIA plot) was more likely to be found in the chronic group. (Nayani and David 1996, 184)

I do not wish to imply that exactly the same process is at work in all cases. For instance, elaboration of the core experience may involve a distinctive type of change in the modal structure of intentionality, one that encompasses certain kinds of imagining as well as inner speech, while other VHs may involve a more specific disturbance of the boundary between perception and inner speech. And it could be that degree of personification depends on whether and to what extent the relevant emotions originate in distressing events involving particular individuals. The account offered here is thus intended to accommodate a range of more specific phenomena.

4.4 Hypervigilance

Up to now, my discussion has been limited to internal VH experiences, which I have distinguished from external, audition-like VHs. However, in emphasizing the contrast between these two broad categories, there is a risk of oversimplification. It is now time to acknowledge some of the messiness and diversity. First of all, it should be noted that the category "internal VH" accommodates different kinds of experience. It would be wrong to place all the emphasis on perception-like experiences of inner speech. The alienating role of anxiety could apply equally to distressing contents of memory and imagination. Some of these may have more pronounced auditory qualities, thus accounting for VHs that are experienced as both internal and audition-like. Michie et al. (2005) suggest that VHs consist of memory intrusions, rather than misplaced inner speech, although McCarthy-Jones et al. (2014) report that only 39 percent of their subjects acknowledged VH contents resembling memories and even fewer said that their VH contents were memories. So it could well be that the category "internal VH" is heterogeneous, encompassing inner speech, memories, and imaginings, as well as experiences that involve some combination of the three. The prevalence of one or another subtype may reflect individual differences, different life histories, and/or different psychiatric diagnoses. If, as seems plausible, a TI description of experience generally corresponds to "an internal VH involving a perception-like experience of inner speech" rather than "an internal VH of whatever kind," we would expect reports of internal VHs to be more widespread than reports of TI.

We should also keep in mind that social anxiety is not a singular phenomenon but something that would benefit from further analysis. Some first-person accounts emphasize shame and humiliation, others interpersonal threat and helplessness, and others guilt and self-hate. Different variants of social anxiety are likely to be associated with different thematic contents, given that VHs tend to be mood congruent. Again, some of these differences might correspond, at least to some degree, to different psychiatric diagnoses. For example, a person with a diagnosis of psychotic depression may hear voices that mock her and criticize her for her failures (Larøi 2006). Hence my account is able to handle considerable phenomenological diversity, and to distinguish VH characteristics that may be more typical of one or another diagnosis. It is not intended exclusively as an analysis of "inner speech hallucinations"; I am making a more generally applicable point about the modal structure of intentionality and the role played by affective, anticipatory processes.

But what about external VHs? If first-person accounts are to be taken at face value, these are often much more like veridical auditory perceptions. However, social anxiety is plausibly implicated here too, in some cases at least. In addition to inducing internal VHs, pervasive social anxiety could dispose a person to misperceive auditory stimuli, especially in complex, unpredictable social environments where there are plenty of ambiguous utterances and other noises. For example:

> "I was at an airport once and pretending not to listen to a very animate conversation—I was in the midst of a significant period of distress that resulted in psychiatric intervention for psychosis—I was looking down at the floor as I pretended not to listen. The content of the conversation was disturbing and I believed at the time it was directed at me. When I looked up the individuals in question were not speaking, and seemed to be positioned such that they could not have been engaged in such a lively conversation. This type of occurrence is quite common for me in periods of distress. Other times, I have had it confirmed that I really was 'overhearing' real comments and interpreting them in 'paranoid' ways—by sympathetic friends who I asked to listen along with." (25)

As with internal VHs, this could involve cycles of affective anticipation, as opposed to a lack of anticipation. Consider the following account, which concerns voices that appear to originate in the external environment:

> "Due to the murmuring voice experiences being so distressing with each successive occurrence however, I grew to dread ever more either whenever another experience would appear to possibly be forthcoming or, once in the midst of an actual ongoing experience, what would come next; waiting for the next shoe to drop." (31)

Consistent with reports such as these, Dodgson and Gordon (2009) suggest that some VHs, specifically those that seem to emanate from a determinate location in the external environment, are attributable to "hypervigilance." These experiences depend, to some extent at least, on sensory stimulation. However, because the person feels under threat, there is a heightened disposition toward false positives, toward the misinterpretation of environmental stimuli in terms of certain thematic contents. Negative emotions such as shame might then dissuade the voice-hearer from using other people for "reality testing." Vicious cycles can thus develop, involving anxiety, isolation, and an increasing tendency to misinterpret external stimuli in consistent ways. Dodgson and Gordon (2009, 332) therefore distinguish VHs that involve the misperception of inner speech from those attributable to the effects of anxious hypervigilance on auditory perception. It has been noted that VHs occur most often either in noisy social environments or when a person is on her own (e.g., Delespaul, deVries, and Van Os 2002). As Dodgson and Gordon observe, this further supports a distinction between two types of VH that are generated via two different mechanisms. When the person is alone with his thoughts, rather than distracted by the surrounding environment and by tasks he is engaged in, we would expect inner speech VHs to be most frequent. However, in noisy social environments, audition-like VHs would more likely predominate. All of this is consistent with my account of internal VHs. Furthermore, as anxiety is implicated in both cases, it is clear why many people "hear" both internal and external VHs. Incidentally, both types of VH could be said to involve failures of "source monitoring." And, insofar as a source-monitoring approach accommodates but fails to distinguish these importantly different kinds of experience (which also come about in quite different ways), it is insufficiently specific and lacks explanatory power. However, this is not to imply that a consideration of the modal structure of intentionality is irrelevant to an understanding of external VHs. As chapters 5 and 6 will further emphasize, VHs generally occur in the context of a shift in how the person relates to the social world as a whole, something that involves an all-enveloping change in the structure of intentionality. As well as rendering her vulnerable to internal VHs, this can also dispose her to misperceive or misinterpret certain environmental stimuli.

In conjunction with anxious hypervigilance, there is a role for what Hoffman (2007) calls "social deafferentation." In brief, the idea is that voice-hearers are often estranged from others in general and that, when socially isolated to such an extent, one can miss sensory input from others in much the same way that the nervous system comes to "miss" an amputated limb. In a manner that is analogous to the generation of a phantom limb, social isolation leads to the production of "spurious social meaning" in vulnerable individuals, involving "emotionally compelling hallucinations and delusions representing other persons or agents." Noting the association between schizophrenia and social isolation, as well as the correlation between reduced social interaction and the onset of VHs, Hoffman thus appeals to the "repopulating" of a "barren interpersonal world" (2007, 1066–1067). Given the distinction between internal and external VHs, this view requires further refinement. It is applicable to both types, but in different ways. In the case of external VHs, it can be combined with an emphasis on anxiety and hypervigilance. Even in the presence of others, the voice-hearer feels isolated; she needs interpersonal communication and is primed for it. At the same time, she dreads what she will find and is therefore disposed to experience environmental stimuli—especially spoken language—in terms of unpleasant, self-directed utterances. She cannot help seeking something but, in so doing, she ends up finding only the variant of it that she has been trying to avoid. In the case of internal VHs, it could be that, in addition to dreading the linguistic manifestations of self-directed emotions, she feels isolated from other people and thus especially prone to imagining interactions with them. But, as these interactions are shaped by negative, self-directed emotions, she is caught in the conflictual situation of seeking and resisting something at the same time. So we can see why one might have an ambivalent relationship with a "voice." For some, it is comparable to being stuck with a horrible "friend," owing to an absence of alternative company.

To summarize, internal VHs are heterogeneous, and all such experiences are to be distinguished from external VHs. Nevertheless, some external VHs are equally attributable to anxiety. It is thus fruitful to interpret VHs in terms of an overarching internal–external distinction, a distinction that is phenomenologically revealing and also points to different mechanisms. Consequently, it turns out that there is at least something to be said for how Jaspers (1963) distinguishes between hallucinations and pseudo-hallucinations. Granted, the term "pseudo-hallucination" has been and continues to be used in a number of different ways, does not have a clear referent, and is often unhelpful (Berrios and Dening 1996). But here, I am concerned more specifically with Jaspers' formulation of it. According to Jaspers, there are two main differences between hallucinations and pseudo-hallucinations: pseudo-hallucinations are experienced in "subjective space" and also lack the character of "objectivity" or "concrete reality" (1963, 69). This distinction is consistent with that between internal and external VHs.

To quote Jaspers (1963, 74), "we have to differentiate 'inner voices' ('voices of the mind') that is 'pseudo-hallucinations' from 'voices proper.'" Internal VHs are not experienced as externally located phenomena but arise *in the head* or, if you like, in one's own subjective *space*. Furthermore, the sense of presence or reality that they involve is not to be identified with that of *concrete reality*. The voice is taken to be real in a qualitatively different way from that in which a veridical utterance by another person is taken to be real. Nevertheless, I have argued that this does not imply taking it to be *less real*. Different factors contribute to a sense of its presence, and VH content is not present in quite the same *way* as an object of auditory perception. It is not the case that all hallucinatory experiences approximate, to varying degrees, a singular experience of presence or reality. That sense is multifaceted, and sometimes conflicted.

Jaspers (1963, 68) further states that pseudo-hallucinations are not really "perceptions" but, rather, a "special kind of imagery." He construes this in terms of a spectrum of sensory detail, spanning from less developed experiences to others that are comparable, in their content, to a veridical perceptual experience. What these "pseudo-hallucinatory" experiences lack corresponds to what I have called the *sense* of perceiving. However, I have argued that this does not apply to internal VHs. We need to distinguish the sense of having a perceptual experience from the characteristic content of such an experience. Internal VHs involve a perception-like experience of a more usually nonperceptual content, rather than a non-perception-like experience of something that continues to resemble perceptual content. So Jaspers is right to emphasize the distinction between internal and external VHs, as well as how their contents differ. But he is wrong to construe the contents of internal VHs as akin to those of external VHs, and he also fails to acknowledge how internal VHs can have a sense of reality that is, in some respects, *more* pronounced than that of external VHs. Therefore, the term "pseudo-hallucination" is after all a misleading one in this context, as it wrongly suggests that one kind of experience is somehow a poor approximation of another. However, there is another, more accurate way of thinking about pseudo-hallucination. This involves turning our attention away from first-person experience and toward the perspective of the interpreter. Internal VHs are not hallucinations, in the orthodox sense of an experience that resembles, to varying degrees, a veridical perception. Nevertheless, there is a pervasive tendency to misinterpret them as such. So they are pseudo-hallucinations, in the sense that they look like hallucinations of the orthodox variety to an insufficiently attentive interpreter, when they are not like that at all.

Can all VHs be unambiguously assigned either to the "internal" or to the "external" category? Jaspers seems to think so. He describes the difference between inner and outer or subjective and objective as a "gulf," and insists that "there are no transitions" (1963, 70). He does allow that an internal VH can change into an external VH. So, in ruling out transitional phenomena, I take him to be claiming that, although an internal VH might become an external VH, there are no enduring experiences that fall between the two. I doubt that this is the case, though, and my own account does allow for in-between cases. A perceptual stimulus could trigger an imagining, which is experienced as an object of pronounced anxiety, and consequently as alien and perception-like. The same applies to inner speech: an external stimulus with auditory qualities could trigger an increasingly determinate linguistic content that is then experienced as alien. Unlike an internal VH, this would seem to originate in the external environment, given its association with a perceived environmental cause. Auditory properties might also be interpreted so as to cohere with the content of the communication. This is consistent with descriptions of voices as "inside the head" and at the same time elicited by auditory stimuli:

> "They are often triggered by (real) sounds, and they have no meaning. For example, if I hear the words 'do it,' it won't be as if I am thinking of doing something, or feel like I'm being compelled to do something. The voice is also not my voice. And it is more audible than my thoughts, it jumps out over them." (18)

It could well be that many VH experiences straddle the internal–external distinction. Consider the following: "I can interpret an innocent conversation that people are having in my vicinity as a derisory discussion about me, which stops when I challenge it by listening more closely" (34). We might interpret this as a simple hypervigilance hallucination. On the other hand, it could involve something more complicated, such as hearing a conversation, getting a vague sense that it is about oneself, and then imagining things that might be said about oneself, which are themselves the manifestations of negative, self-directed emotions, and elicit anxiety as they crystallize. Thus, while the external–internal distinction serves to distinguish two importantly different phenomena, it is also compatible with there being a range of experiences between the two poles.[19]

4.5 Voices in Context

Although anxiety about one's own thought contents is unusual, it is perhaps more widespread than internal VHs. It could be that many people have disruptive, intrusive, and self-directed thoughts that provoke anxiety but are not experienced as VHs. I do not want to rule out the possibility that internal VHs, of the kind described here and in chapter 3, can occur against the backdrop of a more generally undisturbed modal structure. According to what I have said, an exceptionally pronounced feeling of anxiety with respect to a particular thought content could, in principle, induce such an experience. However, I am concerned with what is generally the case, rather than with what is conceivably the case on rare occasions. And VHs are more usually symptomatic of wide-ranging changes in the structure of experience, which render a person vulnerable to more pronounced, localized disruptions of the kinds so far described.

As discussed in chapter 2, the role of alterations in the overall structure or form of experience is a consistent theme in phenomenological psychopathology. For instance, van den Berg (1982, 103) states that "'a' hallucination, like any other artificially isolated phenomenon, can only be rightly observed in a study of psychical totality, which is disturbed in some way." Others have claimed, more specifically, that the early or prodromal stages of schizophrenia involve phenomenological changes that render a person's thoughts strangely and increasingly perception-like. There are reports of inner dialogue becoming "more pronounced" before the onset of voices, with "subtle pre-psychotic distortions of the stream of consciousness—such as abnormal sonorization of inner dialogue and/or perceptualization of thought" (Raballo and Larøi 2011, 163). A "morbid objectification of inner speech" is thus said to be "essential to the formation" of VHs (Henriksen, Raballo, and Parnas 2015, 172). This is consistent with a gradual, progressive process, one that can culminate in experiences where voices are "almost personified" (Raballo and Larøi 2011, 165).

Such approaches have not sought to account for the primary experience of alienation in terms of social anxiety and social estrangement. Both are regarded as secondary to a more fundamental, schizophrenia-specific disturbance of self-awareness. Of particular interest, though, is what Louis Sass calls "hyperreflexivity": a heightened attentiveness to more usually unreflective aspects of experience, which is most fundamentally involuntary but can include forms of voluntary attention as well. This, Sass maintains, is largely responsible for a wide-ranging experience of alienation from psychological and bodily processes, in the context of which more localized anomalous experiences occur. Anxious anticipation of thought content, as described earlier, can be construed as a form of hyperreflexivity. It involves a heightened, largely involuntary attentiveness toward something, which at the same time constitutes a sense of alienation from its object. According to Sass, hyperreflexivity is bound up with "diminished self-affection," a global diminution of normal emotional feeling that can occur in conjunction with more localized affective responses that are unusually heightened and/or otherwise anomalous (e.g., Sass 2003, 2007, 2014a).[20] Again, this is consistent with the suggestion that unusual forms of affective anticipation can disrupt the sense of which intentional state one is in. That said, I do not wish to suggest that hyperreflexive alienation in psychiatric illness invariably takes this form. There may well be cases where alienation from experiences and thoughts is brought about in some other way and *makes* the person anxious. The anxiety would then feed into and exacerbate the original experience.

Sass maintains that, although the most disruptive forms of hyperreflexivity occur in schizophrenia, its presence is also consistent with other psychiatric diagnoses, including depersonalization disorder and some dissociative conditions (Sass 1992, 1994, 2014a). As we saw in chapter 2, others make the stronger claim that VH/TI originates in a distinctive form of self-disorder that is specific to schizophrenia, and that other types of VH experience are quite different (e.g., Henriksen, Raballo, and Parnas 2015). However, anxious alienation of thought content is diagnostically nonspecific, and the more enveloping phenomenological changes that I go on to describe in chapters 5 and 6 are also common to a range of psychiatric diagnoses. The implications of this for the diagnostic category "schizophrenia" will be considered in chapter 6. So far, I have focused on one of two roles played by social anxiety, that of acting as an immediate trigger for VHs. However, as mentioned in section 4.1, generalized anxiety and social isolation are also disposing factors (which is not to rule out others). People with various different psychiatric diagnoses report all-enveloping feelings of anxiety and estrangement. These, I will suggest, amount to wider-ranging disturbances in the structure of intentionality. In addressing such experiences, it is worth reminding ourselves of a central claim made by the Hearing Voices Movement: VHs originate in traumatic or otherwise unpleasant interpersonal events (e.g., Romme et al. 2009). Anxiety, stress, social estrangement, experiences of abuse, and fear of others are prominent themes in the accounts of many people who experience VHs. For example:

"I was only 9 when I started hearing voices so I don't remember so much. I had a lot of anxiety, OCD, was bullied and had no friends. I was constantly feeling stressed and out of place, kept everyone at a distance." (1)

"Life was very stressful. I was quite often in crisis mode. Lots of agitation present." (20)

"I was lonely and often scared, worried about what I'd done wrong and why I was being treated the way I was." (21)

"I was living in terror the first time it happened. I had been living in terror for a few years. It was a very dark time. I didn't open my blinds for fear of attack for two years. When I heard it first I actually thought it was my children screaming. I was so scared, it took me four years to tell my psych. I was hearing things. I was scared I would lose my children." (22)

"Before I started hearing voices, I was in an abusive relationship for five and a half years. He was mentally abusive, took control of me and banned me from seeing my friends and family. ... I ended up remembering that my ex had raped me and I started hearing voices not long after that." (23)

"I was fourteen years old and was in a period of intense distress: not sleeping, fearful that everyone hated me, that some people were trying to hurt me in some way I didn't understand but needed to figure out." (25)

"First began experiencing voices ... in an abusive church/home situation as a small child. Depression, anxiety, bullying." (38)

"I first began to hear voices during the darkest and loneliest time of my life." (35)

What is often described is a sequence of unpleasant situations and events, such as suffering childhood sexual abuse, followed by abusive relationships and marriage breakdowns in adulthood. In other cases, however, matters are not so clear. Some say that they have always heard voices or that they cannot remember when their voices started:

"I can't remember when it started, I can't remember it not happening." (3)

"I can't remember. I've been experiencing this since childhood." (18)

It should certainly not be assumed that VH/TI is invariably associated with a history of trauma or, at least, unpleasant interpersonal experiences. In an alternative scenario, anomalous experiences, including VH/TI, cause social isolation and disrupt social relationships. Nevertheless, it is plausible to maintain that traumatic events involving other people can and often do bring about changes in the structure of intentionality. Chapters 5 and 6 will address what these changes consist of and how they come about. I will show how traumatic experience can involve loss of a pervasive form of *trust*, *confidence*, or *certainty*, something that is inseparable from one's relationship with the social world and equally inseparable from the modal structure of intentionality. The account I will develop is consistent with work in phenomenological psychopathology, insofar as it emphasizes alterations in the overall structure of experience that envelop even the most basic or "minimal" sense of self. However, it further maintains that the integrity of this structure is dependent on interpersonal relations. In this respect at least, it is consistent with the stance of the Hearing Voices Movement.

5 Trauma and Trust

In chapter 4, I argued that affective anticipation makes a substantial contribution to the sense of being in a given type of intentional state. I focused primarily on episodic, content-specific disturbances of anticipation, but added that these are usually embedded in more enveloping alterations of intentionality. This chapter shows how the latter can likewise be understood in terms of anticipation. What I will call the "global style of anticipation" amounts to a kind of habitual conviction, on which the modal structure of intentionality depends. This style is inseparable from how we experience and relate to other people in general. Hence profound, wide-ranging, and enduring changes in the interpersonal realm, of a kind that are sometimes brought about by unpleasant events involving other people, also amount to changes in the overall structure of intentionality.

I begin by introducing Karl Jaspers' classic account of the "delusional atmosphere" that often precedes symptoms such as delusions and hallucinations. In so doing, I emphasize two points. First of all, wide-ranging phenomenological changes of this nature are not limited to the contents of experience and thought. They also involve alterations in the sense of reality, something that is rooted in perceptual experience rather than consisting of however many "beliefs" or "judgments." Second, seemingly localized, content-specific phenomena, of the kind that might be labeled "hallucinations" and/or "delusions," are often largely symptomatic of more enveloping changes in the sense of reality. While Jaspers suggests that these changes cannot be further characterized in phenomenological terms, I reject that view. However, rather than further addressing delusional atmosphere, I turn first of all to the effects of interpersonal trauma. My reason for doing so is methodological: descriptions of traumatic experience better serve to illustrate how experience incorporates an anticipatory style, and also how that style—and with it the modal structure of experience—relates to the interpersonal. Allegedly unintelligible phenomenological disturbances are easier to make sense of once the interpersonal, relational aspects of human experience are acknowledged. (As we will see in chapter 6, this applies equally to delusional atmosphere.)

I focus on the effects of traumatic experience in adulthood, which make salient the contrast between a previously taken-for-granted sense of confidence, trust, or certainty and the unpredictable, threatening world that one comes to inhabit following traumatic events. (In chapter 6, I widen the scope of the discussion to include childhood trauma.) To formulate a more detailed account of anticipatory style and how it is altered, I introduce some themes in the later writings of Edmund Husserl, which relate both to the modal structure of intentionality and to the nature of minimal self. Finally, by drawing on my interpretation of Husserl, I make clear why the structure of intentionality depends on the interpersonal. Three central themes are then further developed in chapter 6: (a) how the modal structure of intentionality is developmentally and constitutively dependent on other people; (b) what that structure consists of, with particular emphasis on its temporal constitution; and (c) the relationship between delusional atmosphere, as described by Jaspers, and a loss of confidence, trust, or certainty that is often—but perhaps not always—interpersonally caused.

5.1 Delusional Atmosphere

I suggested in chapter 4 that localized VH experiences generally occur against a backdrop of wider-ranging phenomenological changes. This is a prominent theme in phenomenological psychopathology, where there is a particular emphasis on experiences that arise during the early or prodromal stages of schizophrenia. An influential statement of the view is that of Jaspers (1963), who addresses phenomenological disturbances that both precede and fuel the onset of delusions. (As discussed in chapter 2, it has been proposed that these same disturbances are responsible for VH/TI.) Jaspers distinguishes what he calls "delusions proper" from "delusion-like ideas." The latter, he says, emerge in understandable ways from experience, whereas the former originate in what he describes as a "*transformation in our total awareness of reality*" (1963, 95).[1] According to Jaspers, a delusional belief cannot be understood in isolation from its wider phenomenological context. It is a "secondary" judgment that is symptomatic of a more "primary" delusional experience. He refers to this experience as "delusional atmosphere" or "delusional mood," and describes it as follows:

> Patients feel uncanny and that there is something suspicious afoot. Everything gets a *new meaning*. The environment is somehow different—not to a gross degree—perception is unaltered in itself but there is some change which envelops everything with a subtle, pervasive and strangely uncertain light. A living-room which formerly was felt as neutral or friendly now becomes dominated by some indefinable atmosphere. Something seems in the air which the patient cannot account for, a distrustful, uncomfortable, uncanny tension invades him. (Jaspers 1963, 98)

The claim is not simply that delusional atmosphere *causes* delusional beliefs to arise. Rather, primary delusions are intelligible only in the context of such an experience. By analogy, a checkmate situation would not be intelligible outside of a chess game. Thus, to understand the delusion, we also need to understand the more enveloping experience in which it is embedded. Delusional atmosphere involves some sort of perceptual change. But it is not just a change in one or more circumscribed perceptual contents, and its nature is hard to pin down. As Jaspers says, things are "somehow" different, in a way that is "indefinable." In fact, it is seemingly paradoxical, in that "perception" is at the same time "unaltered." In other words, if we somehow managed to compile a complete inventory of perceived properties before and after the onset of delusional atmosphere, everything would be much the same; red things would still be red, squares would still be square, and so on.

What has happened, then? Importantly, Jaspers (1963, 93) states that "the experience within which delusion takes place is that of experiencing and thinking that something is real." By this, he does not just mean that delusions involve taking something to be real when it is not. Ordinarily, when we perceive something, perception incorporates not only a sense of *what it is* but also the sense *that it is*. It appears as *there*, *present*, and part of the same world as the perceiver. Jaspers' proposal, at least as I understand it, is that delusion-formation involves a disturbance of this ordinarily taken-for-granted sense of things as *there*; nothing presents itself in quite the same way anymore. So things look different not because their physical properties have changed but because they have a different kind of presence. In other words, the *sense of perceiving* is somehow diminished or otherwise altered. In this respect, the experience is analogous to the more localized experiences discussed in chapters 3 and 4, where something continues to "look like" the content of a thought but is no longer experienced as thought-like, given that the sense of thinking has been disrupted. However, delusional atmosphere involves a wider-ranging and less pronounced disturbance of intentionality. Another important difference is that, according to Jaspers, perceptual experience has a privileged status over other types of intentionality. It not only incorporates a grasp of distinctions such as "here/not here" and "the case/not the case"; it is also the basis for that grasp. And, as argued in chapter 2, all other forms of intentionality are dependent on these same distinctions. Without any sense of the difference between something being and not being the case, we could not distinguish believing or perceiving from imagining. The ability to distinguish between remembering, anticipating, and various other kinds of intentional state involves a further appreciation of the differences between "what was once the case," "what might be the case," "what will be the case," "what has never been or never will be the case," and so forth. And, without any appreciation of the overarching contrast between being and not being the case, more refined discriminations such as these would be equally unsustainable.

Hence, when we take something to be the case or otherwise in the form of a nonperceptual judgment or belief, the possibility of such an attitude is not autonomous of perceptual experience but dependent on a more fundamental experience of reality. We can, Jaspers says, think up as many definitions of "reality" as we want, but our thoughts about reality will never add up to a sense of what it is to be real. What is needed is "something more that this purely logical concept of reality; there is also *the reality we experience*" (1963, 93–94). Our experience incorporates a kind of bedrock (the nature of which remains unclear), in which some things are embedded and thus taken to be the case, while others are not. It is the nature of this bedrock, and its role in sustaining the modal structure of intentionality, that I seek to explore here.

How might "delusional atmosphere" (and also those delusional beliefs that arise within it) be further characterized? A consistent observation is that it is extremely difficult to describe. Jaspers (1963, 62) states that "description always proceeds by metaphor," and goes so far as to concede that "it is impossible to express the experiences directly." He is surely right that people struggle to communicate them. As Sass (1992, 46) observes, even highly articulate individuals "are usually reduced to helplessly repeating the same, horribly inadequate phrase: everything is strange, or everything is somehow different." That people have difficulty articulating something does not imply that it is impossible to understand or describe. Furthermore, even if the experience cannot be understood in the first person, this does not rule out the possibility of a phenomenologically sensitive interpreter shedding some light on it. Nevertheless, Jaspers (1963, 98) insists that the "primary experiences" underlying delusions proper are forever outside the reach of phenomenological understanding:

> If we try to get some closer understanding of these primary experiences of delusion, we soon find we cannot really appreciate these quite alien modes of experience. They remain largely incomprehensible, unreal and beyond our understanding.

However, he does not make clear where the limits of comprehension lie. There cannot be a total embargo on phenomenological understanding, as Jaspers himself offers a description of delusional atmosphere that surely includes at least some insight into its nature. He also maintains that the transition from atmosphere to delusion is something we can make sense of. Delusional atmosphere involves a pervasive and unpleasant feeling of uncertainty. So those afflicted with it search for some "fixed point," any fixed point, to which they can cling, and delusions are the outcome of that search. Jaspers (1963, 98) adds that this is akin to something we all do on occasion: "Whenever we find ourselves depressed, fearful or at a loss, the sudden clear consciousness of something, whether true or false, immediately has a soothing effect." Thus, it is not the transition from experience to fully formed delusion that resists characterization but the experience itself.[2]

Jaspers' positive account of how delusional atmosphere leads to fully formed delusions shares certain features with the account of VH/TI developed in chapters 3 and 4. In both cases, we have the articulation or linguistic crystallization of something less determinate. Along with this, there is an emphasis on how something seemingly specific depends, at least in part, on phenomenological changes that are more pervasive. However, while I attribute VH/TI to anxious anticipation, which disrupts the modal structure of intentionality, Jaspers emphasizes a felt need to relieve the tension that permeates an indeterminate and unpleasant experience. Nevertheless, the two need not be mutually exclusive. When faced with anxiety-driven VHs, as well as wider-ranging changes in the structure of experience, a person might feel a need to interpret the overall experience in a more determinate, coherent way. The delusional interpretation of experience that consequently arises cannot be a straightforward belief or system of beliefs. While it serves to make sense of, among other things, a modal disruption of experience, it is also embedded in that disruption. It therefore involves a kind of intentionality that differs from clear-cut cases of imagining or believing.

Delusional interpretations of anomalous experience are not so tightly connected with modal disruptions as internal VHs (which, I have argued, just *are* especially pronounced modal disruptions). Even so, they arise against the backdrop of wider-ranging disturbances of intentionality, which culture certain *kinds* of intentional state and shape, to some degree, their thematic contents. This is not to suggest that VHs will always go together with what Jaspers describes, just that the two are compatible and can be understood in complementary ways. Delusional interpretations of anomalous experience are possible in the absence of VHs, and vice versa. Where there are global changes in the structure of intentionality, but without heightened, localized disruptions brought about by anxious anticipation of thought content, we might expect to find delusional interpretations of experience without VHs. Where global phenomenological changes are not so pronounced, but localized disruptions are more extreme, VHs could occur in the absence of delusions.

So we have at least a sketch of how an all-enveloping shift in a perceptually grounded sense of reality might be responsible for certain so-called "delusions" and "hallucinations." However, we can go much further than Jaspers in exploring what changes in the sense of reality consist of.[3] I have already suggested that it is helpful to conceive of them in terms of the modal structure of intentionality. I will now argue that they can be described more specifically still, in terms of anticipation. In brief, my proposal is that the experience of reality Jaspers refers to consists in a dynamic interplay of anticipation and fulfillment. All intentional states, of the form "remembering that *p*," "perceiving that *q*," and "imagining that *r*," presuppose this dynamic, and changes in the modal structure of experience can be understood in terms of its disruption. It follows that these changes are, after all, comprehensible. That said, they present us with a particular interpretive challenge. For the most part, when we seek to understand others' experiences, we take for granted that they inhabit the same modal space as ourselves. It does not occur to us to question whether they believe, remember, imagine, or think in quite the ways we do, whether they experience time as we do, or whether they are rooted in the public world in the way we are. So, to understand modal disruptions, we first have to make explicit and suspend certain assumptions that are more usually made about the commonality of experience. This applies not only to delusional atmosphere but to any phenomenological difference between people that is wholly or partly attributable to differences in the modal structure of intentionality (Ratcliffe 2012).

To address the relevant phenomenology in more depth, I will leave aside delusional atmosphere for now and turn instead to kinds of enduring change in *how one finds oneself in the world* that are sometimes brought about by traumatic events. These experiences better serve to illustrate how the modal structure of experience centrally involves anticipation, and also how it is inextricable from interpersonal relations. This is because they are explicitly attributed to certain kinds of interpersonal cause, which are said to shatter a primitive form of trust. By clarifying the nature of this trust, we come to see how the modal structure of experience depends on a ubiquitous style of anticipation. Chapter 6 will then explore the similarities, differences, and relationships between delusional atmosphere and traumatic loss of trust. As we will see, the line between them is far from clear. And, in both cases, altered interpersonal experience is inseparable from a change in the modal structure of intentionality, rather than unilaterally implied by it or otherwise secondary to it. By recognizing the extent to which, and the ways in which, the integrity of experience depends on being with other people, we come to better understand something that Jaspers took to be incomprehensible.

5.2 Trauma

Like delusional atmosphere, the experiential changes that follow traumatic events can be all-enveloping, profound, and difficult to describe. In both cases, what is affected includes not only however many intentional states but also something that the integrity of intentionality depends on. For now, I focus on traumatic events in adulthood and, more specifically, traumatic events that are deliberately brought about by other people. My aim is to describe a pervasive shift in how the traumatized person relates to others, something that is often referred to in terms of losing trust but can equally be conveyed in terms of losing confidence, security, or certainty. This, I will suggest, centrally involves a pervasive alteration in the sense of time, something that can be construed more specifically in terms of an overall style of anticipation.

Among other examples, I will consider the psychological effects of torture, something that involves a subversion of the trust that ordinarily underlies and regulates encounters with other people.[4] The two psychiatric diagnoses most often associated with the effects of torture are major depression and post-traumatic stress disorder (PTSD), which are difficult to tease apart when diagnosed together (Istanbul Protocol 1999, 45). As the kind of phenomenological change I seek to describe here is not exclusive to torture victims, it might seem preferable to widen the scope of the inquiry to PTSD and depression. However, the diagnostic category "PTSD" admits considerable heterogeneity, and there are also high levels of comorbidity with several other psychiatric conditions (DSM-IV-TR, American Psychiatric Association 2000, 465). The same points apply to "major depression" (Ratcliffe 2015). Furthermore, some forms of trauma, such as "war trauma," involve a wider range of symptoms than those associated with PTSD and/or major depression (Ford 1999; Hunt 2010). The kind of experience I have in mind is better captured by the ICD-10 subcategory of "enduring personality change after catastrophic experience," the symptoms of which include "a hostile or mistrustful attitude towards the world," "social withdrawal," "feelings of emptiness of hopelessness," "a chronic feeling of being 'on the edge,' as if constantly threatened," and "estrangement" (World Health Organization 1992, 209). It is also consistent with Judith Herman's account of what she calls "complex PTSD" or "disorders of extreme stress not otherwise specified" (Herman 1997; Ford 1999). However, it is not reliably associated with any one psychiatric diagnosis.

Given that (a) the experience is not diagnostically specific, (b) many of the relevant diagnostic categories are contested, and (c) all of these categories are also compatible with other—often subtly different—kinds of experience, I do not tie my subject matter to one or another diagnosis. Instead, I focus on the effects of a certain kind of traumatic event, where suffering is deliberately inflicted on a person by one or more others, usually with the intent to do harm. Torture is an extreme example of this, but my discussion applies equally to the potential effects of bullying, sexual assault, domestic violence, prejudicial discrimination, enforced periods of extended solitary confinement, and other forms of physical and psychological abuse.

In referring to "trauma" it is debatable whether the emphasis should be on events that are intrinsically traumatic according to some criterion or whether any event that affects a given person in the relevant way qualifies as traumatic in that instance. In this chapter, I am concerned with occurrences that would cause almost anyone great distress, and so the distinction between traumatic events and the traumatic effects of events is not so pressing.[5] I thus refer both to "traumatic events" and to enduring "traumatic experiences" or "experiences of trauma" that follow them. Of course, people respond in different ways to traumatic events, owing to factors that include age, gender, idiosyncratic dispositions, life history, interpersonal relationships, and how events are interpreted and reinterpreted individually, socially, and culturally. Furthermore, effects of traumatic events can be hard to distinguish from effects of wider social and cultural upheavals, as is often the case in refugee populations.[6] The potentially different effects of discrete traumatic events and repeated or chronic exposure should also be kept in mind (Herman 1997; Ford 1999).

Although the kind of experience addressed here does not invariably follow interpersonal trauma, there is something distinctive about the psychological effects of harm inflicted by others. As Janoff-Bulman (1992, 77) observes, being "singled out for injury ... by another person ... presents particular challenges to the victim's assumptive world. ... Survivors of human-induced victimizations are most apt to hold negative assumptions about themselves and the benevolence of the world." I want to explore the nature of these "challenges" to one's "assumptions," and to show how a pervasive loss of the sense that people are "benevolent" implies a change in the overall structure of experience. So my approach is to demonstrate the manner in which and the extent to which the integrity of experience is vulnerable to other people, by focusing on certain extreme cases. However, the kind of phenomenological disturbance I will describe is not exclusive to such cases. Something very similar could come about through a more subtle and gradual process, involving a sequence of events or perhaps a long-term interpersonal relationship that slowly alters what a person expects from others in general. It should be added that, even in the case of an extreme event, the relevant experience is not simply an effect of the event itself. Causal relations here are complicated, and the effects of traumatic events also depend, to varying degrees, on how other people respond—at the time, immediately afterward, and in the longer term. Furthermore, as the relationship between traumatic events and subsequent phenomenological changes is a causal one, it may be that similar or identical changes arise from other causes as well, including causes of a wholly impersonal nature (a point I will return to in chapter 6). Hence traumatic events are neither necessary nor sufficient for the type of experience described here. Nevertheless, they are frequently associated with it, and there is a clear connection between the nature of the events and the nature of the experience in question. A kind of trust or confidence, consisting of a habitual style of interpersonal anticipation, is disrupted by interpersonal experiences that run counter to it.[7]

5.3 Projects and Narratives

To see how traumatic experience can alter anticipatory style, let us start with the more general observation that the experience of time is somehow affected. The Istanbul Protocol, a United Nations guide for investigating and documenting cases of torture, describes one of its long-term effects as follows:

> The victim has a subjective feeling of having been irreparably damaged and having undergone an irreversible personality change. He or she has a sense of foreshortened future without expectation of a career, marriage, children or normal lifespan. (1999, 47)

A "sense of foreshortened future" is also mentioned as a symptom of PTSD in the fourth edition of the *Diagnostic and Statistical Manual of Mental Disorders* (DSM-IV-TR, American Psychiatric Association 2000, 468). In DSM-5, there is a more general statement about negative expectations concerning the future. But what, exactly, does this sense of foreshortened future or change of attitude toward the future consist of; what is it that people describe in these terms? The DSM and Istanbul Protocol do not provide any further clarification, and the cursory descriptions that they do offer are compatible with various interpretations.

On one account, a sense of foreshortened future involves a cluster of interrelated judgments about what the future most likely holds, such as "I will die young," "I will not have a family," and "I will not have a successful career." These either comprise or originate in a more general evaluation of future events, the content of which is something like "Bad things are going to happen to me and good things are not going to happen to me." In conjunction with this, negative emotions toward the future predominate: one fears that *p* and *q*, rather than hoping that *r* and *s*. If this is right, then a sense of foreshortened future is to be distinguished from an experience of time itself or, if you prefer, from an experience of temporal properties. The traumatized person continues to distinguish past, present, and future, to anticipate the arrival of future events, and to experience temporal passage. Regardless of whether she anticipates future event *p*, where *p* is evaluated negatively (most notably, her own premature death), or future event *q*, where *q* is evaluated positively, both are experienced as "future" in the same way. So a foreshortened future is a matter of *what* is anticipated, a negative evaluation of what the future holds rather than an altered sense of the future itself. However, such as interpretation would be mistaken. Instead of a change in what is anticipated, arising against a backdrop of intact temporal experience, there is an altered sense of temporal passage, of "moving forward" in time, along with a change in how past, present, future, and the relationships between them are experienced. (In chapter 6, I will suggest that posttraumatic "flashbacks" can also be understood in these terms.)

A sense that the future is bereft of positive, meaningful life events is equally a sense that one's meaningful life is in the past, finished. So remarks to the effect that the future has nothing to offer are sometimes accompanied by the claim that one has died, that part of one has died, or that one persists but no longer "lives": "I felt as though I'd somehow outlived myself" (Brison 2002, 9). This corresponds to a wider phenomenon that Freeman (2000, 89) has called "narrative foreclosure," defined as "the premature conviction that one's life story has effectively ended: there is no more to tell; there is no more that *can* be told." It is not just that the person believes she does not have much time left. The traumatic event somehow disrupts her ongoing life story in such a way that the story ceases to be sustainable. (A "life story," for current purposes, is a meaningful, largely coherent interpretation of past activities, relationships, achievements, and failures, which also includes a sense of where one is heading—what one's cares, commitments, and projects currently consist of, and what one seeks to achieve.) Even if something like this is right, it does not tell us *why* a life story has collapsed. Consider three possible scenarios:

1. Loss of a life narrative is constitutive of a sense of foreshortened future.
2. Loss of a life narrative is symptomatic of a loss of projects, cares, and commitments upon which that narrative is founded.
3. Both (1) and (2) are symptomatic of losing something that is presupposed by the intelligibility of life narratives and life projects.

I doubt that a sharp distinction can be drawn between (1) and (2), as the ability to develop, sustain, and revise projects and commitments plausibly includes the ability to situate them within a cohesive, purposive, forward-looking narrative, one that is told and retold to oneself and others. I do not deny that some instances of narrative foreclosure are attributable largely or wholly to a combination of (1) and (2). Life projects and commitments depend on a wider social and cultural environment, and are therefore vulnerable to collapse in the event of changes in that environment. For example, if universities ceased to exist after some major social upheaval, a life focused around excelling as a university professor would be unsustainable. Numerous projects would collapse, along with a broader, purposive narrative into which they are integrated; a life story would be cut short. Lear (2006) describes how cultural changes can lead to loss of meaning structures that the life stories and purposive activities of whole communities depend on. This amounts to a form of narrative foreclosure, a sense that meaningful events can no longer transpire, that nothing can "happen." However, it is to be distinguished from a superficially similar but importantly different kind of experience.

Interpersonal trauma can lead to narrative foreclosure even when the relevant social and cultural structures remain largely intact. Indeed, reestablishing a sense of connection with these structures has been identified as an important goal of rehabilitation (Herman 1997). Furthermore, trauma is often experienced as specific to oneself; it is something that "I" and "I alone"—rather than "we"—have endured and continue to endure. In such cases, it involves a kind of isolation from others that distinguishes it from shared meaning loss (although the distinction is certainly not clear-cut, and the kind of experience I describe can also involve shared meaning loss). In at least some cases, I suggest, what is lost is not just (1) and/or (2) but also (3). In the scenario described by Lear, an open and meaningful future remains; what is lacking is a more determinate sense of which meaningful possibilities that future includes. However, for some, even this much is lost. There is a change in the structure of temporal experience and, to be more specific, in the overall style of anticipation. We can begin to understand its nature by turning to the closely related theme of "trust."

5.4 Trust

First-person accounts of severe trauma, especially interpersonal trauma, tend to emphasize the loss of trust. There are references to this in diagnostic manuals as well. For instance, DSM-5 (American Psychiatric Association

2013, 271) refers to "exaggerated negative beliefs" such as "no one can be trusted" and "the world is completely dangerous." But what, in this context, is "trust"? Use of the term is easily misunderstood. Trust is sometimes construed by philosophers as a three-place relation, of the form "A trusts B to do *z*." So the philosophical task becomes that of identifying criteria with which to distinguish trusting B to do *z* from various other attitudes, such as hoping that B will do *z* and thinking that B will probably do *z*.[8] However, this does not exhaust the scope of trust. Three-place trust can be distinguished from two-place trust, where "A trusts B" full stop, without reference to a specific situation or action. There is also what we might call "one-place trust," where one trusts other people in general rather than trusting a specific individual or group of individuals: one "trusts B to do *z*" because one "trusts B," and one trusts B because one simply "trusts." The latter might also be described as "having trust" and is thus analogous to "having hope," something that need not relate to a particular hope content (Ratcliffe 2015, chap. 4).

Although one-place trust is seldom remarked on in mundane, everyday discourse, its loss is a conspicuous theme in first-person accounts of traumatic experience. It might be objected that the term "trust" is misleading here, as "trust" ordinarily refers to the three-place and perhaps also the two-place relation, both of which are quite different. One-place trust is at least closely related to the others: one must first *have trust* in order to trust B to do *z* or to trust B more generally. Even so, that *p* is a condition of possibility for *q* does not imply that *p* and *q* are of the same type. And nothing really hinges on whether we insist on the word "trust." A reason for retaining it, though, is that people generally *do* refer to what I describe as a form of trust. However, a host of related terms are also at play. Jones (2004) calls it "basal security," while Herman (1997) refers to "basic trust" and also to a sense of "safety in the world." Améry (1999) describes an enduring loss of "trust in the world" that he experienced after torture and subsequent incarceration in Auschwitz, but also emphasizes the broader theme of "security," which includes an "entire field" of related words, such as "loyal, familiar, confidence, to trust, to entrust" (47).[9] In what follows, I will suggest that a loss of "trust" in people in general also implies a wider loss of "trust" in the world, but that both can equally be construed in terms of losing habitual confidence, losing a distinctive and seldom explicitly acknowledged form of certainty, or losing a sense of security. So I do not wish to be too prescriptive with regard to terminology.

"Having trust" might be construed as a nonphenomenological disposition to adopt certain attitudes and have certain kinds of experience. However, it also has a phenomenology in its own right; "losing trust" involves losing a habitual confidence that more usually permeates all experience, thought, and activity. Many accounts of traumatic experience support this view. The effects of trauma are sometimes described in terms of finding oneself in a different world, a world where people in general seem somehow different: "the entire world of people becomes suspect" (Janoff-Bulman 1992, 79).[10] Traumatic events are often said to shatter a way of experiencing the world and other people that was previously taken for granted:

> We experience a fundamental assault on our right to live, on our personal sense of worth, and further, on our sense that the world (including people) basically supports human life. Our relationship with existence itself is shattered. Existence in this sense includes all the meaning structures that tell us we are a valued and viable part of the fabric of life. (Greening 1990, 323)

What, exactly, does this "shattering" involve? It could be that experiencing significant suffering at the hands of another person leads to a negation of engrained beliefs such as "people do not hurt each other for the sake of causing pain," "people will help me if I am suffering," and so on. Then again, through our constant exposure to news stories and other sources, most of us are well aware that people seriously harm each other in all manner of ways. One option is to maintain that we do not truly believe such things until we endure them ourselves, and various references to loss of trust as the overturning of deeply held "assumptions" lend themselves to that interpretation. For example, Herman (1997, 51) states that "traumatic events destroy the victim's fundamental assumptions about the safety of the world," and Brison (2002, 26) describes how interpersonal trauma "undermined my most fundamental assumptions about the world." An explicitly cognitive approach, which construes these assumptions as "cognitive schemas" or fundamental beliefs, is adopted by Janoff-Bulman (1992, 5–6), who identifies three such beliefs as central to one-place trust: "the world is benevolent"; "the world is meaningful"; and "the self is worthy."

However, it seems implausible to insist on something like this: B thinks that B believes that *p*, when in fact B believes that not *p* until B suffers greatly at the hands of other people and really does come to believe that *p*. It could be argued that the term "belief" encompasses more than one type of attitude (a position I will endorse in chapter 8). So one *a*-believes that *p* but later comes to *b*-believe it too.[11] Another option is to note that the belief "People have done *p* to other people and will do so again" is distinct from "Someone might do *p* to a particular person, me." Hence the deep-rooted belief that is overturned is of the form "*p* won't (or even can't) happen to me." One, the other, or both might well be right, but it would be a mistake to construe loss of one-place trust solely or even principally in these terms. Although it clearly does involve changes in attitude toward oneself, other people, and the world more generally, it also involves something else.[12]

What is eroded is a habitual, nonpropositional *style of anticipation*, which cannot be exhaustively characterized in terms of however many propositional attitudes of the form "B believes that *p*." It is something that could be described in terms of the negation of any number of different propositions, including "The world is safe," "Others will help me when I am in trouble," "People generally mean well," "Good things will happen in the future," "I will live a long time," "There are worthwhile projects," "I am worthy," and "I have friends." However, such utterances do not just convey distinct, thematically related belief contents. They are also used to express a unitary and more enveloping phenomenological change, the nature of which can be made clearer by emphasizing the theme of unpredictability:

> Massive deconstruction of the absolutisms of everyday life exposes the inescapable contingency of existence on a universe that is random and unpredictable and in which no safety or continuity of being can be assured. (Stolorow 2007, 16)

A previously ubiquitous anticipatory style is lost, rather than anticipation pure and simple. The traumatized person may retain a consistent style of anticipation, but one that is quite different from before. Rather than anticipating things in general with a kind of unthinking confidence, she constantly anticipates something dreadful, the nature and arrival-time of which are variably indeterminate. And, where other people were previously taken for granted as dependable and predictable (at least for the most part), they now appear threatening and unpredictable. Many of us anticipate most things in the guise of habitual certainty. It does not occur to us that we will be deliberately struck by a car as we walk to the shop to buy milk or that we will be assaulted by the stranger we sit next to on the train. This is not to suggest that we naively trust everybody or feel safe all the time, regardless of circumstances. The point is that, when we do feel unsafe in a certain situation or explicitly distrust a particular person, this involves a departure from our default attitude.

Our sense of security can be so engrained that we are oblivious to it. Indeed, the more at home we are in the world, the less aware we are that *feeling at home in the world* is even part of our experience (Bernstein 2011; Baier 1986). It is not itself an object of experience but something that operates as a backdrop to our perceiving that *p*, thinking that *q*, or acting in order to achieve *r*. To lose it is not just to endorse one set of evaluative judgments over another. It is more akin to losses of practical confidence that all of us feel on occasion, in relation to one or another performance. Suppose, for instance, one starts to feel that one can no longer teach well. Granted, evaluative judgments have a role to play, but loss of confidence need not originate in explicit judgments about one's performance, and its nature is not exhausted by however many judgments. The lecture room somehow *looks* different—daunting, oppressive, unpredictable, uncontrollable. Along with this, one's actions lack their more usual fluidity and one's words their spontaneity. The experience centrally involves feeling unable to engage in a habitual, practical performance. And loss of confidence can remain resistant to change even when one explicitly endorses propositions such as "I am a good teacher." Experiences like this can be fairly circumscribed, relating primarily to certain situations. However, human experience also has an all-enveloping *style* of anticipation, and this is what is disrupted in trauma; there is a global change in what is anticipated from other people and, by implication, from the world in general.

5.5 Habitual Certainty

To further clarify what a style of anticipation consists of and how it relates to the structure of intentionality, I will now draw on some themes in the writings of Edmund Husserl. Some of Husserl's later work points the way toward a detailed analysis of the relationships between style of anticipation, the modal structure of intentionality, and our most primitive sense of self. In addition, it can help us to see why the structure of experience depends on interpersonal and social relations. I will suggest that Husserl's account is consistent with and further illuminates the nature of hard-to-describe phenomenological disturbances, such as those associated with trauma. In turn, its applicability to these experiences serves to corroborate it and to indicate ways of further developing it.

Of central concern here is how we experience *the possible*. Husserl proposes that perceptual experience of an entity is imbued with possibilities, some of which take the more specific form of anticipation. This is not to suggest that we can *see* possibilities in the way we see chairs and tables. Rather, perception of something as present includes a sense of the possible, which partly constitutes our appreciation of *what that entity is* and also our appreciation *that it is*. So possibilities are not added to our experience of what is "here, now"; they are integral to it. These possibilities are not experienced in isolation from one another. The claim is that perceptual experience of a given entity is inextricable from a characteristic *horizon* of possibilities, a structured system of potentialities for ongoing perceptual access:

> Everywhere, apprehension includes in itself, by the mediation of a "sense," empty horizons of "possible perceptions"; thus I can, at any given time, enter into a system of possible and, if I follow them up, actual, perceptual nexuses. (Husserl 1952/1989, §15, p. 42)

An entity's "horizon" is intersensory in structure. When we perceive something through one sense, it also offers us possibilities for accessing it through other sensory modalities (1952/1989, §18, p. 75). For example, a cup might appear visually as something you could reach out and touch. Importantly, the horizonal structure of experience also involves an appreciation of entities as perceptually available to other people. According to Husserl (e.g.,1952/1989, §18, pp. 86–87), the phenomenological difference between encountering something as *really there*, independent of my own perspective on it, and experiencing it as self-generated is constituted by a sense of whether or not it is actually or potentially accessible to others. The horizonal structure of experience is also inextricable from the feeling (as opposed to the felt) body—the body is not merely an object of perception; it is also an organ of perception, *through which* we experience our surroundings. To be more specific, an appreciation of how to gain additional perceptual access to an entity is also an awareness of how to move in order to actualize perceptual possibilities. Hence the possibilities we experience as integral to the environment are, at the same time, felt bodily dispositions.[13]

If this much is accepted, we might wonder whether the horizonal structure of experience is limited to potential *perceptions* and associated bodily dispositions. I have argued elsewhere that we should conceive of it in a more encompassing and elaborate way, to include possibilities for goal-directed action and the many, subtly different kinds of *significant* possibility that relate, in different ways, to our activities. For instance, something might appear relevant insofar as it is urgently required in the context of a project, obstructs one's activities, appears immediately enticing, or threatens. These different kinds of possibility also implicate the feeling body in different ways. For instance, the experience of something as immediately threatening and certain to occur is bound up with dispositions to retreat from it, to hide, or to protect oneself, whereas the sight of a cold drink when very thirsty on a hot day exerts a bodily pull—one feels drawn toward the object. It can be added that other people offer a range of further possibilities, from emotional communion to specifically personal forms of threat. I have further argued that certain kinds of experience are best interpreted in terms of changes in the *types* of possibility that are phenomenologically accessible to a person. For instance, it might be that nothing appears tangible or practically accessible anymore, or that other people in general cease to offer the potential for certain kinds of interpersonal connection (Ratcliffe 2015, chap. 2).

For current purposes, the emphasis is more specifically on experiences of possibility that take the form of immediate anticipation, the sense that something will happen shortly, will probably happen, might happen, might not happen, or might not unfold as previously anticipated. Many experienced possibilities are to be understood in this way. However, it is not clear that all of them are. For instance, some interpersonal possibilities arguably take the form, "If someone *were* there now, that person would also be able to see this." Something similar may also apply to certain impersonal possibilities: "If I were to turn this cup around, then I would see something along the lines of *p*, even though I do not anticipate turning the cup around and, by implication, do not anticipate seeing *p*."

Experiences of anticipation are to be construed in a dynamic way: as possibilities are actualized (through one's own actions, the actions of others, and/or impersonal events), other possibilities are revealed, and so on. Husserl suggests that, for the most part, this process proceeds in a way that is "unobstructed." In other words, perceptual expectations are fulfilled, generating further expectations, which are themselves fulfilled, facilitating an experience of something that is both consistent and increasingly specific: a "progressive fulfilment of expectations, a fulfilment which is at the same time always an ever more precise determination of the object" (Husserl

1948/1973, §21, p. 87). We do not merely anticipate things; we are also *drawn into* situations, solicited to actualize certain possibilities, in ways that yield increasingly refined perceptions of entities. Some experienced possibilities entice us and cannot be extricated from a felt bodily inclination to actualize them. There is, as Husserl says, a "striving 'to come ever closer' to the object" that belongs to "normal perception," as well as a sense of "satisfaction" as it progresses and our perceptual access to the object is enhanced (1948/1973, §20, pp. 85–86).[14] Hence perceptual experience is riddled with practically engaged anticipation.

Should we think of possibility and, more specifically, anticipation, in terms of the content of the experience or its attitudinal phenomenology? One option is to maintain that what we anticipate from an entity is integral to our experience *of it* and thus enriches experiential content. It could be added that, when we set aside experiential content and seek out a wholly separate experience of anticipation, there is nothing to be found—experience is transparent. So, in response to the argument of chapters 3 and 4, one might object that there is, after all, nothing more to the sense of being in a given type of intentional state than its characteristic content. The problem is just that the scope of content has been understated and that there has been a failure to acknowledge the possibility of conflict between different types—or perhaps different aspects—of content, including what we anticipate from things. This way of thinking presupposes, from the outset, a neat separation between intentional attitude and content. We first split them off from each other. Then we describe experiential content. Then we set aside anything that is attributable to content, ask what is left of the attitude, and conclude that there is nothing to be found. However, the sense of the possible described by Husserl does not respect an attitude–content distinction; it cuts across it. The possibilities we experience as integral to entities in the surrounding environment are at the same time felt as bodily dispositions, as phenomenologically accessible movement tendencies of various kinds. When an entity says "Turn me around to reveal my hidden side," we feel drawn toward it in a specific way. It is not that we experience the possibilities and also the bodily dispositions; they are one and the same thing. The relevant bodily dispositions are not themselves objects of experience, at least not ordinarily. It is through these dispositions that we experience possibilities as inherent in things.[15] Felt dispositions have a dual-aspect structure; they manifest themselves as possibilities that are integral to what we experience, and they contribute, at the same time, to the experience of encountering it in a given way. The latter contribution, I will show, is central to the sense of being in one or another type of intentional state with respect to a given entity.

To appreciate the relevance of Husserl's work to the phenomenology of trauma and the modal structure of intentionality, we need to make clear what form the experience of anticipation ordinarily takes. Husserl maintains that there is a sense of confidence or "certainty" inherent in perceptual activity. We do not just recognize something as possible; we anticipate it with such confidence that no alternatives present themselves. What we anticipate is variably determinate, and so confident anticipation does accommodate what he calls "open" uncertainty. For example, when I reach to turn around an object, such as a cup or an ornament, what I anticipate might be "a side with the same shape and the same color," or it might be something less specific, such as "the currently unseen side of a solid, three-dimensional object of an approximate size." When perception proceeds confidently, the resolution of open uncertainty takes the form of filling in the blanks, yielding a more specific appreciation of the object and its properties that is consistent with what was anticipated (Husserl 1948/1973, §21, pp. 96–98). Thus, a habitual, bodily confidence or sense of certainty, which allows for varying degrees of indeterminacy, is what we might call the "default mode" of anticipation: "Original, normal perception has the primordial mode, 'being valid simpliciter'; this is what we call straightforward, naïve certainty. The appearing object is there in uncontested and unbroken certainty" (Husserl 2001, §8, p. 75).

Husserl contrasts confident anticipation with what he calls "problematic" uncertainty. Here, what is anticipated is not just indeterminate; there is also an experience of "doubt," which involves conflicting systems of anticipation and eventual resolution in favor of one system or the other. In unproblematic cases, it is not that all potentially conflicting possibilities are ruled out. Rather, they are not salient to begin with and do not interfere with the sense that a certain possibility will inevitably be actualized: "Nothing speaks in favour of them in this given moment; the expectations are straightforward certainties that are not inhibited" (2001, §13, p. 91). In the problematic case, however, alternative possibilities are phenomenologically conspicuous. Take the example of seeing a figure in a shop window and being unsure whether it is a man or a mannequin, something that involves two competing systems of anticipation:

> Perhaps we see a figure standing in a store window, something which at first we take to be a real man, perhaps an employee working there. Then, however, we become hesitant and ask ourselves whether it is not just a mere mannequin. With closer observation, the doubt can be resolved in favour of one side or the other, but there can also be a period of hesitation during which there is doubt whether it is a man or a mannequin. (Husserl 1948/1973, §21, p. 92)

In such cases, there is a perceptual experience of doubt, where an original system of anticipation is undermined by an alternative system: "the visual appearance, the spatial form imbued with color, was until now provided with a halo of anticipatory intentions which gave the sense 'human body' and, in general, 'man'; now there is superposed on it the sense 'clothed mannequin'" (Husserl 1948/1973, §21, p. 92). Problematic uncertainty can also take a less determinate form, along the lines of "this might turn out to be different from what I am anticipating"; "things might not be quite as they seem." It does not have to involve a more specifically focused doubt, where the original system of anticipation competes with an equally determinate alternative. Husserl adds that systems of expectation can be "disappointed" rather than "fulfilled," regardless of whether or not disappointment was anticipated in the guise of problematic uncertainty. Hence we can distinguish different modes of anticipation (certainty, doubt, and degrees of problematic uncertainty) and disappointment (the various ways in which something can appear not quite as expected: it might have different properties, turn out to be a different kind of entity, or be present or absent in a way that conflicts with expectation).

According to Husserl, the perceptual experience of disappointment, of something turning out to be other than anticipated, includes a recognition of *negation*. Moreover, it constitutes our most fundamental grasp of the phenomenon of negation. Our sense of what it is for something to not be the case originates not in propositional thought but in the experience of negated anticipation. This experience has an essentially temporal structure, involving confident anticipation, perhaps followed by problematic uncertainty, and finally by a lack of fulfillment. When the original expectation is overridden and updated, an awareness is retained of it *as* something that has been displaced. The anomaly need not be wholly surprising, as it may have been anticipated to some extent and with varying degrees of determinacy. The sense of negation is more a matter of its incongruity or inconsistency with a wider system of anticipation that preceded it. So, if Husserl is right, the "original phenomenon of negation" is embedded in perceptual experience. If we did not experience negation perceptually, we would not be able to form judgments as to whether something is or is not the case, as we would lack all sense of the relevant distinction: "*It thus appears that negation is not first the business of the act of predicative judgment but that in its original form it already appears in the prepredicative sphere of receptive experience*" (1948/1973, §21, p. 90).

Importantly, when we experience something as negated, only part of the anticipation-fulfillment pattern is disrupted. Experience as a whole continues to be structured by confident, unproblematic anticipation: "In order for a unity of an intentional process to be maintained ... a certain measure of thoroughgoing fulfilment must be presupposed under all circumstances" (Husserl 2001, §6, p. 67). What is crucial, for current purposes, is Husserl's observation that it is only against a nonlocalized, dynamic backdrop of confident anticipation and fulfillment that we are able to encounter a localized occurrence as anomalous. To be anomalous is to stand out against something that remains more generally cohesive. So Husserl does not conceive of habitual certainty, problematic uncertainty, and specifically focused doubt simply as different modes of anticipation, otherwise on a par with each other; certainty is the "primal mode" (1948/1973, §21, p. 100). He adds that this nonlocalized sense of certainty is not something we acquire within a pregiven experiential world. It is itself our most fundamental sense of being rooted in a world, in a realm where things are able to show up as potentially or actually discrepant in one or another way: "For us the universal synthesis of harmonizing intentional syntheses corresponds to 'the' world, and belonging to it is a universal belief-certainty" (2001, §23, p. 146).

If this is right, then a form of certainty is presupposed by the modalities of intentionality. Taking something or other as "not" presupposes a wider context of practical and perceptual confidence. Importantly, this applies equally to an explicit sense that something "is." Acceptance of *p* rather than *not p* only makes sense given the possibility of doubt and its resolution in favor of the original rather than the competing system of anticipation. So this is not a point about what the specific *content* of perceptual experience must include or whether some contents are more fundamental than others.

The claim is that, for us to encounter things—regardless of what they might be—in one or another way, experience must have a global *form*, a temporal structure whereby coherently organized possibilities are actualized in line with confident anticipation. Husserl notes that perceptual experience and nonperceptual belief share the same modal structure. Belief can involve taking something to be the case or not the case, possible or doubtful, and these same modalities are available to us in perceptual experience. It is, he says, "no coincidence that perception and judgment have these modalities in common" (2001, §6, p. 67). The reason is that the modal structure of belief is parasitic on the anticipation-fulfillment structure of perception. The differences between taking something to be the case, not the case, possible, or doubtful are intelligible to us only because perceptual experience supplies us with a sense of these alternatives as distinct from one another:

> It is not only the original phenomenon of negation which is already to be found in the prepredicative sphere; the so-called *modalities* of judgment, which constitute a central element of traditional formal logic, also have their origin and their foundation in the occurrences of prepredicative experience.
>
> … We understand *modalizations as obstructions in the procession of the original perceptual interest.* Such an elucidation of the origin reveals that the *simplest certainty of belief* is the *primal form* and that all other phenomena, such as negation, consciousness of possibility, restoration of certainty by affirmation or denial, result only from the modalization of this primal form and are not juxtaposed, since they are not on the same level. (Husserl 1948/1973, §21, pp. 91, 100–101)

As I understand Husserl, he seeks to generalize from the case of belief to other types of intentional state. And, even if he does not, this direction is implied by his analysis. To be able to distinguish the various types of intentional state from each other, we must have a sense of reality that includes the relevant modal distinctions (Ratcliffe 2015). Therefore, all kinds of intentionality depend (in ways that of course require considerable further elucidation) on a background of practical, habitual certainty, without which a grasp of these distinctions could not be sustained. To be more specific, I will argue in chapter 6 that different kinds of experience, such as imagining and remembering, incorporate different patterns of anticipation and fulfillment. Our sense of which type of intentional state we are in is largely constituted by these patterns and by a recognition of them *as* departures from the anticipation-fulfillment pattern of perceptual experience.

So, although Husserl describes presupposed certainty as a kind of "belief," what he is referring to does not involve taking something to be the case in the way we do when we perceive a cup in front of us or believe that the Eiffel Tower is in Paris. Our grasp of what it is for something to be present or not present, and, more generally, for it to be the case or not the case, presupposes a habitual style of immersion in a situation. This immersion is not the object of an intentional state and neither is it an intentional attitude. It is something that the ability to direct oneself toward an object, via belief or any other kind of attitude, presupposes. We can now see what is meant by the "global style of anticipation." I conceive of this in much the same way as Merleau-Ponty, who, drawing on Husserl, writes of a "style" that shapes all perception and thought, a "universal style of all possible perceptions" (Merleau-Ponty 1964, 16).[16] Our sense of belonging to a world is not a matter of perceiving some *thing* or adopting the belief that some entity exists. It is not an attitude with content at all, but a habitual way of anticipating, a temporal pattern that pervades experience:

> The natural world is the horizon of all horizons, and the style of all styles, which ensures my experiences have a given, not a willed, unity beneath all of the ruptures of my personal and historical life; the counterpart of the natural world is the given, general, and pre-personal existence in me of my sensory functions, which is where we discovered the definition of the body. (Merleau-Ponty 1945/2012, 345)

Experiencing something as *there* involves its integration into this style, and the sense of confidence or certainty constituted by the dynamic actualization of possibility just *is* our most fundamental appreciation of being situated in a world.[17] There is nothing beyond or before it that we can appeal to in order to secure our convictions, to convince ourselves that something is the case. This has the interesting implication that if we could somehow actualize all possibilities, comprehend everything as it is in its entirety, without anticipating anything more in the guise of open or problematic uncertainty, we would not succeed in comprehending reality as a whole. Instead, we would be completely uprooted from the very temporal dynamic in relation to which taking something to be the case, taking it to be *real*, is an intelligible possibility. Comprehending something in that way would involve deprivation of the modal structure that is needed to comprehend anything at all. Thus a "view from nowhere," at least if conceived of in this manner, is plain incoherent. As Merleau-Ponty (1945/2012, 347) puts it:

> If spatio-temporal horizons could (even ideally) be made explicit and if the world could be conceived from nowhere, then nothing would exist. I would survey the world from above, and far from all places and times suddenly becoming real, they

would in fact cease to be real because I would not inhabit any of them and I would be nowhere engaged. If I am all and everywhere, then I am never and nowhere.

To be taken as real, as the case, is to be integrated into a wider-ranging style of experience; there is nothing more to ask for. So, phenomenologically speaking, the "is" of existence is equivocal. Our appreciation of being immersed in a world does not rest upon a deeply entrenched proposition concerning the existence of some entity or upon some kind of distinctive sensory content. It consists in a distinctive pattern of anticipation and fulfillment, something that is inseparable from habitual, bodily immersion in the world. This kind of certainty cannot be coherently doubted in propositional form, as it is presupposed by the intelligibility of doubt.

It is worth noting how Husserl's position complements Jaspers' remarks about the sense of reality. Jaspers similarly indicates that belief is possible only if one is already experientially rooted in a world: "conceptual reality carries conviction only if a kind of presence is experienced, provided by reality itself." Our grasp of reality, he says, is grounded in "the practice of living." So we need to distinguish an "*immediate certainty of reality*" from a "*reality-judgment*" that depends on it (1963, 93–94). What Husserl says is also consistent with descriptions of traumatic experience and can, I suggest, serve to further illuminate its nature. However, a small addition to his account is first required. In chapter 4, I distinguished (a) the content of what is anticipated, which may be more or less determinate, from (b) the mode of anticipation, which may be doubt or uncertainty but is more usually certainty. Both are covered by Husserl's account. However, what Husserl does not acknowledge is (c) the *affective* style of anticipation, and it is here that his discussion needs to be supplemented. When we anticipate events that matter to us in one or another way, we might do so with excitement, hope, curiosity, fear, panic, or dread. Habitual certainty has its own affective style: a confident, comfortable engagement with what is coming next, something that is incompatible with fearing or dreading it. Even when we dread *p* (regardless of whether *p* is anticipated in the mode of certainty, problematic uncertainty, or doubt), we generally do so within a wider context of confidence, in relation to which *p* is experienced as an anomaly or disruption.

Were this wider style of anticipation to break down entirely, we could not anticipate localized conflicts in the modes of problematic uncertainty or doubt. The result would be a complete loss of experiential structure.

What, though, if the anticipatory structure of experience were altered in some way, rather than altogether lost? This is what traumatic loss of one-place trust involves. A confident style of anticipation gives way to pervasive and nonlocalized uncertainty and doubt, where a sense of potential danger predominates. We can thus begin to see why a traumatized person might describe herself as living in a different world. When the realization of some indeterminate threat is anticipated, things *look* foreboding. And when the overall style of anticipation takes this form, a sense of being confidently immersed in the world, at home in it, is lost. One feels uprooted; the world as a whole appears strangely and disturbingly different. With this, there is at least some degree of modal change. The overall style of experience, in which the distinction between being the case and not being the case is embedded, has shifted. Even though it does not break down entirely, things no longer seem the case or not the case in quite the same way they did before.

At this point, one might object that a loss of trust arising due to interpersonal trauma specifically concerns what is expected from other people, rather than from the world as a whole. So, even if other people in general seem menacing, unpredictable, and no longer dependable, the impersonal environment survives intact. But, as the remainder of this chapter will show, that is not the case—the effects of losing interpersonal trust are far more pervasive. I acknowledge that loss of confidence or one-place trust can take a number of more specific forms. When faced with chronic illness, one's bodily experience can involve a pervasive feeling of what Carel (2013) calls "bodily doubt"; one ceases to habitually trust in various bodily capacities and capabilities, and the default style of anticipation becomes that of anxious uncertainty. Other losses of trust, confidence, or certainty are focused more so on the impersonal world. After an accident or natural disaster, an environment that once seemed dependable may seem dangerous and unpredictable. Loss of trust can also concern one's own abilities, perhaps even the reliability and coherence of one's own thinking. Hence it might appear that the term "one-place trust" is misleading. Given that it can have different emphases, "trust in *p*," "trust in *q*," and so on, it actually falls under the category "two-place trust." However, "having trust in the context of domain *p*" is to be distinguished from "trusting *p*." The former is not a relation of trusting but a precondition for one or another kind of trust relation. So, although one-place trust has more circumscribed domains, it is not itself an attitude toward something.

Another concern that might be raised is that the term "trust" properly applies only to the interpersonal domain and that its extension to other forms of practical confidence is inappropriate. In response, it should be noted that the term "trust" is sometimes used in the more permissive way, and that victims of trauma often refer to a wider-ranging "loss of trust in the world." Furthermore, the relevant experiences are structurally similar, with all of them involving changes in the anticipation-fulfillment structure of experience. Even so, I suggest that having trust in other people has a kind of primacy over others forms of one-place trust. This is because its loss entails a wider-ranging loss of confidence in oneself, one's abilities, and one's surroundings. We might conceive of a nonsocial creature, for which the anticipatory structure of experience (if we grant it a capacity for experience) is largely independent of what it anticipates from conspecifics. But it is a contingent fact that human beings are not like that. Human social development involves becoming increasingly immersed in a shared world, where what we anticipate from the world in general cannot be disentangled from our expectations regarding other people. The overall coherence of a system of anticipation is, in effect, *entrusted* to others. In pursuing our projects, we depend on others in all manner of ways—they assist us, advise us, work alongside us, share our goals, commission projects, and act as suppliers and recipients. In walking around a city center, we expect and rely on others to respect traffic lights, to maintain safe public transport systems, to sell food that is not poisoned, and not to attack us at random.

We thus take for granted that most people will abide by a plethora of social norms, which shape to a substantial degree what we anticipate from them and from the social environment more generally. Many of the things we anticipate also depend, more specifically, on our relations with particular individuals, such as partners, friends, and work colleagues. Even when we are not directly concerned with the actual or potential actions of however many people, what we anticipate from the impersonal environment continues to depend on interpersonal expectations. Trusting that a device will work properly or that your train or plane will not crash is incompatible with experiencing people in general, including designers and operators, as unpredictable and menacing. It follows that any change in what is anticipated from other people will envelop experience more generally. Even when walking in an untouched wilderness, there remains the possibility of encountering others and of anticipating such encounters in one or another way. Thus, when interpersonal relatedness is profoundly disrupted, so is one's confidence in the wider world.

We can now see how interpersonal trauma might bring about a change in the overall structure of experience. Traumatic events can elicit a shift in the global style of anticipation. What makes interpersonal trauma distinctive is the *subversion* of interpersonal trust it involves. The other person recognizes one's vulnerability and responds to it by deliberately inflicting harm. For instance, the aim of torture has been described as the complete psychological destruction of a person: "The torturer attempts to destroy a victim's sense of being grounded in a family and society as a human being with dreams, hopes and aspirations for the future" (Istanbul Protocol 1999, 45). It is a "calculated assault on human dignity," more so than an attempt to extract information (Amnesty International, 1986, 172).[18] The victim is confronted by a kind of interpersonal relation that exploits her vulnerability in an extreme way. Améry (1999, 29) describes how, when one is hurt, there is ordinarily an "expectation of help" from others, something that is engrained from early childhood. Torture therefore involves a radical conflict with habitual styles of interpersonal anticipation. It is not just that others fail to offer help; they are themselves the agents of harm, and there is nobody else to intervene on one's behalf. Furthermore, many forms of torture involve taking familiar, homely items that would more usually be encountered in a confident, purposive way, and using them to cause harm. For instance, household utensils are sometimes used to inflict pain (Scarry 1985, 40–41). So it is not just that an interpersonal situation fails to offer what is habitually anticipated; it offers something utterly opposed to it.[19]

Given the extent to which our expectations in general depend on what we expect from others, a loss of trust in other people (of the kind that can be brought about by events that challenge or subvert what was previously taken for granted) permeates everything. Without the assumption that others will offer assistance in moments of need, the impersonal environment also seems less safe. What was once anticipated with habitual confidence is now anticipated with uncertainty and dread:

> When you think about everything on a deep level … you see that nothing in life follows any rules; you can't rely on anything to be always true, ever. Nothing is constant and nothing is reliable, so nothing is "safe" to just simply believe in and be done with it. You are constantly looking at everything around you and re-assessing it, re-evaluating it as you get new information about it.[20]

The point applies to trust in one's own abilities as well, even to the reliability of one's own judgments and thought processes. More usually, when there is doubt we turn to others for reassurance and support. Importantly, when trust in the impersonal environment or in one's own abilities is damaged, trusting relations with others can help one to negotiate what has happened and move on. They establish a sense of contingency, opening up new possibilities and facilitating new interpretations. When interpersonal trust is lost, the prospect of entering into an interpersonal process that might otherwise have nurtured changes in anticipatory style is lost along with it. As Laub (2001, xv) observes,

> The survivor of torture feels completely alone. He—or she—no longer believes in the very possibility of human communication; he envisages no one who will be present to him and for him if he returns in his mind to the places of horror, humiliation, and grief from which he barely emerged and which continue to haunt him.

Without any anticipation of self-transformative interpersonal relations, one's predicament seems inescapable; the world no longer offers anything else. To this, we can add that almost all projects, cares, and concerns are sustained interpersonally. When others in general cease to be dependable, when the world is unsafe and one's own abilities are in doubt, projects collapse. What is lacking is not merely a condition of possibility for however many *specific projects*; it is something that the intelligibility of *projects in general* depends upon. In a world where other people appear unpredictable and threatening, everything else is riddled with uncertainty and doubt as well: "The fact that other, qualified people have built this device gives me no reason to think it will work"; "This object could be used by someone to harm me"; "Others might do any number of things with this." In the most extreme case, one comes to inhabit a world where the possibility of meaningful, progressive, goal-directed activity is absent. Other kinds of concern may be affected in different ways. For instance, care for certain other people might endure, but a pervasive sense of the world as unsafe, unpredictable, and inhospitable to human relationships would render it fragile and vulnerable. Interpersonal care is thus coupled with the anticipation of impending and inevitable loss, with dread and anticipatory grief.

Hence we can further see how such experiences implicate the sense of time. One no longer experiences the actualization of significant possibilities in the way one once did. The future may appear largely or exclusively in the guise of threat, while the past may seem oddly closed, something that can no longer be built on, positively developed. Given an inability to anticipate and actualize certain kinds of possibility, one cannot *move on* from what has happened. How the traumatized person relates to others thus shapes how the world as a whole is experienced, in a way that centrally involves a change in the global style of anticipation. Another reason why loss of safety, security, certainty, confidence, or trust amounts to an alteration in the modal structure of intentionality is that the bedrock relative to which things are more usually taken to be the case or otherwise is not just *mine* but *ours*. Taking something to be the case ordinarily involves taking it to be rooted in a public world, to which one also belongs. And the sense of being part of a public world is inextricable from how one anticipates and relates to other people in general (a point I will return to in chapter 6). By rendering the global style of experience dependent on other people to such an extent, we also render ourselves vulnerable to them, as cases of traumatic experience serve to illustrate. Husserlian certainty, and with it the modal structure of intentionality, is thus inseparable from trust in other people; its integrity is entrusted to them.

In some of the texts discussed earlier in this chapter, Husserl indicates that a largely confident anticipation-fulfillment structure is integral not only to the modal structure of intentionality but also to what I referred to in chapter 2 as the "minimal self," our most primitive sense of being a singular locus of experience.[21] Were that dynamic to break down completely, he suggests, the unity and singularity of consciousness would be altogether lost:

> But here, so that in all events the unity of an intentional process can still be maintained, a certain measure of continuous fulfilment is presupposed. Correlatively, a certain unity of objective sense must be upheld throughout the flux of successive appearances. It is only in this way that we have, in the process of lived experience and its appearances, the unanimity of *one* consciousness, one unified intentionality spreading over all phases. (1948/1973, §21, p. 88)

> Every expectation can also be disappointed, and disappointment essentially presupposes partial fulfillment; without a certain measure of unity maintaining itself in the progression of perceptions, the unity of the intentional lived-experience would crumble. (2001, §5, p. 64)

This is consistent with my view that even the most primitive sense of self is inextricable from the modal structure of intentionality. However, it should be added that erosion of the sense of being a singular locus of experience is not attributable solely to a loss of specifically *perceptual* cohesion. The reason even "minimal self" does not survive is that the coherence of perceptual experience underlies the ability to distinguish between modalities of intentionality. If the other modalities of intentionality could be sustained independently of perceptual experience, then some sense of subjectivity would endure even the most profound of perceptual disruptions, given that one would still remember, believe, and imagine, and distinguish between such experiences. It is *because* perceptual experience includes something more encompassing, something essential to the structure of intentionality, that breakdown of the anticipation-fulfillment dynamic is incompatible with retention of self-experience, with any kind of perspectival structure.

6 Intentionality and Interpersonal Experience

This chapter further explores how interpersonal relations shape and regulate the structure of experience. In so doing, it develops the position introduced in chapter 5, according to which perceptual experience incorporates a distinctive kind of anticipation-fulfillment dynamic, upon which the modal structure of intentionality depends. My central claims are as follows: (a) disturbances of *global anticipatory style* are inextricable from changes in how one experiences and relates to other people; (b) these disturbances can lessen differences between the characteristic *temporal profiles* of intentional states (where a temporal profile is the anticipation-fulfillment pattern that is typical of one or another type of intentional state); and (c) temporal profiles are central to, but not exhaustive of, the sense of being in a given type of intentional state.

The chapter begins by addressing how perceptual experience is interpersonally regulated, after which it considers the implications of this for our understanding of belief. The discussion of belief draws on themes in the work of Jaspers and the later Wittgenstein, which complement and enrich the position attributed to Husserl in chapter 5. This is followed by a brief consideration of the anticipatory structure of memory. I then bring together the various strands of argument from this and earlier chapters in order to offer a full statement of my central thesis, according to which the sense of being in a given intentional state is largely attributable to its distinctive temporal profile. Next, I turn to the links between trauma (in particular, childhood trauma) and psychosis, to further support my position. In so doing, I ask whether and how certain forms of experience associated with trauma are distinguishable from those associated with schizophrenia diagnoses. I also offer an interpretation of the text *Autobiography of a Schizophrenic Girl* (Sechehaye 1970), to illustrate how a greater emphasis on the relational structure of experience can prompt us to reinterpret first-person accounts. The chapter concludes with some tentative remarks on how a phenomenological account of the modal structure of experience and its vulnerability to disruption can be brought into mutually illuminating dialogue with neurobiological research on predictive coding.

6.1 The Interpersonal Regulation of Experience

During the course of everyday life, interpersonal interactions shape our wider experiences of the world in various subtle ways. How our surroundings appear is partly a reflection of whether we are with others, what they are doing, and how we relate to them. This is not to suggest that whether or not we see a cup or a car, a red thing or a green thing, depends on our interpersonal situation. Rather, what appears salient to us and the kinds of significance things have for us depend, in part, on our relations with others. By implication, what we anticipate from our surroundings is interpersonally shaped. The point applies both to relations with specific individuals and to relations with other people in general. Regarding the former, van den Berg (1972, 65) makes the following observations:

> We all know people in whose company we would prefer not to go shopping, not to visit a museum, not to look at a landscape, because we would like to keep these things undamaged. Just as we all know people in whose company it is pleasant to take a walk because the objects encountered come to no harm. These people we call friends, good companions, loved ones.

Interaction with a particular person can drain the surrounding world of its significance or, alternatively, enrich it with salient possibilities that would otherwise be lacking. The point is not exclusive to perceptual experience; it applies equally to interpreting and finding significance in past, present, and anticipated events, to anything that matters to us:

> We all know people with whom it is best not to share anything that matters to us. If we have experienced something exciting, and if we tell it to those people, it will seem almost dull. If we have a secret, we will keep it safe from those people, safe inside us, untold. That way it won't shrivel up and lose all the meaning it has for us. But if you are lucky, you know one person with whom it is the other way around. If you tell that person something exciting, it will become more exciting. A great story will expand, you will find yourself telling it in more detail, finding the richness of all the elements, more than when you only thought about it alone. Whatever matters to you, you save it until you can tell it to that person. (Gendlin 1978/2003, 115)

Of course, the reliability of casual phenomenological reflection can be challenged, but it is not our only source of evidence. Such observations are consistent with the results of empirical studies on the interpersonal effects of gaze and expression. For instance, Bayliss et al. (2007, 644) found that another person's emotional reaction to a target object influences one's own appraisal of it: objects looked at with a happy expression by someone else are subsequently liked more than those looked at with disgust. Evaluation does not seem to require a nonperceptual judgment, made on the basis of a prior perceptual experience. These and other findings better complement the view that evaluative properties are experienced as inherent in objects: "observing another person gazing at an object enriches that object of motor, affective and status properties that go beyond its chemical or physical structure" (Becchio, Bertone, and Castiello 2008, 254). Consistent with this, explicit consideration of other people's reactions is not needed; the effect is something we are susceptible to even when we are unaware of it. Hence other people's responses to features of the shared environment are not just objects of perception; they also shape our own experiences of the environment.[1]

How we experience our surroundings is also influenced by an appreciation of potential interactions with others who are co-present. How something appears salient and significant is often symptomatic not just of *what I could do* but of what might be achieved in cooperation with others, *what we could do together*. This is especially so when immersed in shared tasks of whatever duration and complexity, where the perceived significance of things reflects what others are doing, what they ought to be doing, and what they are expected to do (e.g., Sebanz, Bekkering, and Knoblich 2006; Sebanz and Knoblich 2009). To extrapolate from this, how others affect one's experience presumably depends more specifically on the affective style of actual and anticipated relations with them. How the surrounding world appears when one is with a group of good friends surely differs markedly from how it appears when one is confronted by a gang of knife-wielding strangers.

It has been further proposed that what we anticipate from other people influences our perceptual experiences in much the same way as our own anticipated actions. When we initiate actions, their predicted sensory consequences usually attenuate incoming sensory signals. Although the postulated mechanisms are largely nonconscious, there are corresponding phenomenological differences between the effects of self-produced and non-self-produced changes in sensory stimulation. For instance, most people cannot tickle themselves; the experience is less intense than that of being tickled by someone else, and perhaps qualitatively different as well (Blakemore, Wolpert, and Frith 2000). Now, in this case, there is a contrast between the effects of self-produced and other-produced sensory stimulation. All the same, this is compatible with there being further differences between the sensory effects of anticipated and unanticipated other-produced stimulation, between an anticipated tickle and an unanticipated one. In fact, differences between experiences of self- and other-produced stimulation may be largely attributable to the fact that exactly what the other person will do and when she will do it is usually less clear. To anticipate being tickled is not to anticipate precisely how you will be tickled. In addition, self-tickling and being tickled by someone else are likely to involve different patterns of affective anticipation. And, as argued in chapter 4, affective anticipation can shape what is subsequently experienced. Another possibility to consider is that differences between self- and other-produced sensory changes may be especially pronounced in the case of self-touch, but not when it comes to the perceived effects of acting on the surrounding environment.

Thus, where experiences of self- and other-produced action involve the same style of affective anticipation, and where there is a similar degree of indeterminacy concerning the nature and timing of an anticipated outcome, it is possible that perception of the surrounding environment is affected in a similar way. According to Sebanz and Knoblich (2009, 358), this is indeed the case: one's own actions and those of a "co-actor" are "represented in a functionally equivalent way." For instance, when you press a button to produce a tone, the tone is perceived as less intense than when it occurs without prior anticipation, and the same applies when you see someone else pressing it.[2] The point extends to the regulation of action. What others do and when they do it can be "as effective for anticipatory action control" as "internal signals about one's own actions" (Sebanz, Bekkering and Knoblich 2006, 74). If this is right, our encounters with other people have a significant influence on our wider perceptual experience. Whether and how something appears salient depends in part on what is anticipated from others: how they act, how they are likely to act, and what effects their actions are likely to have. Even when nobody else is actually present, experience is plausibly shaped by the anticipated presence of others and by what one expects from them, as illustrated by the contrasting styles of affective anticipation when walking around a deserted cemetery on a dark night and when walking through an empty public park in a safe area on a sunny morning.

It might be objected that none of this concerns our *sensory* perceptions of things. First of all, we have a sensory experience of *p*. Then we register someone else's presence, direction of attention, and emotional reaction, perhaps along with her actual and potential relationship to oneself. Finally, we make a value judgment that is separate from the earlier perceptual experience of *p*. However, there are reasons to prefer the view that we *experience* our surroundings as we do in virtue of how we have related to others (specific others or others in general) in the past, how we currently relate to them, and how we anticipate relating to them. For the most part, we *do* experience the significance of an entity as inherent in it: a pen appears relevant to us in the context of writing; an ice cream looks enticing on a hot day. We do not usually have to make a separate value judgment. It would be implausible to maintain that we must resort to this in all those cases where other people are somehow implicated. Consistent with this view, the empirical studies I have mentioned take themselves to be exploring a low-level phenomenon, involving an involuntary effect that occurs even when we are not encouraged to attend to or reflect on what others are doing.

Of course, it could still be maintained that the experience includes more than just sensory perceptual content, according to one or another theory of content. But my concern here is with *how the world appears to us*, as distinct from what we might explicitly infer from appearances. And this contrast can be maintained without having to insist that immediate experience of our surroundings is exclusively a matter of sensory perception. In referring to perceptual experiences and what they incorporate, I am thinking simply of those experiences that present their objects as "here, now," as present. The relevant phenomenology can be addressed without getting dragged into debates over how to individuate sensory modalities and how to distinguish perceptual from nonperceptual content, debates that also encompass various nonphenomenological considerations. Nevertheless, as we will see, the aspects of experience considered here are inseparable from an anticipation-fulfillment structure that is specific to perceptual experience, and thus inseparable from the *sense* of perceiving. So any account of sensory perceptual experience that excluded them would also have to exclude this sense. And, as argued in chapter 2, the sense of perceiving is more plausibly regarded as partly constitutive of both "perceptual experience" and "perception."

The view that we regulate each other's perceptual experience and activity in a range of ways, often without the mediation of propositional thought, is consistent with recent "enactivist" approaches to intersubjectivity, according to which coordination and understanding between two or more parties often depends on patterns of interaction between them that cannot be reduced to the cognitive achievements of separate individuals (e.g., De Jaegher and Di Paolo 2007; Fuchs and De Jaegher 2009). For instance, Froese and Fuchs (2012, 205) describe a kind of "inter-bodily resonance between individuals" that generates "self-sustaining interaction patterns." Face-to-face interaction with another person can assist us in understanding (and perhaps, to some extent, experiencing) her mental life. At the same time, it also shapes how we experience the surrounding world. And, even when we are not explicitly attending to and seeking to make sense of another person's activities, interaction continues to influence how our surroundings are experienced. As Gallagher (2009a, 298, 303) observes, these two aspects of interpersonal experience are closely related but distinguishable:

> Making sense of the world together (in a social process) is not the same thing as making sense of another person within our interactive relationship. … The presence of others calls forth a basic and implicit interaction that shapes the way we regard the world around us.

Take the example of reading a book to one's child. In his absence, the book might appear tedious, devoid of significance. Yet, as he smiles, frowns, gestures, and expresses curiosity, and as one responds in complementary ways, a shared experience of the book develops. One continues to distinguish "my experience of the book" from "his experience of the book" and might well direct one's attention toward the latter. But there is also "our experience" of the book, a sense of its significance "for us," which is sustained and regulated by interaction between the two parties.[3] Similarly, when walking through a city with him, the salience of one's surroundings is partly a reflection of his needs, vulnerabilities, and concerns, and how these relate to one's own actual and potential activities. A road appears hazardous, a steep escalator treacherous, and a box of Star Wars Lego in a shop window conspicuous. One does not have to think "He likes Lego," or somehow come to like Lego oneself, in order to experience a Lego Millennium Falcon as immediately relevant in the context of a shared situation.[4]

There are also stronger claims in some of the enactivist literature, concerning the dependence of subjectivity itself on interpersonal interaction. For instance, McGann and De Jaegher (2009, 430) write that "a subject is not fully constituted outside of the interaction, independently of it. A subject, instead, is partly constituted in and through the interaction." Complementary claims have been made about intersubjective development, to the effect that infant–parent interactions are integral to a developmental process through which the sense of self is formed. According to Reddy (2008, 149), the self is "a dialogic entity, existing only in relation and therefore knowable only as a relation. Other-consciousness, therefore, is inseparable from self-consciousness, and perhaps both should be called self-other-consciousness." Zeedyk (2006, 321) similarly claims that "subjectivity arises out of intimate engagement with others," that emotional interaction with caregivers enables the development of capacities including self-awareness and consciousness.

Zahavi (2014, 27–28) rightly responds that such claims are often unclear about the kind of "self" at stake. For instance, in suggesting that self is formed through interpersonal processes, Maclaren (2008, 65) refers to capacities for "agency, self-possession, and self-governance." These arguably do not relate to the most primitive or "minimal" sense of self but to a richer conception, one that goes beyond merely being a subject, to further include reflective self-regulation or "governance" of conduct. For similar reasons, it must be conceded that what I have said up to this point is importantly lacking: even if we accept that interpersonal processes can enrich, diminish, and transform the nature of *what* a person perceives, remembers, or imagines, it remains the case that she perceives it, remembers it, or imagines it. In other words, the modal structure of intentionality, the sense of being in state *x* rather than *y*, is unaffected by these processes. If I am right in associating minimal self with the modal structure of intentionality, then minimal self is equally unaffected.

However, it is arguable that interpersonal processes (and their absence) can further contribute to the sense of which intentional state one is in or was in, at least in certain exceptional situations. If something looks somehow odd, you might rub your eyes or shake your head to confirm that you are seeing it right, and our checking procedures often rely on other people in much the same way. In addition to or instead of adjusting our own perceptual apparatus, we seek out others in order to interpret and validate our experiences. Suppose you see something utterly strange and surprising, such as a person walking past on the street, wearing a Darth Vader costume, pulling a zebra on a lead, singing "House of the Rising Sun," and kicking passers-by. A first reaction might be to wonder "What is happening?" or even "Is this really happening?" and to look for similar reactions of surprise from others. The feeling of bewilderment would be even more pronounced in a situation where everyone else on the street appeared utterly indifferent to the situation, as though nothing out of the ordinary were happening or nothing were happening at all. After an unusual event, there may also be a felt need to tell people about it, something that can involve interpreting and reinterpreting your experiences in cooperation with others. In the absence of certain kinds of interpersonal process, at the time and/or afterward, you might start to wonder, "Did I actually see that?," "Did I misperceive?," "Have I imagined it?," "Am I really remembering this?," "Did that actually happen?"

Even if this much is conceded, such indeterminacies and doubts are surely rare. So it might seem that interpersonal situations only occasionally influence the sense of one's intentional state. Importantly, though, I am not concerned exclusively or even primarily with how a particular situation is experienced—a meeting with B or a journey with C. How we experience any such situation is also attributable to the global style of interpersonal anticipation introduced in chapter 5. Ordinarily, this takes the form of habitual confidence or trust. Even when we feel threatened or otherwise unsafe, the situation is experienced as anomalous, as a departure from what is more usually the case. To assess whether and how changes in interpersonal experience can affect the modal structure of intentionality, we also need to consider the potential impact of all-enveloping shifts in how one anticipates, experiences, and relates to other people in general.

In reflecting on how interpersonal encounters are more usually shaped by a deep-rooted and nonlocalized form of trust, I find it helpful to draw on the work of Løgstrup (1956/1997). According to Løgstrup, whenever we enter into a relationship with someone, of a kind that might open up significant possibilities and thus enrich our experience, we inevitably render ourselves vulnerable to being affected in other ways too, to having our world somehow diminished. Likewise, we cannot avoid having some effect on the other person, some degree of "power" over him. The world-shaping effects of interpersonal interaction can be subtle and short-lived or pronounced and enduring:

> By our very attitude to one another we help to shape one another's world. By our attitude to the other person we help to determine the scope and hue of his or her world; we make it large or small, bright or drab, rich or dull, threatening or secure. We help to shape his or her world not by theories and views but by our very attitude toward him or her. (Løgstrup 1956/1997, 18)

Relating to someone in a distinctively *personal* way thus involves exposing ourselves to the possibility of harm, while anticipating that we will not be harmed. Løgstrup refers to this combination of vulnerability before another person and openness to being affected by her as *trust*:

> Trust is not of our own making; it is given. Our life is so constituted that it cannot be lived except as one person lays him or herself open to another person and puts her or himself into that person's hands either by showing or claiming trust. (1956/1997, 18)

Consistent with the discussion of chapter 5, trust of this kind is not just an attitude adopted toward some people on some occasions, perhaps friends rather than strangers. Instead, it is our default attitude toward other people in general, an overarching style of anticipation that determines how we relate to people and, consequently, how they shape our wider experience. Granted, we depart from it on occasion, when we distrust someone in particular or exercise caution. However, as with Husserl's "problematic uncertainty" (introduced in sec. 5.5), such occasions are localized departures from something that is more usually taken for granted.

Løgstrup further suggests that socially decontextualized encounters between people would involve an uncomfortable experience of vulnerability and overexposure. So it is not just a matter of trust. Most interpersonal encounters and relations are further regulated by shared practices and conventions, which facilitate the development of trusting relations by reducing mutual exposure. On the other hand, they also provide ways of avoiding interpersonal openness by allowing one to hide behind behavior-prescribing norms and standardized performances. I suggest that trust is equally implicated in the sustenance of this support structure. A global breakdown of trust in others would also impact on the acceptance of norms and conventions. If others in general are not to be trusted, then practices that depend on their behaving in certain ways are not to be trusted either.

So everything would be tainted with an air of unpredictability, and interpersonal encounters would be anticipated in the absence of mediating social structures that more usually help to frame and regulate them.

Experience of our surroundings is thus shaped by (a) habitual trust in other people in general, (b) the anticipated and actual effects of encounters with specific individuals, and (c) wider social structures that regulate interpersonal encounters. The global anticipatory style of interpersonal experience (a) influences all of our experiences of particular individuals and social situations, and a change in (a) therefore implies changes in (b) and (c). With this in mind, let us consider what would happen if there were a substantial shift in the balance between vulnerability and trust. Suppose others in general were anticipated in the guise of threat, where the source, nature, and timing of any anticipated harm remain ill-defined, thus amounting to a pervasive feeling of vulnerability and uncertainty.[5] As we saw in chapter 5, experiences like this can arise due to traumatic events, especially those that involve being deliberately harmed by others, and they may come about in other ways as well. Take an extreme case: suppose the prospect of confirming, sharing, interpreting, and reinterpreting experience through relations with others were altogether absent from one's world; they no longer present such possibilities and instead appear menacing and unpredictable. This, I maintain, would indeed affect the modal structure of experience, and in a profound way. There are several contributing factors to consider, and it is when we take into account their combined effects that a compelling case emerges.

First of all, where there is no prospect of interpersonal validation or challenge, one might be more inclined to accept the deliverances of unusual experiences. More importantly, though, alienation from others in general would erode the sense of being firmly rooted in a shared, consensus world. The contrast between what is there for all of us and what is not would therefore be less pronounced. Nothing would be experienced as *there for all of us* in quite the way it was. So, although one might be more inclined toward accepting certain things, this would involve a different way of "taking something to be the case," a different kind of acceptance. I will return to this point in section 4.2, when I discuss belief.[6]

What we anticipate from the world is also shaped by projects of whatever duration, along with associated configurations of equipment. Confident anticipation of events depends largely on the integrity and coherence of projects and wider concerns, which specify to varying degrees what will happen and when, what ought to happen, and what effects one's actions are likely to have. Almost all projects implicate others in one or another way. Hence, as mentioned in chapter 5, an inability to trust other people in general would impact on what is anticipated from the world as a whole. In a world where others offer only uncertainty and threat, shared projects would collapse and various activities would present themselves as effortful, perilous, and perhaps doomed to failure.[7] Furthermore, equipment would no longer appear dependable, insofar as it is designed, constructed, used, and maintained by other people. Given the role that interrelated projects more usually play in grouping things together into salient, cohesive, and predictable patterns, the structure of experience would be to some extent degraded. The world would have a different affective tone, where things that were once anticipated with habitual confidence now seem unsafe, uncertain, and less coherently organized. This would also add up to a pervasive experience of *passivity*. Rather than being comfortably immersed in a social world, where situations invite effortless responses to meaningful possibilities, one would feel helpless, incapable, and disengaged from everything. Loss of trust thus involves what we might call "diminished agency" (Ratcliffe 2013a,b, 2015; Benson, Gibson, and Brand 2013). And, I suggest, where there is a constant, all-enveloping experience of disengagement, passivity, and lack of control over one's situation, the phenomenological distance between *actively* initiating something and *passively* receiving it from elsewhere will be lessened to some degree. This could increase one's susceptibility to more pronounced, localized disruptions of phenomenological boundaries such as that between thinking that *p* and perceiving that *p*. Returning to a theme of chapter 3, this is where we should be appealing to loss of the sense of agency, rather than trying to account for VH/TI (verbal hallucination/thought insertion) more directly in those terms.

Another factor to consider is the interpersonal regulation of emotion and feeling. Chapter 4 argued that internal VHs occur due to a certain *way* of affectively anticipating one's own thought contents, something that is embedded in wider-ranging disturbances of affective anticipation. More generally, both localized and wider-ranging changes in the structure of intentionality involve altered affective anticipation. As I have further argued in this chapter, the affective tone of experience is inextricable from anticipated and actual interactions with particular people, and also from a wider style of interpersonal anticipation. That view is complemented by recent discussions of emotion regulation. Gross (1999, 2001) makes an overarching distinction between "antecedent-focused" and "response-focused" regulation strategies, where the former involve acting before an emotional response is generated and the latter involve influencing an emotion that is already occurring. There is also a distinction to be drawn between reflective or effortful and nonreflective strategies. All of these strategies can be, and often are, interpersonal or social in nature. Whether and when a given type of emotion occurs is partly attributable to interpersonal processes. Indeed, it has been suggested that, when studying emotion regulation in humans, it may be more appropriate to treat the "dyad" as a "unit of analysis" than the individual (Diamond and Aspinwall 2003, 146). As Griffiths and Scarantino (2009, 445) remark, society depends on people having "the right emotions at the right times, and it is not left to individual psychological processes to ensure that this occurs." It is arguable that emotions are socially regulated to such an extent that certain *types* of emotion could not occur at all outside of interpersonal processes. Slaby (2014, 41), for instance, maintains that nothing else is "as emotionally engaging as the expressivity of fellow humans," and that "individuals as well as groups can draw us into emotional experiences that we would not be able to experience on our own." These experiences plausibly include distinctive patterns of affective unfolding, which take shape as we are drawn into interpersonal interactions and become comfortably immersed in them. With a pervasive loss of trust, others are no longer experienced as offering the possibility of such interactions.

Colombetti and Krueger (2015) point out that emotion regulation also involves trusting various impersonal environmental resources, meaning that we habitually depend on their having certain effects. Trusted regulators for a given individual might include clothes, cinemas, art galleries, churches, charms, mementos, letters, smoking, drinking coffee, and listening to music. It is clear that our confidence in most of these resources, perhaps all of them, implicates other people in one or another way. If one could not feel at ease in the presence of others, one could not become comfortably immersed in a film at the cinema or in the communal atmosphere of a church service. And, to the extent that one enjoys drinking and smoking with other people in a given social environment, the regulatory effects of these pastimes depend on who else is there and how one relates to them. As for the effects of music, these can involve the elicitation of all sorts of interpersonal feelings. Changes in the style of interpersonal experience could thus influence which feelings, if any, a piece of music elicits.[8]

When we combine (a) lack of interpersonal validation, (b) loss of phenomenological coherence, (c) disengagement from practical activity, and (d) wide-ranging disruptions of affect regulation, it becomes clearer how changes in interpersonal experience could affect the modal structure of intentionality. Among other things, the anticipation-fulfillment structure of perceptual experience would become closer to that of imagination. It would be isolated to some degree from the public world, disengaged from practical activity, no longer regulated by shared concerns, less coherent in structure, and its deliverances would not be subject to interpersonal scrutiny. This, I suggest, could render a person susceptible to more localized and intense disruptions in the structure of intentionality, of the kind detailed in chapters 3 and 4. It could also nurture hypervigilance hallucinations. Where the integrity of perceptual experience is disrupted, there is more noise—more ambiguity and indeterminacy. This is accompanied by a disposition to interpret noise in a particular way, in line with an overarching style of affective anticipation.[9]

6.2 Ways of Believing

A pervasive alteration in what is anticipated from other people and from the world in general also affects the *form* of belief, the *way* in which a person believes. As we saw in chapter 5, Husserl (2001, §6, p. 67) notes that perception and belief share the same modalities, and suggests that this is no coincidence: the modal structures of both belief and perception depend on an overarching anticipatory style that is integral to practically engaged perceptual experience. Now, taking something to be the case in the form of a belief does not involve integrating it into the anticipation-fulfillment structure of perceptual experience, in the way that encountering it as present does. However, it does at least involve taking it to be part of a world in which one is rooted. And the sense of being rooted in a world is constituted by the global style of perceptual experience. Hence disturbances of perceptual style affect one's grasp of what it is to be the case or otherwise, and much of what applies to perceptual experience applies equally to belief. In chapter 5, I considered both delusional atmosphere and traumatic experience, but left unresolved the issues of how (a) delusional atmosphere involves the interpersonal, and (b) delusional atmosphere is to be distinguished, phenomenologically, from traumatic experience. One might think that Jaspers' account of schizophrenic delusions crystallizing out of an all-enveloping atmosphere is best construed in individualistic terms: a difficult-to-describe endogenous disturbance induces an unpleasant feeling of indeterminacy and tension, which is resolved through the formation of delusions with more determinate contents. However, in a short section entitled "Psychological Digression," he offers the following remarks, which indicate the need to place more emphasis on the interpersonal and the social:

> Normal convictions are formed in a context of social living and common knowledge. Immediate experience of reality survives only if it can fit into the frame of what is socially valid or can be critically tested. ... The source for incorrigibility therefore is not to be found in any single phenomenon by itself but in the human situation as a whole, which nobody would surrender lightly. If socially accepted reality totters, people become adrift. ... Reality becomes reduced to an immediate and shifting present. (Jaspers 1963, 104)[10]

At least three interrelated themes can be discerned here and further developed. First of all, beliefs are ordinarily formed in the context of relations with others, who provide testimony, instruction, confirmation, clarification, and correction. So, in the absence of these relations, belief-formation processes would be quite different. Second, where beliefs are not formed through interpersonal processes that align them with shared knowledge, their contents will differ. Third, and most important, the attitude of belief itself presupposes a grasp of the distinction between p being the case and p not being the case. Someone who lacked the usual sense of that distinction could not *believe* in quite the same way as those who take it as given. And Jaspers maintains that taking something to be the case ordinarily involves taking it to be part of a publically accessible, consensus world. If none of one's beliefs developed in the context of that world or were ultimately embedded in it, one's sense of the contrast between being the case and not being the case would be altered or diminished. This, I take it, is why Jaspers (1963, 105) goes on to remark that "reality" for the patient "does not always carry the same meaning as that of normal reality." The boundaries between intentional state types are configured differently. More specifically, reality becomes "an immediate and shifting present." The temporal consistency of belief depends on its being anchored in an enduring, structured, public world, in which one has a largely consistent set of ongoing practical concerns. Isolated from the social world, from coherent patterns of shared, goal-directed activities, and from accountability to others, one's convictions would become more ephemeral, transient, and idiosyncratic. Importantly, belief would lack a certain *temporal* coherence that is more usually integral to our sense that something is the case. The contrast between being integrated into a pattern of confident, coherent anticipation and fulfillment, and standing out in contrast to such a pattern, would therefore be diminished or otherwise altered. As with perceptual experience, this would render belief closer in structure to the temporal profile(s) of imagining.

It follows that delusions, at least in this scenario, are not simply anomalous beliefs. Like internal VHs, they have a type of intentionality that differs from mundane experiences of believing, remembering, imagining, and perceiving. This is consistent with the observation in chapter 3 that delusions can involve a form of double-bookkeeping: the person seems both to believe that *p* and not to believe that *p*. The kind of intentionality at play is neither belief nor something wholly different from belief. It does not conform to neat, tidy, categorical distinctions between a few established intentional state types. Moreover, until it is made sufficiently clear which of many subtly different kinds of intentionality the term "belief" does encompass and which it does not, there can be no fact of the matter as to whether or not delusions of this kind are beliefs. Although the *attitude of belief* is altered, such that it is more transient and no longer grounded in a public world of shared concerns, this is compatible with the inflexible endorsement of delusional "beliefs." Where delusions are concerned, stubborn conviction and recalcitrance to change can be symptomatic of a *kind* of conviction that is importantly different from that more usually involved in firmly held belief. In the more usual case, a belief is firmly held because it is integrated into a shared, public world to such an extent that it is taken for granted. At the very least, it is shared by a group of people with whom one identifies in some way. Delusional beliefs are inflexible precisely to the extent that they are *not* anchored in a shared world and are therefore impervious to the influence of social, regulatory practices. So, in one scenario, certainty is symptomatic of being comfortably immersed in a shared world while, in the other, it is symptomatic of precisely the opposite. What we have are different *kinds* of conviction, rather than a singular way of taking something to be the case that accommodates varying degrees of confidence.[11]

6.3 Becoming Unhinged

I have already noted a convergence between Husserl and Jaspers, on the view that the certainty of "belief" presupposes a different kind of confidence or certainty. This same position can be arrived at through a consideration of themes in Ludwig Wittgenstein's later writings. And I think it is instructive to see how different philosophical routes lead us to the same place, to the conclusion that the attitude of belief depends on a nonpropositional form of confidence, trust, or habitual certainty that is inextricable from the social world. In *On Certainty*, Wittgenstein (1975) maintains that some of our beliefs are immune from doubt. Where this is so, we cannot be said to *know* that *p*, partly because *p* was never doubted in the first place and partly because we are unable to supply any grounds for the belief that *p*. Some things have to be taken for granted; they are not objects of inquiry but "hinges" on which our inquiries hang: "We just *can't* investigate everything, and for that reason we are forced to rest content with assumption. If I want the door to turn, the hinges must stay put" (OC, 343).[12]

Campbell (2001) seeks to account for certain delusions by appealing to the view that our various beliefs rest on an unquestioned bedrock of "hinge" or "framework" propositions. In short, if delusions are themselves hinge propositions, it is no surprise that they are recalcitrant to change and largely insulated from rational debate. I agree that Wittgenstein's discussion is highly relevant here. However, it is a mistake to construe hinge propositions as beliefs, of the kind that involve adopting a linguistically expressible attitude toward a specific content. Furthermore, certain kinds of delusion do not consist of or depend on something being accepted in the form of a hinge. They instead involve what we might call a *loosening of the hinges*.

According to some interpreters, Wittgenstein takes hinges to consist not of unwavering propositional beliefs, but instead something practical, habitual, and nonpropositional, something that such beliefs presuppose (e.g., Moyal-Sharrock 2005; Rhodes and Gipps 2008). I agree with that interpretation.[13] Now, Wittgenstein gestures at different kinds of certainty in the text and it is not always clear quite what he has in mind. Consider the following: "If you tried to doubt everything you would not get as far as doubting anything. The game of doubting itself presupposes certainty" (OC, 115). There are various ways of interpreting this, some or all of which may be at play at one or another stage in his thinking. The weakest claim is that particular doubts are always expressed against wider backgrounds of acceptance. So, where one doubts that *p*, one also accepts that *q*. In a different situation, one could just as easily doubt that *q*; but this would be a situation where one does not doubt that *p*, at least not in the same way. For example, it would be peculiar, and perhaps even incoherent, to state "I do not know whether B will marry C or D, and I do not know whether B exists," as the first doubt takes for granted the existence of B. All the same, this does not prohibit doubting the existence of B in another scenario; it is merely that some doubts are contextually incompatible.

However, Wittgenstein is also concerned with a more fundamental kind of certainty. Some propositions are not just immune from doubt in some situations or relative to a subset of our practices. They are taken for granted in all situations, perhaps by an individual, by a culture, during a historical period, or even by all typical human beings in all cultures at all times. Even if this is accepted, it remains tempting to think in terms of deeply entrenched propositions that are immune from doubt thanks to some combination of the following: (a) we do not ordinarily make them explicit and subject them to critical scrutiny; (b) some or all of our other beliefs depend on them; and (c) we are unable to supply grounds for them, at least not in the way we do for contestable empirical claims. But, whatever the case, Wittgenstein is clearly addressing something else as well. It is something he explicitly struggles to articulate, not just because it is more usually accepted without question but also because it is different in kind from propositional belief. At one point, he remarks, "I am inclined to believe that not everything that has the form of an empirical proposition *is* one" (OC, 308). One might interpret this as "Some propositions that look like empirical propositions are in fact propositions of a different kind." Alternatively, it could be read as "Some things that look like empirical propositions are not propositions at all." I suggest the latter reading.

Wittgenstein later refers to a "comfortable" certainty, which he describes as a "form of life," only to concede, immediately afterward, that this is "very badly expressed and probably badly thought as well" (OC, 357, 358). Even if it is badly expressed, the reference to a form of life indicates that what he has in mind is nonpropositional in nature. Whatever "forms of life" might be, they are not propositions. Rather, the emphasis is on a background of shared linguistic and nonlinguistic practice that meaningful propositions presuppose. For instance, in his earlier *Philosophical Investigations* (Wittgenstein

1953), he writes: "the *speaking* of language is part of an activity, or of a form of life" (PI, 23). At the very least, it seems that such certainties are not usually explicitly *endorsed*. Instead, their acceptance is constituted by and expressed in practice, in a way that somehow lends itself to linguistic articulation in terms of the belief that *p* or *q*. And articulation or expression is not the same as translation; neither the attitude nor the content are wholly preserved or replicated in propositional form. But this is still not terribly exciting. It is not clear why the habitual acceptance of something cannot be identified and articulated (to at least some extent) by spoken language, and subsequently challenged. After all, many largely or wholly nonlinguistic practices remain normatively accountable. What is accepted in a habitual way can be made explicit, held accountable to whatever norm, criticized, and finally revised, perhaps via retraining.

Of course, it can be added that some practical acceptances are both deeply entrenched and indispensable to wider contexts of linguistic and nonlinguistic activity. However, even if this is sometimes what Wittgenstein has in mind, I think he is also struggling to articulate something else, something importantly different. Wittgenstein writes that comfortable certainty is to be conceived of as "something that lies beyond being justified or unjustified; as it were, as something animal" (OC, 359). He adds that, in grappling with it, he wishes to construe the human being as "an animal," a "primitive being to which one grants instinct but not ratiocination," a "creature in a primitive state" (OC, 475). This "animal certainty," I suggest, is most plausibly identified with the kind of habitual, confident immersion in the world described by Husserl. While Husserl offers a clearer and more detailed analysis of its structure, in terms of anticipation and fulfillment, Wittgenstein places more emphasis on its social embeddedness. In both cases, though, what we have is not a practical or theoretical attitude toward something or the content of such an attitude but a condition for the possession of any kind of intentional state, something that our grasp of the distinction between *what is* and *what is not* rests on.

What is needed is a reading of "the game of doubting itself presupposes certainty" that emphasizes the *form* of doubt, rather than the *content* of doubt. The claim is not merely that a doubt with a given content makes sense only in a particular linguistic or nonlinguistic situation, or that all doubts happen to operate within one or another stable context of acceptance. In addition, the form of doubt, the intelligibility of the attitude of doubt, depends on grasping something as potentially anomalous *relative to* a wider backdrop of acceptance. This grasping is first and foremost habitual and practical rather than propositional. By implication, the same applies to negation, as well as to affirmation in the face of potential negation. Hence certainty, in the relevant sense, is not a matter of taking something to be the case. It is presupposed by the modalities of belief: by doubt, negation, and affirmation. And this is why it does not consist of "belief," at least not in the way that a propositional or even nonpropositional attitude might be thought of as a belief.

Wittgenstein emphasizes that certainty of this kind is inseparable from immersion in a *shared* world. He states that "in order to make a mistake, a man must already judge in conformity with mankind" (OC, 156), and also describes our "picture of the world" as an "inherited background against which I distinguish between true and false" (OC, 94). Again, I do not think such remarks are to be interpreted merely in terms of conformity with a wider body of knowledge or a contingent set of linguistic and nonlinguistic practices. Also at play is the recognition that uncertainties, doubts, and errors make sense only against a backdrop of shared certainty. Furthermore, it is only in the face of potential doubt or uncertainty that we take something to be the case in a propositional way. So, if you point to any particular belief or, indeed, any combination of beliefs, you will not capture the underlying sense of certainty. It consists instead in a kind of habitual, *animal* confidence.

This reading is consistent with some of Wittgenstein's remarks on certainty in *Philosophical Investigations*. There, he appears to explicitly identify certainty with a kind of affective anticipation:

> The belief that fire will burn me is of the same kind as the fear that it will burn me.
>
> I shall get burnt if I put my hand in the fire: that is certainty. That is to say: here we see the meaning of certainty. (What it amounts to, not just the meaning of the word "certainty.") (PI, 473, 474)

One might object that this kind of expectation is itself propositional in nature. However, other passages make clear that Wittgenstein is concerned with something practical, affective, and habitual: "What kind of reason have I to assume that my finger will feel a resistance when it touches the table?" (PI, 478). There is no *reason*, and there is no *assumption*; such expectations instead form part of a wider, cohesive pattern of anticipation. As

Wittgenstein acknowledges, "An expectation is imbedded in a situation, from which it arises" (PI, 581). An expectation, whether it takes the form of unproblematic acceptance or doubt, makes sense only relative to a wider situation in which it is embedded; confident expectations are consistent with that situation, while doubts are potential deviations. So, whenever we take something to be the case or otherwise, our doing so always rests on another kind of certainty, a coherent system of confident, habitual anticipation. This is what it is to *have certainty*, to be able to take something or other as certain.

Moyal-Sharrock (2005, 66) suggests that hinges can also be thought of in terms of "blind trust," an unthinking reliance on things that serves as our "default attitude." Wittgenstein mentions trust at various points in the text. For example:

> How does someone judge which is his right and which his left hand? How do I know that my judgment will agree with someone else's? How do I know that this colour is blue? If I don't trust *myself* here, why should I trust anyone else's judgment? Is there a why? Must I not begin to trust somewhere? That is to say: somewhere I must begin with not-doubting; and that is not, so to speak, hasty but excusable: it is part of judging. (OC, 150)

Again, references to trust are consistent with an emphasis on anticipatory style. To start trusting "somewhere" is not to accept some content of experience or thought as certain. It is only because we habitually trust and are already immersed in "comfortable certainty" that a distinction between being the case and not being the case is intelligible to us. We must inhabit the world in a certain way, have a certain style of anticipation, for "judging" to be possible at all; that is "part of" what it is to judge. One might ask whether I first trust myself in this way, first trust the world, or first trust other people. In chapter 5, I argued that trust in others has a certain priority. It is through this that trust in ourselves, our activities, our abilities, and the world as a whole is sustained and restored. With this in mind, it is informative to consider the notion of a "moral hinge." In *On Certainty*, Wittgenstein does not explicitly address moral beliefs. Nevertheless, it has been argued that some of our moral beliefs behave in a way that is consistent with his discussion. Pleasants (2008, 2009) makes a case for "basic moral certainties," such as "killing people is wrong." His argument involves showing how, when philosophers attempt to explicitly defend claims like this, their attempts come across as empty, absurd, amusing, or offensive. We cannot supply grounds for knowledge claims here, as the relevant propositions do not operate as potential objects of doubt to begin with, other than in a few exceptional circumstances. The wrongness of killing is rooted in our practices, in such a way that it is ordinarily beyond question:

> Because of the role and significance that death, and hence killing, has for us as embodied, finite, vulnerable beings, the statements "death is bad" and "murder is wrong" are not moral propositions but expressions of basic moral certainty. Just as no-one in non-extraordinary circumstances is in a position to say *how* they know that they have hands, so no-one can say what the badness of death and wrongness of killing consist in. (Pleasants 2009, 677)

The concept of a moral hinge can be related to traumatic experiences, where a person faces the task of describing the loss of something that is more usually taken for granted, even by the language she has to rely on in order to convey her loss (Kusch forthcoming). Again, there is a distinction to be drawn between convictions with specific contents, however deep-rooted they may be, and something more pervasive, which is not propositional at all. Specific moral convictions, however entrenched, are distinct from an overarching way of relating to other people. And something that looks like a proposition could turn out to be an expression of the latter. For instance, "Other people will not harm me," "The world is generally safe," "Others will help me when I am suffering," and so forth, can be expressive of the global style of anticipation. Propositions such as "Killing people is wrong" are at least partly attributable to it as well (although more needs to be said about the relationship between habitual expectation and normative judgment). Assuming one's experiences and thoughts arise within a world where reciprocal trust is taken as given, it does not even make sense to consider whether killing other people might be an appropriate way to act. For that reason, a clear distinction should not be made between moral hinges and hinges more generally. A style of interpersonal relatedness, which some moral judgments can also express, is inextricable from having a world at all, from being rooted in a realm where some things are and some things are not.

Our most confident beliefs therefore turn out to be different in kind from a confidence that makes belief possible. I concede that not all of Wittgenstein's examples of hinges express the latter. "The Earth exists" and "There are physical objects" are good candidates. These are arguably inextricable from the sense of being embedded in a shared world. But propositions such as "The Earth is round" and "I have a brain" fall into a different category. Whereas the former are expressions of something that is inextricable from the style of experience, from the possibility of perceiving and believing, the latter look more like deeply entrenched belief contents. Even so, the erosion of ingrained beliefs can affect experiential style. For example, if I somehow discovered that the Earth was only thirty years old and that I had been cloned from a Martian, this would have such a profound and disruptive effect on my habitual confidence that it might well precipitate a shift in the overall form of anticipation, in the structure of intentionality. Thus, while only some "hinge propositions" are integral to the modal structure of experience, those that are not remain intimately associated with it. This applies especially to the interpersonal sphere. Even when our most entrenched beliefs and expectations are challenged, we can turn to others for reassurance and recalibration. But suppose the challenge to belief were such as to compromise precisely those interpersonal relations that would otherwise aid restoration of habitual confidence. Here, in particular, we would expect an erosion of entrenched beliefs, brought about by revelations or deeds, to impact on the overall structure of experience.

Wittgenstein remarks, at one point, that "the difficulty is to realize the groundlessness of our believing" (OC, 166). On one reading, this concerns belief content: we inevitably take some things as given without being able to supply any further grounds for them. However, there is another way of understanding the remark. There is a sense in which the attitude of believing is itself groundless. Once we have acknowledged a kind of confidence that constitutes our sense of what it is to be the case or otherwise, there is nothing more we can ask for, no further bedrock buried beneath a fragile system of habitual expectations. So, when the default pattern of anticipation and fulfillment breaks down, we face a peculiar kind of disturbance. It is not just that something is missing, lacking, or otherwise different. An erosion of the modal structure of intentionality is also an erosion of perspective, of being open to a world where some things are and others are not, where the imaginary is distinct from the real. This amounts to a profound experience of groundlessness and helplessness. We become, if you like, unhinged from the consensus world, and any certainty that remains is different in kind.

6.4 The Anticipation of Memory

One might worry that an emphasis on the anticipatory structure of experience does not accommodate experiences of remembering, which concern what is past rather than what is to come. However, the content of a memory is to be distinguished from a sense of that content *as* remembered. And the experience of remembering something does, I suggest, involve a characteristic pattern of content-anticipation that contributes to a sense of it *as* past.

To illustrate this, let us consider post-traumatic flashbacks, which are said to involve perception-like experiences of unpleasant past events. Flashbacks involve autobiographical memories that are not exclusively propositional in nature, by which I mean that one remembers the event rather than just remembering *that* the event happened. These memories are also self-involving. Remembering what happened in a television program that you watched some time ago is not self-involving in the relevant way, while remembering something that happened to you is. When we remember life events, we do not experience the coming of those events but we do anticipate the coming of our memories, in a way that differs from the anticipation of perceived events, imagined events, and our own inner speech. Often, we remember something that relates, in however tenuous a manner, to what we are currently thinking, doing, attempting to do, or actively trying to recall. In addition, remembered events tend to be experienced as significant, as mattering to us in one or another way. How they matter to us is a reflection of our current commitments, concerns, projects, and values—what we care about and why. A remembered event might involve something that is to be further developed, compensated for, or left behind. Hence the autobiographical past is constantly renegotiated, reinterpreted, in light of where we are heading:

> The future is the site of both anticipation and the unexpected, planning and the changing of plans. This predominant orientation toward a changing future also means a fluid or unfixed past, because the past is continually being reassessed as one moves into the future. (Havens 1986, 21)

Where the possibility of moving forward in a purposive, progressive, structured fashion is compromised, so is that of contextualizing, interpreting, and reinterpreting past events in light of current concerns. As we saw in chapter 5, traumatic events can bring about a shift in the anticipatory structure of experience—a loss of trust, confidence, or certainty. Projects collapse; other people appear threatening and unpredictable; and there is no prospect of relating to others in such a way as to open up new possibilities and reinterpret one's predicament. So one cannot *move on*. We can thus begin to see why traumatic memories might be experienced as vivid, intrusive flashbacks, why they are relived more so than recalled (e.g., Hunt 2010, 70). They are not integrated into a coherent, dynamic, and meaningful life story. So the traumatized person does not first recall another, related part of the story and, in the process, anticipate their coming. They are triggered or cued in a different manner. Difficulties in voluntarily recalling traumatic memories may be similarly attributable to this lack of contextualization. Other autobiographical memories would not be affected in quite the same way. Those that were formed before the traumatic event would still be integrated into a life, albeit a life that now seems strangely distant. Granted, if one feels dislodged from the social world and disengaged from goal-directed projects, memories of events that occurred after the trauma will lack cohesion as well. However, it can be added that traumatic memories are not altogether bereft of anticipation; their coming is anticipated with anxiety and dread, which alienates one from them still further. So, what we have is the anxious anticipation of something unpleasant that is not contextually embedded in the way that memories more usually are. Like the inner speech VHs addressed in chapter 4, traumatic memories are thus experienced in a perception-like way, as something unpleasant that a person might seek to avoid but is forced to confront. This does not imply that a traumatic memory endures as a wholly uncorrupted record of how the event was experienced at the time. The point is that it is not anticipated in any of the *ways* that memory contents more usually are.[14]

The effects of trauma can also include a more general erosion of the modal structure of intentionality. As discussed in section 6.1, perceptual experience may become permeated by passivity and detachment, lack of cohesion, and varying degrees of removal from the consensus world. With this, a sense of memories as distinct from perceptions will already be diminished, rendering the person more susceptible to pronounced, episodic disruptions, in the guise of distressing, decontextualized contents. An account along these lines may well capture some internal VH experiences. Michie et al. (2005) suggest that VHs sometimes occur because of a failure to inhibit irrelevant memories. If that is right, then the terms "flashback" and "verbal hallucination" could refer to a common experience. Such an account would not accommodate all traumatic memories, given that their contents need not be predominantly verbal. Even so, it is consistent with cases where distressing memories centrally involve speech, perhaps that of an abuser.

There are potential implications here for our understanding of dissociation in trauma. The term "dissociation" is used to refer to various different kinds of experience. These include experiences of *derealization*, involving a sense of detachment from the world and from one's body. Loss of trust, as described in chapter 5, is consistent with something along these lines. In brief, the person feels disconnected from other people and from the whole a world—she is not quite *there*. And, as she lacks certain feelings of anticipation and associated bodily dispositions, her body feels different too. Traumatic memories, as I have described them, involve another kind of dissociation; they are not integrated into a person's life and, owing to their lack of context, she may also have trouble accessing them voluntarily. Inner speech VHs, as described in chapter 4, can similarly be conceived of in terms of dissociation: anxious anticipation of inner speech content involves an unusual degree of detachment from one's own self-directed emotions, which are then confronted in the guise of "voices."

On the other hand, an experience of post-traumatic dissociation could also involve preserving some degree of trust by not confronting the relevant events, by actively resisting their integration into one's life and, in the extreme case, striving to go about one's business as though nothing has happened. The extent to which a person tries (successfully or otherwise) to avoid contemplating past events, and the extent to which she succeeds in retaining a sense of trust, confidence, or certainty, are both likely to vary considerably. So, while some experiences of "dissociation" are largely attributable to disturbances of the modal structure of intentionality, others may owe more to the attempt to sustain that structure (where this attempt could involve a range of different strategies, into which a person has varying degrees of insight). Both ends of the spectrum are consistent with memories that are decontextualized, anxiously anticipated, and consequently experienced as variably perception-like.[15] This complicates discussion of the relationship between dissociation and "reality discrimination" (e.g., Varese, Barkus, and Bentall 2012), given that the modal structure of intentionality, and thus the sense of reality, will not always be affected in the same way or to the same extent. Thus, as this brief consideration of traumatic memory further illustrates, an emphasis on the modal structure of intentionality can assist in illuminating various kinds of anomalous experience, while also pointing to more specific analyses that distinguish them from each other.

6.5 Intentionality and Time

I have argued that the sense of being in a given type of intentional state depends, to a significant extent, on the temporal structure of experience and, more specifically, on patterns of anticipation and fulfilment. Chapters 3 and 4 addressed content-specific, episodic disturbances in the structure of intentionality, which can be understood in terms of changes in anticipatory style. Chapter 5 added that these experiences usually occur against a backdrop of wider-ranging phenomenological disturbances. So it is not merely that the anticipatory structure characteristic of intentional state *x* with content *p* is disrupted such that *p* is experienced as the content of a *y*-like intentional state. While experiences of this kind could in principle occur in isolation, they are more usually symptomatic of nonlocalized changes in the modal structure of intentionality. But how, exactly, do the two relate to each other? Drawing the various strands of discussion together, the overall position arrived at is as follows:

The sense of being in a given intentional state depends largely on its having a distinctive temporal profile. This includes a sense of whether and how the relevant temporal profile differs from that of other intentional state types. An appreciation of such differences is inseparable from the global style of anticipation. Perceptual experience ordinarily has a cohesive, tightly structured anticipation-fulfillment profile, on which the attitude of belief is also parasitic. Changes in the overall style of perceptual experience therefore imply changes in *how* one believes; things are no longer taken to be the case or not the case in quite the same way. The temporal profiles of imagining and remembering are experienced *as* departures from that of perceptual experience, insofar as they involve lesser degrees of structure. A change in how a person relates to others in general can erode the structure of perceptual experience by uprooting it from the consensus world, generating widespread unpredictability, dysregulating affective anticipation, and insulating her from interpersonal processes that more usually sustain or repair experiential cohesion. In so doing, it alters the modal structure of intentionality, lessening the gulf between temporal profiles. For instance, perceptual experiences that lack cohesion, have no bearing on life projects, are isolated from the public world, and do not solicit activities are, in these respects, similar in structure to certain imaginings. Consequently, the person is more susceptible to modally ambiguous experiences.

I think this position is consistent with where Husserl was heading in some of his later work. More generally, though, very little has been written on anticipation-fulfillment profiles and how they contribute to the sense of being in one or another type of intentional state. An exception is Straus (1958, 162–164), who explicitly states that some experiences, including certain hallucinations, "*originate in the medium of distorted modalities*." Different kinds of intentionality, he observes, have different temporal structures. For instance, "In my recollection I can transport myself to past decades; in waking sensory experience I can only advance from present to present into the future." When it comes to imagination, "I can cross the ocean in one leap; in sensory experience there are no leaps." So a principal difference between perceptual experience of one's surroundings and remembering or imagining is that perception involves a distinctive, more tightly structured pattern of anticipation and fulfillment: "Waking experience has its own peculiar order and precision. Every moment is directed to the following one in a meaningful anticipation. … In the continuum of anticipation we grasp our wakefulness." It is not *because* one already experiences oneself as perceiving rather than imagining that certain things are anticipated rather than others, and that certain things are taken to be anomalous that would be unproblematic if imagined. Rather, these anticipatory patterns constitute the sense of one's intentional state.

Merleau-Ponty (1945/2012, 338) makes some complementary observations regarding the experience of imagining:

> In imagination, I have hardly formed the intention to see before I already believe that I have seen. Imagination is without depth; it does not respond to our attempts to vary our points of view; it does not lend itself to our observation. We are never geared into the imagination. In each perception, however, it is the matter itself that takes on sense and form. … The real stands out against our fictions because in the real sense surrounds matter and penetrates it deeply. … The real lends itself to an infinite exploration, it is inexhaustible.

Thus, as well as having more consistency than imagination, perception differs in the range of possibilities that are anticipated and the ways in which they unfold. When you imagine something, the imagined entity does not call out for further exploration in the way that a perceived entity does. It is not experienced in terms of various different perceptual and practical possibilities that might be actualized. There is also a sense in which the contents of our imaginings are more fully present: there is less indeterminacy, less that calls out for exploration. Yet it is precisely because of this that an entity is experienced as imagined rather than as perceptually present. Remembered situations also unfold in ways that are removed from the cohesive, consistent anticipation-fulfillment structure of perceptual experience; one can dart from one time and place to another. On the other hand, memories are constrained in ways that imaginings are not. For instance, a specific event, as remembered, cannot be moved from one past situation to another; it cannot be swiftly erased and replaced with an alternative scenario; and it retains some degree of consistency with other remembered events. Memories also implicate other people in ways that imaginings do not. A remembered event can be something *we* saw or did; something that others could in principle corroborate; and something that had or will have repercussions for others. More generally, memory contents are constrained by their integration into a cohesive, consensus world, in a way that the contents of counterfactual imaginings are not. Hence the anticipatory styles of imagining and remembering involve distinctive privations of what I have called "global anticipatory style." As they run alongside perceptual experience, they are experienced as departures from it, as temporal patterns that are disengaged in different ways from one's rootedness in the present.

Alfred Schutz (1945) conceives of the modal structure of intentionality in what I take to be a compatible way. He addresses the view of William James (1889) that, during the course of our daily lives, we inhabit a number of different "sub-universes," such as the world of perception, the world of science, and the world of the supernatural. For James, which of these we regard as authoritative, as our ultimate reality, is not the outcome of reasoning or evidence, but a reflection of whether and how it relates to our lives, to what we care about. It is not always clear whether these different sub-universes are to be thought of in terms of different kinds of content, different kinds of intentionality, or a combination of the two. However, Schutz's development of the view suggests the latter. For instance, when he contrasts the world of science with the worlds of dreaming and imagination, it is clear that the difference is not just one of content but also one of form; different kinds of intentionality are at work. Schutz prefers the term "province of meaning" to "sub-universe," and maintains that the province of everyday experience has priority over others. It is "marked out as ultimate or paramount reality," in virtue of the "unity and congruity of the world." Other meaning-provinces are all *derived* from the world of everyday, practical, social life by means of selective abstraction: "The world of working in daily life is the archetype of our experience of reality. All other provinces of meaning may be considered as its modifications" (Schutz 1945, 552–554).

Interestingly, Karlsson (2008, 370) explicitly relates Schutz's discussion to VH experiences, observing how participants in a study "described how the voice hearing was enacted in another reality, or in an enclave of the ordinary life that the participants spiritually visited." It can be added that the difference between consensus reality and this other "reality" should not be construed solely in terms of their respective experiential contents. Consider Schutz's inclusion of the imaginary as a province of meaning. This inclusion might at first seem misplaced: when we imagine something, we retain a sense of our imaginings *as* imaginings that arise in the context of a world that we continue to take as given. So an isolated imagining does not constitute a cohesive sub-universe or meaning-province in its own right. However, this does not apply so obviously to extended imaginative exercises, where we take things to be the case and act accordingly within wider-ranging make-believe realms. For Schutz, these realms are distinguishable from the world of everyday life in virtue of their relative lack of structure. They are not constrained by objects that resist us or by projects that we are committed to, and are liberated from the regimented spatiotemporal structure of the consensus world:

> Living in one of the many worlds of phantasy we have no longer to master the outer world and to overcome the resistance of its objects. We are free from the pragmatic motive which governs our natural attitude toward the world of daily life, free also from the bondage of "interobjective" space and intersubjective standard time. (1945, 555)

So it is not just a matter of taking something to be the case in one meaning-province that is not taken to be the case in another. The world of imagination involves a kind of abstraction from the everyday; it is prereflectively experienced *as* a privation, as a withdrawal from something. Our sense of it *as an imagined world* therefore continues to presuppose our habitual immersion in a consensus world.

This is not to suggest that different kinds of intentionality unfold in parallel, in complete isolation from each other. As I contemplate what I will write next, perceive the computer screen, and imagine seeing my children this evening, these aspects of experience are co-present and easily distinguishable from each other. Yet they also interact in various ways, and certain kinds of interaction are anticipated. My imagining might take my writing in a new direction; something I remember might prompt me to do something else; and an incident in my environment might distract me from my task. Like the temporal profiles of the intentional states concerned, these interactions are structured in characteristic ways. I experience the influence of my imaginings on the flow of my thoughts as distinct from the influence of my memories. The way in which a type of intentional state interacts with others, such as the way in which a memory can drift into an imagining and vice versa, is also integral to its anticipation-fulfillment profile. The task of describing, in detail, all of the various temporal profiles and how they relate to each other amounts to a substantial philosophical and interdisciplinary endeavor. It is not my intention to complete the project here. Instead, my aim is to develop a way of thinking about human experience that opens up the possibility of pursuing a wider-ranging project of this nature. I am also inclined to think that the cohesive modal structure of intentionality (which, as pointed out in chapter 5, is inextricable from the feeling body) is both necessary and sufficient for "minimal self," for the having of a singular, cohesive perspective. Perhaps there is more to minimal-self experience than this. But, if so, we are owed a clear account of what the additional ingredients consist of, rather than appeals to a more primitive experience of subjectivity about which no more can be said.

If the world of everyday life were lacking in structure, in ways described earlier in this chapter, the sense of an imaginary world as a privation of it, and as unfolding alongside it in a different way, would no longer be so clear. Hence VHs can be thought of not just as localized modal disruptions that are imaginatively embellished, but—at least in some cases—as experiences that are embedded in wider-ranging imaginings, where those imaginings are no longer experienced in clear contrast with a consensus reality. The person enters a world in which her voices are experienced, akin to entering a dark wood where things might jump out at you. And again, the line between hallucination and delusion is unclear. Adrift from consensus reality, she does not *believe* in quite the same way anymore. So a clear-cut distinction cannot be drawn between cases where B experiences *p* but does not believe that *p*, and cases where B experiences *p* and further adopts the belief that *p*. Susceptibility to becoming lost in imaginary worlds, like susceptibility to more localized VH experiences, is attributable to changes in global anticipatory style, which weaken the experienced boundaries between "meaning provinces," as well as between more specifically focused intentional states. Both localized and wider-ranging disruptions of intentionality can be short-lived or more enduring. A "voice" could last for seconds or for longer periods, and a person could also become immersed in an imaginary realm for varying periods of time. Even global changes in the structure of intentionality are by no means consistent over long periods of time, and may be more pronounced in some social situations than others. Consider this observation, by Aggernaes (1972, 236):

> The present author found during seven days and nights of living among chronic schizophrenic patients ... that, as to most practical matters and a lot of interpersonal matters, they actually functioned without conspicuous defects in their evaluation of reality.

Perhaps these patients were engaged in a kind of double-bookkeeping, and their anomalous experiences ran alongside their abilities to engage in practical tasks without interfering. But it could just as well be that localized and more pervasive disturbances of intentionality were lessened by sustained exposure to a certain kind of social environment.

Alterations of the modal structure of intentionality differ in three respects from more mundane experiences of moving from one "world" to another. First of all, they involve forms of intentionality that do not respect the usual distinction between what is and is not the case. Second, as the anticipation-fulfillment structure of perceptual experience has been disrupted, they are no longer experienced as unambiguous deviations from what is the case; they are no longer anchored to consensus reality. Third, those that are most likely to be associated with a psychiatric illness diagnosis involve losing some degree of control over when one enters into and withdraws from a "world." This need not amount to a complete absence of control. A person might choose, at least to some extent, to detach himself from the consensus world and inhabit a different kind of reality.[16] On other occasions, though, the transition is involuntary. Consider the following account:

> One time when I was forcibly taken to the hospital, the paramedics stayed with me while I waited and talked to me the whole 6 hours or so. I still heard it, but it felt like it had less power over me because I was aware of the outside world. They were conversing with me even though it was difficult, and kept that line open between me and the outside. But the moment I was transferred to the psychiatric emergency room I was locked in a tiny, bare room by myself for hours. I withdrew and the voice seemed like the only reality and got stronger because I had no distractions. (4)

Here, the authority and reality of the voice is enhanced by physical isolation from other people, something that exacerbates a lack of rootedness in the consensus world, a loss of "awareness" of the "outside world." The "line" between "me and the outside" is lost, and without it, there is no longer a reality with which to contrast the voice, a world that it remains tethered to but, at the same time, distinct from.

6.6 Schizophrenia and Trauma

My account of the relationship between interpersonal experience and the modal structure of intentionality is consistent with a substantial body of research on the links between trauma and psychosis. It also offers a way of interpreting these findings, showing not merely *that* the two are related but *how* they are. This section reviews some of the relevant evidence, after which it addresses the difficult question of how, if at all, modal disruptions that are symptomatic of trauma differ from those associated with schizophrenia diagnoses. In considering the relationships between trauma and psychosis, it is important to distinguish trauma during development, which interferes with the formation of trusting relations, from trauma in adulthood, which disrupts an already established interpersonal style. Various combinations of childhood and adulthood trauma should also be considered, which may be associated with a range of different trajectories and outcomes. Furthermore, how a given individual reacts to traumatic events is not just attributable to the nature of the events in question, combined with level of vulnerability. Outcomes also depend on the responses of other people, responses that are influenced, to varying degrees, by wider social and cultural structures.[17] While some responses may help to sustain a degree of trust and to repair trust, others may erode it still further. Hence patterns of causation are both complicated and highly variable.

Of course, traumatic experiences are not always associated with psychosis or, more specifically, with schizophrenia diagnoses. Nevertheless, a substantial literature points to strong links between adverse experiences, particularly those involving other people, and subsequent diagnoses of psychotic illness. Contributing factors can include prejudicial discrimination, feelings of being socially disempowered, and lack of social support (Bentall and Fernyhough 2008). There are especially strong links between traumatic events in childhood and psychosis. Some studies indicate that around 85 percent of adults diagnosed with schizophrenia have suffered some form of childhood abuse, with sexual abuse in half these cases, figures that are far higher than the population base rate. Abuse and trauma in adulthood also increase vulnerability to psychosis, and some symptoms are most reliably associated with combinations of childhood and adulthood adversity. One might question the extent to which self-reports of abuse are reliable. However, where corroboration is possible, reliability is high (Read et al. 2003, 2005, 334; Larkin and Morrison 2006; Bentall and Varese 2013).

To go into a bit more detail, a study conducted by Kilcommons and Morrison (2005) involved thirty-two people diagnosed with psychosis. Ninety-four percent of them reported at least one traumatic lifetime event and 53 percent met the criteria for post-traumatic stress disorder. There were also correlations between severity of trauma and severity of symptoms, between physical abuse and positive symptoms, and between sexual abuse and hallucinations. Focusing specifically on the effects of childhood trauma, Varese et al. (2012, 669) conducted a meta-analysis of forty-one studies (all judged to be methodologically sound), which together point to the conclusion that "childhood adversity is substantially associated with an increased risk of psychosis." Mueser et al. (2002, 126) report that rates of past trauma are high not just in schizophrenia but in severe psychiatric illness more generally, and that a history of physical and sexual abuse is specifically associated with "severe symptoms," including "hallucinations and delusions, depression, suicidality, anxiety, hostility, interpersonal sensitivity, somatization, and dissociation." The contents of hallucinations often resemble, in one or another way, the nature of traumatic events.[18] In a review of published studies, Morrison, Frame, and Larkin (2003) ask whether psychosis can cause post-traumatic stress disorder, whether trauma can cause psychosis, and whether psychosis and post-traumatic stress disorder both fall within a spectrum of responses to trauma. Their answer is that there is good evidence for all three. Although they acknowledge methodological problems with some studies, they conclude that, when all of the available evidence is taken into consideration, the association between trauma and psychosis is "undeniable." There is also evidence pointing more specifically to a dose-response relationship between trauma and psychosis (Larkin and Read 2012).[19]

Such findings do not imply a causal connection but are at least suggestive of one. How, though, might episodic and/or sustained traumatic experiences cause severe psychiatric illness, including symptoms such as VHs? It is plausible, I suggest, that diminution or loss of trust plays a central role. Rather than focusing solely on the *loss* of trust, as I did in chapter 5, we also need to consider scenarios where its formation is disrupted during development, such that a person never comes to relate to others in ways that many of us take for granted. To reiterate, "trust," in this context, is not a matter of however many intentional states with propositional content. It is a habitual, affective style of anticipation, which shapes how a person experiences and relates to others and, by implication, to the world as a whole. This is consistent with the view that it first arises in infancy, as a set of interpersonal expectations that form through interactions with caregivers and later come to regulate encounters with other people in general. As discussed in chapter 2, a substantial body of literature on child development maintains that psychological development depends on types of patterned interaction between infants and caregivers, which cultivate habitual expectations concerning how interpersonal interactions unfold (Hobson 1993; 2002; Trevarthen 1993; Stern 1993; Reddy 2008). Judith Herman, in her influential study of trauma, similarly suggests that a primitive, nonlocalized form of trust originates in interpersonal relationships during infancy: "The sense of safety in the world, or basic trust, is acquired in earliest life in the relationship with the first caretaker." She adds that, when this form of trust is lost, a "sense of connection" with other people is "shattered," something that also amounts to the loss of a "basic sense of self" (Herman 1997, 51–54).

Among other things, a child's sense of other people in general as unpredictable, uncaring, and potentially or actually hostile in one or another way would interfere with what Csibra and Gergely (2009, 148) call "natural pedagogy." Human communication, they propose, is adapted to facilitate the reliable transmission of generalizable, cultural knowledge during development. The social transmission of knowledge depends on a system of expectations concerning how others will behave, which assume the "communicative cooperation and epistemic benevolence of the communicative partner." Even in infancy, there are patterns of attention and expectation, along with interpretive biases, which render infants receptive to social signals such as ostensive gestures and dispose them to extract generalizable knowledge from these signals. Drawing on this work, Fonagy and Allison (2014) offer an account of the social-developmental process through which trust is formed and consider the cognitive effects of deviations from it. They suggest that the extent to which an infant comes to trust sources of communication is a reflection of attachment style:

> Attachment security, rooted in a history of feeling recognized, appears to increase the likelihood of trust in a source of communication when it is reasonably credible. A secure attachment history also generates confidence in one's own experience and belief and empowers one's judgment. (2014, 374)

Secure attachments in early life foster a trust in others that later generalizes, disposing a person to accept credible communications. We also depend on this trust to instill confidence in our own judgments and abilities, given that self-confidence is reliant on feedback from others. So those who are unable to relate to others in the relevant way are left in a "state of interminable searching for validation of experience." This is accompanied by "epistemic hypervigilance"; they are constantly on the lookout for potential dangers. Attachment insecurity in adulthood is also associated with epistemic biases, including intolerance of ambiguity, inflexible and dogmatic thinking, and a tendency to make judgments based on early and insufficient information (Fonagy and Allison 2014, 374).

It is easy to see why a wide-ranging lack of trust in other people might be associated with these biases, especially in the more extreme cases. As noted by Mueser et al. (2002, 129), "most violence in the lives of people with SMI (severe mental illness) is interpersonal in nature," and so "*avoidance of trauma-related stimuli* often extends to close relationships, leading to reduced social contacts and social isolation." Where a person seeks to avoid other people in general, she will also avoid those types of interpersonal relation that more usually regulate experience and belief formation. To be more specific, as she does not regard others as credible sources of information, she will not be inclined to interact with them in ways that would otherwise serve to challenge her opinions, draw attention to alternative possibilities, and thus foster recognition of ambiguities. Intolerance of ambiguity is also partly symptomatic of how the world as a whole is experienced: an all-pervasive air of insecurity and unpleasant unpredictability precludes the comfortable acceptance of uncertainty and ambiguity.[20] As for dogmatic thinking, if a person is cut off from interpersonal processes that more usually shape the formation of belief, her thinking will be impervious to the influence of others. In addition, she will be more likely to arrive at judgments without consulting all the relevant information. Recognizing information as relevant involves respecting the testimonies of others, something that is inconsistent with a predicament where the interpersonal world is bereft of trusting relations. Furthermore, as argued earlier in this chapter, the effects of social estrangement are not limited to the contents of beliefs and how they are formed. The attitude of believing is itself affected, to varying degrees. A grasp of the distinction between what is and what is not the case depends, in part, on an appreciation of the contrast between what is embedded in a consensus world and what is not. To the extent that one is adrift from the consensus world, the sense of that contrast is diminished.

Descriptions of phenomenological changes that precede the onset of psychosis often point to something very similar. For example, Conrad (2012, 177) attempts to convey the early "trema" phase of schizophrenia through the analogy of walking through a dark forest:

> Nothing is "taken for granted" anymore. Nothing is experienced as "natural." In the darkness, precisely where one cannot see, there lurks something, behind the trees—one does not ask what it is that lurks. It remains undefined. It is the lurking itself. In that area between what is visible and what is "behind" the visible (e.g. the particular tree), what we call the background, where what we cannot grasp becomes uncanny. The background, from which the things we do grasp stand out, loses its neutrality.

In the case of traumatic experience, we might add that what lurks is, more specifically, a sense of *interpersonal* menace. Even so, this would also permeate one's wider experience of the surrounding world, given that how things appear salient and significant depends on what is anticipated from other people. Therefore, it is not so clear whether or how the two types of experience differ from one another. The relationship between trauma, trust in other people, and the integrity of world experience is not a prominent theme in phenomenological psychopathology. However, it is at least explicit in the work of Wolfgang Blankenburg (1969/2001, 1971/2012). He describes how localized symptoms of schizophrenia, such as delusions and hallucinations, arise within wider-ranging disturbances of "commonsense" (a background of habitual confidence that our experiences, thoughts, and activities more usually presuppose). One of his patients describes the predicament as follows:

> What is it that I am missing? It is something so small, but strange, it is something so important. It is impossible to live without it. I find that I no longer have footing in the world. I have lost a hold in regard to the simplest, everyday things. It seems that I lack a natural understanding for what is matter of course and obvious to others. (Blankenburg 1969/2001, 307)

Blankenburg makes clear that this "commonsense" is inextricable from how a person relates to others. It is "primarily related to an intersubjective world (*mitweltbezogen*)." He adds that certain patterns of interpersonal development fail to nurture a "basic trust" on which commonsense is founded (1969/2001, 307, 310). As before, the kind of trust in question is not simply trust in persons A, B, and C to do *p*, *q*, and *r*. Global "loss of natural self-evidence" (*Verlust der natürlichen Selbstverständlichkeit*), of the kind that Blankenburg associates with schizophrenia, is inextricable from the *ability* to trust in anyone or anything (*Vertrauenkönnen*). When a person is incapable of trusting relations with others, nothing is anticipated in an unproblematic fashion anymore; nothing is seamlessly integrated into a cohesive, confident pattern of anticipation and fulfilment. Consequently, nothing seems quite *there*, and nothing is taken to be *the case* in an unhesitant, unthinking way. This lack of confident, habitual acceptance extends to objects of perceptual experience and belief, the names and functions of familiar artifacts, and even word meanings.

Loss of natural self-evidence is closely related to the "hyperreflexivity" that Louis Sass takes to be central to self-disturbance in schizophrenia. To recap, hyperreflexivity is a largely involuntary attentiveness to aspects of experience and thought that are more usually unproblematic and inconspicuous. In Sass's words, it is "a condition in which phenomena that would normally be inhabited, and in this sense experienced as part of the self, come instead to be objects of focal or objectifying awareness" (Sass 2003, 153). Where there is affectively charged uncertainty over the nature of *p* and what to expect from it, *p* will stand out in a way that it would not if it were encountered in a habitually confident manner. Loss of basic trust therefore involves wide-ranging alterations in what appears conspicuous and how. More usually, perception of our surroundings is shaped by confident patterns of anticipation and fulfillment. In addition, our everyday activities are regulated by the unreflective acceptance of shared norms and practices, which prescribe, with varying degrees of determinacy, what is to be done in a given situation. And the habitual confidence we have in our own beliefs is partly a reflection of their being affirmed by others and integrated into a consensus world. I have further argued that an unproblematic sense of being in intentional state *x* rather than *y* depends on a style of anticipation that is inseparable from basic trust. With the erosion of trust, ordinarily inconspicuous features of the environment become uncomfortably salient, as do one's own activities, experiences, and thoughts. The resultant anticipatory style thus incorporates a form of hyperreflexivity.

My position is equally compatible with the insistence of the Hearing Voices Movement that "voices" and other troubling, anomalous experiences are essentially interpersonal, relational phenomena. The cumulative effects of a sequence of traumatic events can lead to increasing social isolation and, with it, a pervasive alteration in the sense of reality, sometimes resulting in a solitary, delusional world:

> I lived in fear of the barrage of abuse that would follow any action of mine. I became increasingly anxious about mixing with others. I retreated into a solitary world as I endeavoured to make sense of what was happening to me. A complex and mystical explanation developed in which I believed that I had been chosen to receive a message from God. This message would relieve mankind of war and conflict and peace would prevail. (Romme at al. 2009, 130)[21]

So it seems that traumatic loss of trust and the phenomenology of schizophrenia have much in common. But what, exactly, is the relationship between them? Drawing on Blankenburg and others (including Wittgenstein), Thomas Fuchs argues that loss of trust is integral to the experience of schizophrenia. He adds that there are looping effects, where erosion of trust impacts on social relations in such a way as to exacerbate loss of trust. And delusions, he suggests, are not "individual false beliefs" but instead "correspond to an intersubjective situation bereft of the basic trust and attunement to others that could help to restore a consensual understanding of the situation and to co-constitute a commonsensical reality" (2015, 208). Hence the relevant phenomenology is to be understood in relational rather than individual terms. Nevertheless, Fuchs continues to prioritize disturbances of minimal self over disturbances of intersubjectivity. Alteration of a "pre-reflective, embodied self," he says, "must necessarily" affect social relations; disruption of habitual, bodily immersion in the world "will result in a fundamental alienation of intersubjectivity," of a kind that is inextricable from loss of trust (2015, 199). So, in the case of schizophrenia, delusional mood comes first, eroding trust and compromising social relations. If that is right, while the effects of trauma might well be similar to certain effects of self-disturbance in schizophrenia, the two predicaments remain distinct: schizophrenic self-disturbance implies loss of trust, whereas loss of trust does not imply self-disturbance. In contrast, I have suggested that the relationship is one of mutual implication: changes in how one relates to people *are* changes in the modal structure of intentionality. As that structure is inseparable from minimal-self experience, they are also changes in minimal self. It is therefore plausible to suggest that causation goes in the other direction as well: loss of trust, brought about by events involving other people, can disrupt the structure of experience and weaken modal distinctions. And this, I maintain, is sufficient for the cultivation of certain kinds of hallucination and delusion.[22] So my position is consistent with the view that schizophrenia diagnoses are often associated with disturbances of minimal self (so long as we concede that minimal self—in humans, at least—depends constitutively on the interpersonal). However, the kind of self-disturbance I have described is not specific to schizophrenia.

Traumatic experiences are implicated in a range of different psychiatric conditions (e.g., Mueser et al. 2002). In fact, Read et al. (2005, 341) go so far as to suggest that whether a person receives a diagnosis of post-traumatic stress disorder or a diagnosis of schizophrenia sometimes depends on whether or not the symptoms are interpreted in the light of distressing past events. Where one clinician sees a "hallucination," another may see a "flashback." Hence it is arguable that some cases of "schizophrenia" are phenomenologically (and more generally) indistinguishable from some cases of "post-traumatic stress disorder": "Psychotic symptoms in patients with posttraumatic stress and dissociative disorders pose continual diagnostic challenges. Many such patients present with disorganized thinking, impaired reality-testing, paranoid ideation, and hallucinations in multiple sensory modalities" (Allen, Coyne, and Console 1997, 327). Doubts have also been raised about the more general distinction between "neurosis" or affective disorder and "psychosis" (e.g., Freeman and Garety 2003). Of course, even if phenomenological differences are unclear or even nonexistent, one could still seek to draw a distinction on the basis of etiology. However, any such proposal would most likely involve substantial revision of current diagnostic practices, given that schizophrenia diagnoses are so often associated with troubled interpersonal histories and experiences of unpleasant events.

An alternative approach, advocated by Bentall (2003, 2009), among others, is to abandon syndrome-based classifications altogether and instead concentrate on explaining and treating individual symptoms, many of which are common to a number of different psychiatric diagnoses. On one reading, this runs contrary to what I have said so far. Experiences such as VH/

TI are not phenomenologically isolable *symptoms*. They involve changes in the overall structure of intentionality, which are bound up with social relations and have numerous more specific effects on a person's experiences, thoughts, and activities. However, Bentall (2003, 141–142) also suggests that what "psychiatrists describe as *symptoms* ... might be better labelled as *complaints*," where the term "complaint" refers to any experience or behavior that is "singled out as sometimes troublesome." Given such a permissive conception, changes in the modal structure of experience, and in how a person relates to the social world as a whole, would equally count as complaints. Hence, if such an approach were adopted, my phenomenological analysis could still be applied, but without any regard for current diagnostic categories. The initial identification of a complaint could be followed up by a more discerning examination of the relevant experiences, one that is sensitive to the differences between anomalous experiential contents and local or global changes in the structure of intentionality.

On the other hand, the phenomenological distinctiveness of schizophrenia should not be dismissed prematurely. Parnas (2013, 222) warns us against this, raising the concern that attempts to "merge" affective disorder and schizophrenia amount to an "ongoing massive simplification of psychopathology." I have argued that symptoms such as VHs are not specific to schizophrenia and are to be understood in terms of changes in the interpersonal sphere, the modal structure of experience, and thus the minimal self that are common to various psychiatric conditions. Even so, this does not rule out the possibility that certain more specific or more pronounced phenomenological changes are most often associated with schizophrenia diagnoses. DSM criteria and the like are far too cursory to draw reliable phenomenological (or more general) distinctions between schizophrenia spectrum disorders and diagnostically nonspecific losses of trust (see DSM-5, American Psychiatric Association 2013, 87–122). So, if "schizophrenia" is to be identified with its DSM characterization, then we do not have a principled way of distinguishing the two predicaments. For instance, here is what DSM-5 has to say about VHs: "Auditory hallucinations are usually experienced as voices, whether familiar or unfamiliar, that are perceived as distinct from the individual's own thoughts" (American Psychiatric Association, 2013, 87). It is added that experiences had while a person is falling asleep or waking up are to be discounted. This, of course, does not help us to distinguish between the many different phenomena encompassed by the label "VH," let alone to reliably associate one or another of them with a specific diagnosis. Nevertheless, there remains the possibility of refining our understanding of the phenomenology, so as to apply the diagnosis in a more discerning way. As Sass (2014a, 5) remarks:

> With all its flaws, the construct "schizophrenia" does seem to indicate some subtle but underlying factor at the core of a psychiatric condition that is perhaps best conceived as a syndrome (and probably represents a final common pathway with diverse etiological origins).

One characteristic that might distinguish schizophrenic self-disturbances (or, to put it more cautiously and accurately, a distinctive subset of self-experiences accommodated by most current applications of the diagnostic category "schizophrenia") is a degree of salience dysregulation and temporal fragmentation that goes beyond what I have so far described. Consider again the delusional "mood" or "atmosphere" described by Jaspers (1963, 98), which involves one's surroundings appearing salient in ways that are unfamiliar and strange. For example, a sofa that should present itself as something to sit on and offer comfort may appear oddly menacing, or significant in some otherwise incongruous manner. A wide-ranging and unstructured mismatch between entities and types of significance would amount to a more specific and also more profound kind of disturbance (Ratcliffe 2015, chap. 10).[23] As such, it would involve a different degree and/or kind of self-disorder. It remains the case that other kinds of phenomenological change are equally sufficient to bring about some of the associated symptoms, such as VHs consisting of modal disruptions. But, to speculate further, perhaps some *kinds* of localized modal disruption are more typical of schizophrenia. For instance, in chapter 4 I raised the possibility that disturbances of inner speech, memory, and imagination may be more often associated with one or another diagnosis.

A position along these lines would not commit us to the view that endogenous self-disorder precedes and causes social distress. It is just as plausible to suggest that wide-ranging salience dysregulation can come about through interpersonal processes, but as a *potential* outcome of the loss of trust rather than something *necessitated* by it. Loss of trust could estrange one from interpersonal regulatory processes and erode the structure of intentionality, in such a way as to render one vulnerable to further disruptions of salience and significance. However, it is likely that something along the lines of "delusional atmosphere" can also arise as a result of largely endogenous or at least impersonal processes. And nothing I have said is inconsistent with the view that both genetic and nongenetic biological causes play a role in some instances, where the latter might include malnutrition, infection, and injury in utero. Kilcommons and Morrison (2005, 352) hypothesize that there are two distinct pathways to psychosis: an endogenous route, involving a predominance of negative symptoms, and a trauma-driven route, where positive symptoms are more conspicuous.[24] Myin-Germeys and van Os (2007) also propose a specific "affective pathway" to psychosis, involving childhood trauma as a significant risk factor. They add that a vulnerability-stress model applies here, according to which some individuals are more vulnerable than others when faced with distressing events. I would add that vulnerability, in this context, should not be conceived of simply as a trait of the individual. The extent to which and the manner in which we come to depend on particular people and others in general to regulate experience, thought, and activity no doubt vary considerably. There are different ways of *entrusting the integrity of our experience to others*. Some of these will carry more risk than others. The effects of trauma will also depend, in part, on whether, when, and how others assist in the preservation and restoration of trust. So we should think of different responses to trauma not only in terms of comparative individual vulnerability and resilience to adverse events but also in terms of the diverse interpersonal regulative processes that both precede and follow traumatic events.

All sorts of in-between scenarios are possible too, which do not conform to a neat distinction between endogenous and trauma-driven psychoses. For instance, certain endogenous symptoms, combined with the stigma of potential or actual diagnosis, might generate social anxiety. This then further disrupts relations with others and erodes interpersonal trust (Birchwood et al. 2006). Ways in which others respond (which are socially and culturally mediated) could in turn exacerbate a loss of trust, leading to growing isolation from the social world and from interpersonal regulatory processes. For example, involuntary detention on mental health grounds can itself be traumatic. As Beveridge (1998, 116) observes, the "experience of being declared a suitable case for compulsory treatment often leads to a crisis of self-identity."[25] More generally, a pervasive loss of trust is likely to interfere in various ways with treatment efforts, and it has been reported that a history of trauma impedes the ability to engage with and benefit from treatment (e.g., Bentall and Fernyhough 2008, 1013). Other factors that shape how experiential changes develop can include negative stereotypes about psychiatric illness and the "fear of going crazy" (Morrison, Frame, and Larkin 2003).[26] The dynamics are thus likely to be complicated and varied, with vicious cycles often developing. And all of this does not depend solely on how *individuals* behave and respond to each other. Wider social and cultural structures have a role to play too. For instance, they might incorporate quite different ways of responding to trauma, as well as different practices of affect regulation (Hinton and Kirmayer 2013).

In summary, everything I have said is compatible with the view that schizophrenia diagnoses are often associated with disruptions of minimal self. I also accept that a certain type of self-disturbance may be specific to schizophrenia. Having said that, a diagnosis of schizophrenia is equally compatible with other kinds of experience. Hence, if schizophrenia is to be identified with a distinctive type of self-disorder, current diagnostic practices will need to be revised. While I remain open to that possibility, the approach developed here can get along just as well without recourse to the category "schizophrenia." Even if the category is to be retained, it remains the case that self-experience is equally interpersonal experience. There are insufficient grounds for postulating an additional, *even more minimal*, presocial sense of self in adult humans. Some self-disturbances are more profound than others, and some are qualitatively different from others, but the differences between them are not to be conceived of in terms of interpersonal and preinterpersonal selves.

6.7 Renee Revisited

In the light of my discussion, it is instructive to revisit a classic text, one that is often quoted in support of the view that schizophrenia involves a distinctive kind of phenomenological disturbance: *Autobiography of a Schizophrenic Girl* (Sechehaye 1970).[27] Once we emphasize the themes of (a) loss of trust, (b) changes in the affective style of anticipation, and (c) distressing events involving other people, some of the experiences described by the author, known only as "Renee," appear in a new light. While Renee's account might at first seem to describe experiential changes undergone by an individual, which *then* alter her relations with others, there is also an interpersonal backstory that is less often remarked upon. Renee refers to "a disturbing sense of unreality," which began when she was five years old (21). She goes on to offer more detailed descriptions of pervasive phenomenological changes, which involve everything seeming strange, distant, and unfamiliar:

> Everything was exact, smooth, artificial, extremely tense; the chairs and tables seemed models placed here and there. Pupils and teachers were puppets revolving without cause, without objective. I recognized nothing, nobody. It was as though reality, attenuated, had slipped away from all these things and these people. (26)

One could identify this with the "delusional mood" that often arises in the early stages of schizophrenia, a wide-ranging phenomenological disturbance that both precedes and fuels the onset of delusions and hallucinations. While I do not wish to dispute that interpretation, I do want to supplement it, so as to emphasize the interpersonal, relational dynamics of the experience. Consider the following passage:

> Little by little I brought myself to confide to my friends that the world was about to be destroyed, that planes were coming to bomb and annihilate us. Although I often offered these confidences jestingly I firmly believed them and, to feel less alone, I wanted to share the fears with others. Nonetheless, I did not believe the world would be destroyed as I believed in real facts. Vaguely I had some misgivings that this belief was linked to my own personal fear, that it was specific and not generally held. (34)

Here, two ways of believing, two kinds of intentionality, come into conflict. There is the belief that the world is "about to be destroyed" and there is the belief in "real facts." The realm of real facts is identified with the shared world, while the belief that horrible things are about to happen is associated with a "personal fear" and recognized, albeit ambivalently, as self-specific and adrift from consensus reality. Also evident here is a need to convey such "beliefs" to other people in whom Renee confides (implying a degree of trust in those people), to share them with others and, in so doing, "feel less alone." Relating to others enhances the sense of being part of a shared world, a world with which the apocalyptic realm of bombing and annihilation is to be contrasted. Yet, as we read on, the kind of interpersonal contact she so desperately seeks out presents itself as impossible. Other people no longer offer the possibility of interpersonal connection. In fact, they are sometimes not experienced as people at all: "I look at her, study her, praying to feel the life in her through the enveloping unreality. But she seems more a statue than ever, a mannikin moved by a mechanism, talking like an automaton. It is horrible, inhuman, grotesque" (38).

Earlier in the text, we see that phenomenological disturbances (which later intensify) are consistently accompanied by extreme "anxiety" (22).

Furthermore, their initial onset is associated with troubling life events: "it was during this same period that I learned my father had a mistress and that he made my mother cry. This revelation bowled me over because I had heard my mother say that if my father left her, she would kill herself" (22). This situation impacts on Renee's sense of confidence in other people and in the world more generally. It "bowled her over," bringing about—I suggest—a shift in anticipatory style. In place of confident anticipation and fulfilment, there is an all-enveloping feeling of anxiety and unpredictability, exactly what I described in terms of the loss of trust, confidence, or certainty. The ensuing phenomenological disturbances themselves induce even more pronounced feelings of anxiety and estrangement, which further exacerbate the sense of unreality, and so forth.

Throughout the remainder of the text, there are numerous references to intensifying feelings of anxiety and interpersonal isolation, all of which are consistent with a process of unraveling that begins with the erosion of basic trust: "I was seized with panic" (23); "an inexpressible anguish pressed in on me" (25); "profound dread overwhelmed me" (26); "ghastly fear gripped me" (27); "[singing] lessons aroused an immeasurable anxiety quite disproportionate to the cause" (29); "an awful terror bound me" (30); "for the first time I felt *real fear*" (32); "suddenly Fear, agonizing, boundless Fear, overcame me, not the usual uneasiness of unreality, but real fear, such as one knows at the approach of danger, of calamity" (32). Changes in how things and people appear to Renee, and more enveloping changes in her sense of reality, are inextricable from a kind of affective anticipation, an all-enveloping but inchoate sense that something terrible is about to happen:

> Then everything seemed to stop, to wait, to hold its breath, in a state of extreme tension, the tension of the needle in the haystack. Something seemed about to occur, some extraordinary catastrophe. An overpowering anxiety forced me to stop and wait. (30)

Loss of practical familiarity is also a consistent theme: "I lost the feeling of practical things" (29). Again, this can be understood—at least in part—in terms of losing trust. Estranged from a consensus world and from the possibility of trusting relations, projects collapse and the prospect of meaningful activity is gone. Loss of trust in others erodes confidence in the world more generally, given that the salience, utility, and reliability of artifacts and other features of the social environment implicate other people in one or another way. Renee's confidence in her own practical and intellectual abilities, and even in the names and functions of everyday entities, is also lost. Guilt and sin become consistent and conspicuous themes: "In my fantasy, entire cities lay in ruins, rocks crushed in fragments, all a consequence of my execrable crime, the sin of Cain" (117). This is not so directly attributable to loss of trust and anxious anticipation. Nevertheless, I think it is plausible to suggest that a sense of passivity, helplessness, loss of interpersonal connection, all-enveloping dread, and exclusion from the consensus world might coagulate into elaborate delusions of guilt, involving a kind of intentionality that differs in kind from that of mundane belief.

As Renee becomes more and more unhinged from the consensus world, we see again how the structure of experience, the sense of reality, and the sense of self are inextricable from an ability to enter into certain kinds of relation with others. Her therapist is the only remaining life-line, which she depends on to maintain a sense of reality: "then I recognized her, she was again herself, my refuge, my life, my very reality, the precious little oasis of reality in the desert world of my soul" (46); "She alone could break through the unreal wall that hemmed me in; she alone kept me in some contact with life" (54). But eventually even this connection is lost and, for a time, Renee comes to inhabit "unreality"—a modal structure, sub-universe, or meaning province that is completely adrift from the consensus world.

None of this is to challenge phenomenological interpretations of the text that do not interpret Renee's account in such an explicitly interpersonal way. Neither is it to assume that the account is reliable. After all, Renee describes how certain experiences struck her as anomalous at the age of five, from the perspective of an adult who has since recovered from severe psychiatric illness. Even if the account is largely reliable, I do not want to insist that my interpretation is the right one. Rather, the point of the example is to show how an emphasis on the modal structure of experience and its inextricability from interpersonal relations opens up the possibility of interpreting first-person accounts in new ways, of understanding forms of experience that otherwise seem obscure, and of seeing how interpersonal events that might at first appear incidental to a first-person narrative can turn out to be central. In Renee's case, there is another story to be told, involving unsettling events, interpersonal estrangement, loss of trust, and social anxiety. It is plausible to situate her departure from consensus reality, and the eventual onset of anomalous experiences with more specific contents, in this context.[28]

6.8 Phenomenology Meets Predictive Coding

I have focused principally on the phenomenology of psychiatric illness, emphasizing the modalities of intentionality, how the integrity of experience implicates other people, and also the dynamic, temporal structure of experience. I have suggested that the sense of being in a given type of intentional state is constituted—at least in part—by a characteristic temporal profile and its departure from the profile of perceptual experience. To conclude the chapter, I want to draw attention to some affinities between this approach and some recent developments in neurobiology. Phenomenological findings have the potential to inform neurobiological research. For instance, if one wishes to study the neurobiology of VHs, and if I am right, then one will get nowhere by regarding VHs as a unitary kind and failing to distinguish hypervigilance VHs from internal VHs, or inner speech VHs from memory VHs. So phenomenology can assist neurobiological research by clarifying *what it is* that requires explanation. Conversely, we can corroborate or fail to corroborate phenomenological claims via neurobiological studies. For instance, the distinctions drawn here between types of VH would be supported, at least to some extent, by the discovery of associated neurobiological differences. On the other hand, if no study, however ingenious, could detect any discernible differences between external and internal VHs, which I claim to be quite different in kind, this would give us compelling grounds for reconsidering the phenomenology.

What I have said also relates to more specific developments in cognitive science. Chapter 4 discussed how mechanistic explanations of VHs are usually premised on the view that they involve thoughts that are unanticipated. This is inconsistent with the observation that VH experiences often include conscious long-term and short-term anticipation. Hence, if we wish to account for them in terms of a lack of anticipation, we need to supply a more detailed account of which anticipatory processes remain intact, which are lacking, and why the lack of some processes but not others leads to an experience of thought content as alien. Nevertheless, there remains considerable affinity between my account of the phenomenology and a much wider-ranging approach in cognitive science, known as "predictive processing" or "predictive coding." As summarized by Andy Clark (2013) in an influential article, the central claim is that brains are "prediction machines," the main task of which is to predict stimuli, match what is predicted with what then occurs, and revise predictions in order to minimize future prediction errors.[29] The process has a complicated, hierarchical structure and involves two-way interaction between the various levels, with no clear line between perception and belief. According to the predictive coding view, perception does not begin with incoming sensory stimulation. What we perceive is largely the achievement of top-down processes that anticipate and thus "explain away" the vast majority of sensory signals, so that we register only those that are in some way unanticipated or anomalous. Clark refers to the nonconscious registration of anomaly as "surprisal." This is to be distinguished from conscious "surprise," as what minimizes surprisal can be very surprising. For example, the most coherent "interpretation" of unanticipated sensory signals might be that there is an elephant in the house, even though finding an elephant in the house is very surprising indeed.

There have been several attempts to account for hallucinations and delusions in these terms. For instance, Fletcher and Frith (2009) maintain that all perceptual and cognitive processes involve prediction, detection of anomalies, and updating of expectations in the light of anomalies. Delusions and hallucinations (which they do not regard as categorically distinct) originate in "false prediction errors." Prediction error signals that should be discounted are disrupted in some way and consequently assigned "undue weight." Errors require that expectations be adjusted, but no amount of adjustment will manage to account for error signals that are false, and so the end result is that false prediction errors are "propagated upwards through the hierarchy" (55). The phenomenological correlate of this is things looking oddly salient and anomalous, in ways that cannot be attributed to anything specific in the environment, and this fuels the formation of delusions and hallucinations. Corlett et al. (2009, 2010) likewise suggest that delusions are the result of misleading prediction error signals. First of all, there is aberrant salience, and the updating processes that responds to it ultimately culminates in delusion:

> During the earliest phases of delusion formation aberrant novelty, salience or prediction error signals drive attention toward redundant or irrelevant environmental cues, the world seems to have changed, it feels strange and sinister, such signals and experiences provide an impetus for new learning which updates the world model inappropriately, manifest as a delusion. (Corlett et al. 2010, 347)

This complements Jaspers' (1963) account of delusion formation, according to which delusional atmosphere generates a kind of tension, which delusions then relieve by making sense of anomalous experiences in more specific ways (Ratcliffe 2013a; Sass and Byrom 2015). Corlett et al. (2010, 351–353) further acknowledge the need to accommodate "affectively charged uncertainty," and also note that "motivational state" can shape what is perceived when signals are noisy and indeterminate, a position that is consistent with what I have said about anxiety and hypervigilance VHs.[30]

Nevertheless, phenomenological research suggests that a more nuanced approach is needed here. Anticipation-fulfillment processes not only shape the *contents* of experience; they are also integral to the sense of undergoing one or another kind of experience, given that different types of affective anticipation are integral to different types of intentionality. So the prediction error approach needs to be widened, to account not only for anomalous experiential contents but also for disturbances in the sense of one's intentional state. Clark (2016) has gone on to offer a more detailed treatment of predictive coding, which draws on a wide range of empirical findings. Even so, his discussion does not account for disturbances of the modal structure of experience. He indicates that the difference between perceiving and imagining is a matter of detail and consistency. Perception involves fine-grained resolution of prediction errors and, with this, a higher degree of stability over time (2016, 98–99). While that is right, it does not explain the sense of something as a percept, rather than a product of the imagination, given that a content more typical of an imagining can be associated with a sense of perceiving. Clark does not acknowledge the possibility of such an experience. Instead, he assumes an orthodox conception of hallucination, according to which "all the machinery of perception is brought to bear," but without the more usual guiding role played by prediction error (2016, 196).

A further complication is that experience involves a range of different anticipatory styles, and what is anomalous in relation to one may be quite consistent with another. There is nothing anomalous about imagining a giant badger turning into a rocket, but this does not apply in the case of perceptual experience. Another consideration is that something can appear incongruous even though it is anticipated, such as a VH experience that one dreads as it crystallizes. It still stands out relative to other aspects of experience, and an account is needed not merely of how surprise relates to surprisal but of how different nonconscious processes relate to all of the various ways in which something might appear incongruous, discrepant, or other than it ought to be, not all of which involve surprise.

Consider also the distinction between "open" and "problematic" uncertainty (introduced in sec. 5.5 of chap. 5), which should apply equally to predictive processing. Failing to anticipate certain details and then filling in the blanks is to be distinguished from having an experience that runs contrary, in one or another way, to what was anticipated. Correspondingly, an account of prediction error needs to distinguish between cases where something is salient because it was not anticipated or not fully anticipated, and cases where it is discrepant. In the problematic case, we can also insist on a further distinction between specific doubts, where two or more systems of anticipation compete with each other, and forms of problematic uncertainty that involve the sense that "it might not be what or how I think it is," in the absence of a competing system. The relations between predictions and error signals will surely be different. In one case, we have "not *p*" and, in the other, we have "*p* rather than *q*."

Even so, the overall approach is broadly consistent with what I have said here, given its emphasis on pervasive patterns of anticipation and fulfillment, upon which the coherence of experience and thought depends. Madary (2012) picks up on Clark's (2013) concession that the world does not look like an "intertwined set of probability density distributions" and that the predictive processing framework therefore needs to account for the considerable gulf between subpersonal processes and what we actually experience. In fact, as Madary points out, it is plausible that perceptual experience is riddled with anticipation, as exemplified by moments of surprise. And this, of course, is also the view we find in Husserl. But the parallels are closer still. For Husserl, experience involves a pervasive sense of certainty; the vast majority of our experiences accord with habitual anticipation, and occasional, localized doubts appear anomalous, calling out for adjustments. In nonphenomenological terms, this is exactly what predictive processing involves. As Clark (2013, 2016) says, much of what we "perceive" is given largely in advance of sensory stimulation—what is consistent with anticipatory processes is filtered out so that only salient differences are detected. And, just as Husserl's account needs to be elaborated in order to distinguish between kinds of affective anticipation and between the distinctive temporal profiles that are characteristic of different types of intentionality, so does the predictive processing framework.

Husserl also offers a more detailed description of the transition from problematic uncertainty, to disappointment, to updating, which is more or less a phenomenological isomorphism of Clark's nonphenomenological account. For both, expectations are not simply updated; the prior system of expectation endures, but *as* updated. Here are some relevant passages from Husserl:

> (In cases of disappointment), the sense of the perception is not only changed in the momentary new stretch of perception; the noematic modification streams back in the form of a retroactive cancellation in the retentional sphere and modifies the production of sense stemming from earlier phases of the perception. (Husserl 1948/1973, §21, p. 89)

> The perceptual sense is changed not merely in the momentary primordially impressional expanse of perception. The noematic transformation radiates back in the form of a retroactive crossing out in the retentional sphere, transforming its accomplishment of sense that stemmed from the previous perceptions. The previous apperception that was harmonized with the consistently unfolding "red" and uniform "round" is "reinterpreted" *implicite* as "green" and "indented" … we are still conscious of the previous sense, but as "painted over." (Husserl 2001, §7, p. 69)

For Husserl, this process of negation and updating is integral to the distinction between past, present, and future. Similarly, correcting a prediction error involves not erasing and rewriting past expectations but updating them and establishing them as past.

Phenomenology can thus enter into dialogue with this kind of research, and aid in refining and distinguishing some of the phenomena to be accounted for. Importantly, my position also implies that predictive coding should adopt a less individualistic approach and place more emphasis on how anticipation-fulfillment processes are interpersonally regulated and even socially distributed. I have argued that this applies at the phenomenological level, and there are no grounds for insisting that things are otherwise at the "subpersonal" level. Consider, for instance, the roles that others' behavior can play in signaling anomalies elsewhere in the world and in interpreting anomalies. If something looks strange or somehow unreal, you might pinch yourself or shake your head. But you are equally likely to turn to others, see what they are doing, and interact with them. Conversely, others' behavior can draw your attention to anomalies elsewhere that you would otherwise have been oblivious to, or give you the sense that something anomalous is happening even if you cannot identify quite what is amiss. Clark (2016, 285) recognizes that an agent's predictive processes can utilize the predictive processes of other agents, and that relationships of "continuous reciprocal prediction" sometimes develop. However, he does not make clear the full extent of this interdependence in the human case. The overall anticipatory structure of experience is interpersonally regulated and sustained. Our brains do not maintain phenomenological coherence on their own, and neither do our organisms. The point applies equally to nonconscious anticipatory processes, which are supposed to account for the relevant phenomenology or at least be consistent with it. As those with a fondness for one or another form of enactivism might put it, we socially enact the modal structure of intentionality, and, with it, the most basic sense of self.

7 Varieties of Hallucination

As we have seen, many of those hallucinations that occur in psychiatric illness resemble neither "philosophers' hallucinations" nor "orthodox clinical hallucinations." To understand these experiences, a more complicated, nuanced conception of intentionality is required. However, I have also acknowledged that other kinds of hallucination may turn out to be quite different. While I cannot do justice to the full range of phenomena that might be labeled as "hallucinations" and make no claim to do so, this chapter addresses at least some of those that have not yet been considered. I begin by identifying a type of hallucination that involves having a sense of perceiving in the absence of perceptual content, but differs from the kinds of modal confusion so far described. While the content of an internal VH (verbal hallucination) might be attributable to imagination, memory, or inner speech, this type of hallucination involves a sense of perceiving that attaches neither to the usual perceptual content nor to a nonperceptual content. So, instead of an experience that is ambiguous and conflicted, there is a less determinate experience, which *lacks* something of the perceptual. Following this, I consider benevolent "voices" and ask whether and how they might be accommodated by the account developed in chapter 4, which emphasized unpleasant experiences. Finally, the chapter turns to bereavement hallucinations, and shows how the phenomenology of grief further illustrates the multifaceted and sometimes conflictual nature of experiencing something as *present*. The example of grief suggests that, in all cases, it is simplistic to conceive of hallucination simply in terms of experiencing something as there when it is not. There is no simple, singular sense of presence. Rather, there are various subtly different ways in which we experience things as present or otherwise.

7.1 Orthodox Hallucinations

An orthodox hallucination involves a kind of mistake that is largely attributable to similarity of experiential content. In short, a hallucinated entity *looks like* (or sounds, tastes, smells, or feels like) something that is present, to such an extent that the two may be confused. Hallucinations of this kind may well occur. For example, Oliver Sacks (2012) discusses a range of experiences, all of which resemble veridical perceptual experiences in one or another modality. These hallucinations, he says, "seem very real" and can "mimic perception in every respect," including "the way they are projected into the external world" (2012, ix). The cases he discusses mostly involve "organic psychoses," and he acknowledges that hallucinations in schizophrenia need to be understood differently. Even so, it is not so clear that the various kinds of experience considered by Sacks do resemble veridical perceptions, at least to the extent that he sometimes indicates. For example, in one case the hallucinations were like a "movie"; they "sometimes fascinated" and "sometimes bored" the person, but "seemed to have nothing to do with her." They were also "silent" and exclusively visual. So the relevant experiences clearly lacked something of the *sense of reality* and, more specifically, the *sense of perceiving*. When this person's hallucinations later seemed "absolutely real" to her, this was associated with their becoming "frightening," something that is consistent with my suggestion that affective anticipation contributes to a sense of perceptual presence (Sacks 2012, 4–8).

Sacks also offers a first-person account of an elaborate drug-induced hallucination, which he took to be real at the time. Although the content of the experience initially consisted of mundane social interaction, he adds that a spider later said "hello," and that it "did not seem at all strange" to him that "a spider should say hello." A conversation with the spider then ensued (2012, 107–109). Although such an experience might *feel real* in some respects, again it surely lacks something of the sense of perceiving. If one's experiences were anchored in consensus reality, conversational interaction with a spider could not seem other than strange. So the anticipation-fulfillment structure of this hallucination differs somehow from that of perception; it does not involve the same sense of potential and actual anomaly. Although it should be granted that such an experience includes something of the sense of perceiving, it is an incomplete sense. And perhaps the content differs too; contents that are more typical of imaginings might be associated with a (partial) sense of perceiving. We should thus be wary of alleged instances of clear-cut, orthodox hallucination.

Earlier, I did concede that some external VHs more closely approximate orthodox hallucinations than the internal VHs that were my primary focus. Nevertheless, they remain at least partly attributable to disturbances in the modal structure of intentionality, which dispose a person to experience sensory stimuli in terms of voices with consistent thematic contents. Hence even an external VH is not experienced in an unequivocally *perceptual* way, as a wider-ranging sense of perceiving as distinct from other kinds of intentionality has been altered. However, what should we say of a case where the content is like that of a veridical perceptual experience and there is *no* modal disruption? Again, the distinction between experiential content and sense is an important one. An experiential content could resemble that of a perception in one or another modality, without being associated with anything of the sense of perceiving. While it might be *as if* one is seeing something, the question of whether one really does see it never arises. Even if the experience comes about in a way that is wholly involuntary, one might retain an unambiguous sense of it as an instance of unusually vivid imagining, an experience *of an image,* or an experience that is otherwise removed from perception of one's surroundings. Its nonveridical nature does not have to be inferred and can instead be integral to the experience from the outset, regardless of level of detail or vividness. So we should not confuse something *seeming real,* meaning that it resembles—in some way and to some extent—the content of a veridical perception, with its having a *sense of reality*. Three kinds of experience can thus be distinguished:

1. A sense of perceiving in the absence of characteristic content
2. Characteristic content in the absence of a sense of perceiving
3. Characteristic content, as well as a sense of perceiving

These are idealizations, and actual cases will approximate one or the other to varying degrees. A hallucination could involve a largely intact sense of perceiving without characteristic content or, alternatively, a content somehow like that of a veridical perception but with little of the sense of perceiving. An experience that is close to (1) is very different in nature from one that is close to (2). Therefore, labeling them both as "hallucinations" and treating them as similar in kind is uninformative and potentially very confusing. With regard to (3), I do not rule out the *possibility* that perfect hallucinations occur, or at least experiences that come close to them. Nothing I have said renders them metaphysically impossible or phenomenologically unintelligible. But whether or not they *actually* occur is another matter. Upon more careful phenomenological scrutiny, it might well turn out that no hallucinations include both an intact sense of perceiving and a content just like that of a veridical perceptual experience.

In fact, some of those experiences that might seem, at first glance, to conform to (3) are actually instances of (1). In earlier chapters, I discussed cases where the characteristic content of a nonperceptual modality is combined with aspects of the sense of perceiving. However, (1) also accommodates another kind of experience. There is a difference between the following:

a. A partial sense of perceiving, associated with an experiential content that is more typical of another kind of intentional state
b. A partial sense of perceiving, but without the more usual content of perceptual experience *and* without experiential content originating in one or another nonperceptual modality

So far, I have only addressed (a). However, the kinds of wide-ranging phenomenological change described in chapters 5 and 6 could equally dispose a person toward (b), and the acknowledgment of (b) thus widens the scope of my analysis. Some "hallucinations," I will now suggest, are unlike perceptual experiences, but not in virtue of their resembling other kinds of experience. There is a partial sense of perceiving something variably specific, which arises in the absence of a complementary sensory experience. The result is a seemingly paradoxical experience of something as *there* and yet quite clearly *not there*.

7.2 Horizonal Hallucinations

The anticipatory structure of experience makes a substantial but not exhaustive contribution to the sense of which intentional state one is in. As already discussed, where the type of anticipatory profile associated with state *x* is associated with aspects of experience more usually associated with state *y*, there is an ambiguous and conflicted experience. But consider another scenario, where the anticipatory profile associated with perceiving a type of entity or token entity is to varying degrees present, but without other constituents of perceptual experience. When I look at a coffee cup, it appears as something I can reach out and touch, and as something I can turn around to reveal a currently obscured side. Importantly, it also appears significant to me in a distinctive way; it is experienced as something for drinking from and, on occasion, it draws me in and solicits me to act. As Husserl would say, perception has a *horizonal* structure, which constitutes both the sense of encountering something perceptually and the sense of encountering one type of entity rather than another. Now, suppose that some aspects of the horizonal structure associated with a particular entity or type of entity were in place, while other aspects of perceptual experience were absent. There would be an ambiguous and partial sense of encountering something, but without the kind of conflict that features in VH/TI, where the content of experience is not merely lacking in some way but also incongruous.

Experiences like this would be just as consistent with the kinds of wide-ranging phenomenological change described in chapters 5 and 6. Suppose the coherence of perceptual experience is disrupted, such that there is widespread salience dysregulation. In conjunction with this, the person is passive and disengaged from the interpersonal world. She thus experiences things as significant in ways that are anomalous, unstructured, and detached from practical concerns. Drawing on Jaspers (1963) and/or recent work on predictive coding, all we need add is a conscious or nonconscious disposition to make sense of anomalous possibilities in a coherent way, in terms of loci around which they cluster. With practical and social disengagement, and a consequent lessening of accountability to the surrounding environment, this would happen in an idiosyncratic fashion. If you like, a kind of perceptual imagination would go to work, but without the constraints more usually supplied by the interplay between sensory input and global anticipatory style. The person would continue to have veridical perceptual experiences as well, albeit with an altered sense of presence. Her anomalous, quasi-perceptual experiences of possibility would run alongside them and be experienced as distinct from them. This scenario differs from one where the sense of perceiving is associated with a content more typical of nonsensory imagining, given that the associative processes in question are also more usually at work in perception and contribute to the sense of perceiving.

What I have just suggested is consistent with Merleau-Ponty's brief discussion of hallucination in *Phenomenology of Perception* (1945/2012, Part II, chap. 3).[1] The intended scope of his remarks is unclear; he refers to "schizophrenia" but does not say whether or not his discussion applies to hallucinations more generally. All I want to insist on is that *some* hallucinations in some contexts, including that of psychiatric illness, plausibly conform to his account. Rather than assuming that hallucinations somehow resemble veridical perceptual experiences, Merleau-Ponty begins by contrasting the two. Patients recognize the difference between their hallucinations and reality. For instance, they might say that "someone speaks to them by telephone or from the radio" in order to convey how the "morbid world" is "artificial," somehow lacking in a way that sets it apart from a "reality" (350). He adds that the objects of hallucination do not impact on other features of the perceived world and are not experienced as available to other people either: "the hallucinatory phenomenon is not part of the world, that is, it is not *accessible*, there is no definite road that leads from this phenomenon to all the other experiences of the hallucinating subject, or to the experience of healthy subjects" (354–355). The world of hallucination and what remains of consensus reality unfold in parallel, involving different kinds of intentionality: "Hallucinations play out on a different stage than that of the perceived world; it is as if they are superimposed" (355).

One of the things that distinguishes hallucinations from veridical perceptual experiences is that they lack the full horizonal structure of perception. An entity, as hallucinated, does not present itself as amenable to various kinds of perceptual, practical, and interpersonal access. For instance, certain *intersensory* possibilities are absent. While a perceived cup of coffee offers the possibilities of touching and tasting, a hallucinated cup of coffee may be experienced in a way that is "mono-modal" (Kraus 2007). Objects of perception are ordinarily experienced as incomplete, not exhausted by our current experience of them, and as part of a wider world. Hallucinations, in contrast, are not fully integrated into the anticipation-fulfillment dynamic of perception: "The hallucination is not, like perception, my concrete hold upon time within a living present. Rather, the hallucination slides across time, just as it slides across the world" (Merleau-Ponty, 1945/2012, 355). On the other hand, Merleau-Ponty also indicates that a hallucination consists *solely* of horizonal structure. Despite its being impoverished, this structure continues to resemble, in some way, that of a perceptual experience. Like Husserl, he claims that an experience of worldly possibilities is also an experience of bodily dispositions. It is through the feeling body that we encounter possibilities in the world: "It is one and the same thing to perceive our body and to perceive our situation in a certain physical and human milieu, and because our body is nothing other than this situation itself insofar as it is realized and actual" (355). When hallucinating, the bodily counterparts of worldly possibilities are exercised without any complementary sensory input from the world, and also in relative isolation from the global anticipatory style into which perceptual experiences are more usually integrated. One experiences a semistructured set of possibilities, characteristic of relating in some way to some entity, but without the level of structure needed to situate that entity in a consensus world. So the body performs a sort of conjuring trick, yielding a partial sense of encountering something as present:

> There are hallucinations because we have, through the phenomenal body, a constant relation with a milieu into which it is projected, and because, being detached from the actual milieu, the body remains capable of evoking a pseudo-presence of this milieu through its own arrangements. (356)

Interestingly, Merleau-Ponty denies that the assignment of a hallucination to a specific sensory modality, such as vision, audition, or touch, is a reflection of modality-specific experiential content. Hallucinations are bereft of sensory content. They are *expressed* in terms of one or another sensory modality because different senses lend themselves to the expression of different kinds of experience: "Each sensory field offers particular possibilities of expression to the alteration of existence. … The worlds of hearing and of touch are best able to represent a possessed, threatened, or leveled-out existence" (357). So a hallucination is actually a nonspecific sense of *being affected in some way by something,* which is then interpreted and articulated in terms of a particular sense: I see it; I hear it; it touched me. That said, I doubt that Merleau-Ponty would endorse a clear distinction between the "expression" of a hallucination through a given sensory modality and its crystallizing into a modality-specific experience. And it is perhaps too extreme to insist that hallucinations, even of this kind, involve no modality-specific phenomenology. Despite their degraded horizonal structure, these experiences need not be wholly bereft of perceptual solicitations such as moving one's head to align one's ear or, alternatively, to bring something into clearer visual focus. Depending on which practical dispositions remain engaged, the horizonal structure may be consistent with one or another sense. This also allows us to retain a contrast between monomodal hallucinations and the multimodal structure of veridical perceptual experience.

Even so, all that remains of perceptual experience is a *feeling of* perceiving something, of being *affected* by something in one or another significant way. Hence such an experience might be described as like perceiving *p* and yet—at the same time—as quite different from perceiving *p*. For example, in a first-person account of mescaline-induced hallucination, the phenomenologist and psychiatrist J. H. van den Berg (1982, 105–106) writes that, in one sense, he saw and heard nothing in addition to what he would more usually have seen or heard. Even so, he really was hallucinating. It was, he says, "as if the hallucination offered itself in the guise of perception so that it could be communicable." Similarly, in *Autobiography of a Schizophrenic Girl*, Renee writes, "I cannot say that I really saw images; they did not represent anything. Rather I felt them" (Sechehaye 1970, 58–59). As in the case of VH/TI, this is consistent with the observation that delusions and hallucinations often involve a kind of double-bookkeeping, where the patient speaks and acts in ways that are in some respects consistent with believing or perceiving that *p*, but also speaks and acts in other ways that distinguish her attitude toward *p* from her ordinary perceptions and beliefs (e.g., Sass 1994; Bortolotti and Broome 2012).

Hallucinations of this kind are perhaps not so far-removed from certain, more familiar kinds of experience. For example, during the last ten years or so, I have increasingly suffered from acrophobia or fear of heights, something that often worsens with age (although my two children have recently cured me through exposure therapy, by repeatedly forcing me onto rollercoasters in Vienna's Prater Park). On one occasion, while standing on a narrow, glass-sided walkway in a shopping center, about fifteen meters above ground level, I paused and tried to reflect on what I was experiencing. It was not so much that I was afraid of falling or of the walkway collapsing. Rather, it was already collapsing. The kinds of possibility consistent with a disintegrating walkway were there: the sense of helplessness, the inclination to cling onto something, a floor that appeared salient as it would if it were breaking apart. Yet, at the same time, it remained quite obviously intact. The one scenario was superimposed on the other. In the consensus world, things continued to unfold in ways that were entirely consistent with an intact walkway. But I was also affected in a way that could be expressed as "it is collapsing; there is nothing to cling onto; I am helpless." The difference between this and a horizonal hallucination is that my sense of being rooted in a cohesive, consensus world ran contrary to the collapsing walkway and was preserved throughout. The collapse-experience was, if you like, phenomenologically quarantined. In contrast, Merleau-Ponty claims that horizonal hallucinations occur against the backdrop of changes in the overarching "style" of experience, something that he also refers to in terms of perceptual "faith" and "primordial opinion." (This is to be identified with what Husserl calls "certainty" and what I have called "global anticipatory style": a way of experiencing possibilities and their actualization that the overall structure of intentionality depends upon.) The perceived world loses its "expressive force," allowing a bodily conjuring of possibilities to assume the "*value of reality*" (358). So, although the hallucinatory world is still superimposed on an ordinary reality, the latter is not wholly intact:

> The existence of the patient is decentered and is no longer accomplished in commerce with a harsh, resistant, and intractable world that is unaware of us; rather, it gradually exhausts itself in the solitary constitution of a fictional milieu. (358)

There remains the question of what, exactly, a person experiences when he hallucinates in this manner. I have suggested that the experience is bereft of some or all characteristic sensory content. It is debatable what, exactly, the missing sensory content consists of in any given case. However, it at least includes a type and level of detail that is accessible only when a cohesive pattern of anticipation is resisted by the environment in ways that are unique to perception in one or another modality. Sense-specific properties such as color may also be absent. Then again, it seems plausible to insist that the contents of some memories and imaginings also include color. So it would be more accurate to say that horizonal hallucinations do not include colors that are integrated into wider situations in a cohesive, dynamic, and perception-specific way. Regardless of the precise details, if I have a horizonal hallucination of my wife standing in front of me, there is a sense in which I do not have a visual experience of my wife. Nevertheless, the experience can still have my wife as its content, insofar as the horizonal structure in question is specific to her, comprising a sense of relating to her and to nobody else. This particularity can remain even when that structure is diminished, when significant possibilities such as addressing her or moving so as to see the back of her head are absent. In contrast, when it comes to a hallucinated cup of coffee, it is doubtful that the horizonal structure would be specific enough to distinguish a particular coffee cup from all other coffee cups. Hence some such hallucinations will involve encountering distinctive particulars, while others involve encountering indistinguishable instances of types.

It is further questionable whether the horizonal structure of the experience is invariably specific enough to identify a type of entity. Take the example of hallucinating a hungry, fast-approaching tiger. Suppose one has the sense that something large, predatory, animate, and threatening is coming. This alone does not add up to an approaching tiger. But such experiences are most likely prone to further interpretation or imaginative embellishment. We also need to distinguish cases where possibilities that are specific to entity A are experienced in the absence of A and do not attach to a perceived entity from other cases where entity B is perceived and something of A's horizonal structure is imposed upon it. Suppose one's perception of an entity, such as a chair, were associated with a horizonal structure more typical of experiencing a hungry tiger. In one sense, the content of the experience would be unchanged: a wooden entity with four identical, cylindrical legs, a flat, horizontal surface, and a vertical back. At the same time, there would be a *feeling* of encountering something different. This could involve two overlapping horizonal structures that are in tension with one another, involving an invitation to sit down and a sense of being threatened by something animate. However, both structures would be importantly incomplete: the chair experience would occur in the context of wider disturbances in the modal structure of intentionality, while the tiger experience would not be embedded in a consensus world at all. In an alternative scenario, the tiger-horizon is not superimposed on anything else. Rather than seeing a chair as a tiger or somehow tiger-like, there is an ambiguous sense of the tiger's presence, a characteristic way of being affected that persists even though it is not associated with a perceived object. Both scenarios differ from the kind of experience described in chapters 3 and 4. There, one does not experience possibilities that are specific to entity A in the absence of A, or experience them as superimposed on B. Rather, in virtue of possibilities that are associated with A, one takes oneself to be in intentional state *x* toward A instead of intentional state *y*. All three types of experience are largely attributable to a common, underlying phenomenological disturbance. It erodes a sense of the differences between intentional state types, rendering one vulnerable to more localized experiences with anomalous anticipation-fulfillment profiles.

7.3 Benevolent Voices

Even if we acknowledge modal confusions, hypervigilance hallucinations, and horizonal hallucinations, the term "hallucination" no doubt admits further diversity. So, to reiterate, the focus of my discussion is not hallucination per se but some of those phenomena that are routinely labeled as hallucinations. Nevertheless, one might object that my account does not succeed in accommodating all of those phenomena that I have sought to address. To be more specific, I have argued that VH/TI and at least some external VHs are attributable to anxious anticipation, which arises against the backdrop of wider-ranging disturbances of intentionality. The contents of these experiences are generally unpleasant and reflect a person's relationship with the social world as a whole. However, not all VHs are distressing. And, even when a person's voices do cause her distress, she may have an ambivalent relationship with them rather than just wanting them to stop. For instance, one questionnaire respondent, who regards her voices as parts of herself with their own personalities, states that "with the parts that mimic my abusers, there's a lot of shame, guilt, self-hatred, and fear. With other parts, there's often fear and vulnerability." But she also writes, "I can't imagine life without my voices—I would be lost, lonely, and empty. I wouldn't want to get rid of my voices" (5). As suggested in chapter 4, this kind of attachment to one's voices may be explicable in terms of a need for interpersonal connection, which persists alongside a sense of other people in general as threatening in one or another way. The voices are anxiously anticipated but at the same time sought out, analogous to unkind "friends" to whom one continues to cling.

However, others report VHs that do not have distressing contents at all (Copolov, Mackinnon, and Trauer 2004; Watkins 2008). People can obtain consolation, support, and/or guidance from their voices, and a voice that was once abusive and distressing can eventually become benign or supportive. Some therapies therefore seek not to eliminate voices but to mitigate the distress they cause, by nurturing more positive relationships with them (e.g., Romme et al. 2009; Corstens, Longden, and May 2012). This also involves gaining or regaining some degree of control over them; more control is associated with pleasant voices, while lack of control is associated with distress (e.g., Nayani and David, 1996). I have argued that the experience of a voice as alien is *constituted* by a sense of passivity, disconnection from the social world, and anxious anticipation. If that is right, then surely voices should simply disappear in the absence of social estrangement and distress. However, anxious anticipation may not be the *only* way of anticipating thought contents that blurs the boundaries between intentional state types. Anticipating consolation and support from one's thoughts may be amenable to a similar analysis. Although not alienating in the same way, it could still amount to an experience of thought content as emanating from elsewhere. Where a person has always "heard" comforting voices, this may well be what is happening. And, where previously hostile voices take on a supportive role, it could be that, once thought contents are already alienated, one is more susceptible to other ways of anticipating them that sustain a sense of their non-self-origin. My aim here has been to formulate a more generally applicable account of the modal structure of intentionality, using certain VH/TI experiences as a case study. This account is compatible with there being a much wider range of experiences that involve a partial sense of being in intentional state *x*, along with other aspects of experience that are more usually associated with state *y*. So, even if once malevolent but now benign voices do turn out to include internal VHs, there is no necessary tension here. Such experiences just point to the need for further analyses of specific phenomena, analyses that can draw on the same account of intentionality and interpersonal relations. Much the same applies to external VHs. Some of these are to be accounted for in terms of anxious hypervigilance, embedded in wider-ranging phenomenological disturbances, but, as the next section will make clear, not all of them take this form.

Another concern is that there are significant cross-cultural differences in voice-hearing experiences, and so my account may apply only to VHs in some cultures. For instance, Luhrmann et al. (2015) compared voice-experiences in groups of subjects from California, South India, and West Africa, all of whom met the same diagnostic criteria for schizophrenia. American subjects tended to use diagnostic labels, reported violent content, disliked their voices, and experienced them as an anomalous mind-thought relationship. In contrast, subjects from West Africa used no such labels, placed more of a spiritual emphasis on their experiences, and often regarded them as positive. In the sample from South India, there were no diagnostic labels and the voices were often experienced as those of relatives. These were interpreted spiritually and offered guidance. Among other things, Luhrmann et al. (2015, 655) conclude that "the voice-hearing experience outside the West may be less harsh." Of course, in the absence of more detailed phenomenological analyses, it is not clear whether these experiences were all of the same broad type: internal or external. Even so, my emphasis on the many ways in which other people shape and regulate our experiences is consistent with there being considerable cross-cultural variation. If all these experiences do involve the modal structure of intentionality, what should we say about the differences between them? It could well be that differing cultural attitudes serve to intensify or diminish a sense of anxiety that is partly constitutive of some VHs. At the same time, it could also turn out that a pronounced sense of social isolation is common to all cases and that this alone is sufficient to alter the modal structure of intentionality. In the absence of heightened social anxiety, the relevant phenomenological change would not result in the kind of VH described in chapter 4, where negative, self-directed feelings are anxiously anticipated and experienced as alien. Nevertheless, it could nurture horizonal hallucinations that lend themselves to expression in VH terms. Certain culture-specific norms, narratives, and practices may even serve to foster these. Thus, although it is far from clear what to say about the full range of historically and culturally diverse experiences that might be labeled "voices," there are no grounds for thinking that an analysis of local and global changes in the modal structure of intentionality is applicable only to a contemporary, culturally specific subset of experiences involving anxiety, alienation, and contingent interpretive practices.[2]

There are also hermeneutic issues to consider. When a voice is said to have become benign rather than to have disappeared, it is not clear that there is always a substantive difference between the two outcomes. In the absence of alienating distress, it could be that the voice is still identified as such by some residual property other than its alien quality and thematic content. So, as it was previously referred to as a "voice," the label sticks. For instance, those whose imagination and/or inner speech always had pronounced auditory qualities might more be inclined to say that the voice is still there, even though it is no longer alien in the way it was.[3] But whether or not a person continues to report *hearing a voice* also depends on how she and others interpret and describe her recovery: "I hear voices but I am not psychotic anymore and it doesn't have the same power over me as it used to. Now, I feel that my voices come from me. They are clouded memories of things that have gone on in my past" (Romme et al. 2009, 273). Where a voice persists without distress, it could well be that what made the original experience anomalous was a blurring of intentional state boundaries, and what gave the voice its alien quality was anxious distress. Once the alien quality and distress are subtracted, what remains, if we still want to call it a "voice," need not differ in a clear-cut way from unproblematic experiences of remembering, imagining, or thinking. It is also notable that people who no longer hear voices are sometimes unable to say when the voices stopped (pers. comm.). Now, it could be that a distressing and salient experience somehow disappears unannounced, like a headache that torments you for most of the day until you notice at some point during the afternoon that it has gone. Alternatively, perhaps there is no fact of the matter. The term "voice" could encompass a range of characteristics, some of which fade while others remain. The referent of the term is probably not stable or consistent enough for us to determine exactly when or why a voice should be declared gone and when it should be said to persist but in a different form. I have sought to account for the experience of a voice as *alien*, as emanating from elsewhere. The object of my analysis is therefore more specific than the full range of experiences that the term "voice-hearing" potentially refers to.

7.4 Relating to the Dead

For the most part, I have been concerned with hallucinations in psychiatric illness. However, another context in which VHs and other kinds of hallucinatory experience are widely reported is bereavement. Some post-bereavement hallucinations will almost certainly fall into categories already discussed. Where a bereavement is especially traumatic, and where the bereaved person feels progressively estranged from the social world as a whole and loses trust, the argument of chapters 5 and 6 will apply. But not all experiences of grief take this form, and perceptual or quasi-perceptual experiences of the deceased occur much more widely. "Sensed presence" experiences are most common; the person feels that the deceased is here, now, in a way that is not attributable to perception in one or another sensory modality. More specific auditory, visual, tactual, and olfactory experiences are also common. For example, a well-known study by Rees (1971) involved 227 widows and 66 widowers in Wales, around half of whom admitted having "hallucinations" or "illusions" of the deceased spouse: 39 percent of respondents reported a sense of presence, 14 percent visual experiences, 13.3 percent voices, and 2.7 percent tactual experiences. In some cases, these had occurred over many years, and the majority of those concerned (but not all) found them comforting and helpful. The likelihood of having such experiences increased with the length of a marriage, and they tended to be associated with happier marriages. Rees's findings are consistent with more recent studies. For instance, Bennett and Bennett (2000, 140) report that perception-like experiences of the deceased are not specific to a particular stage in the grieving process and are often enduring. These can involve a nonspecific experience of "being watched" or "a full-blown sensory experience—olfactory, auditory, visual, and occasionally tactile." Keen, Murray, and Payne (2013, 390) describe the most common type of experience as "a sense or feeling that the deceased person is close by without experiencing them in any sensory modality," while noting that more specific sensory experiences are also common, especially auditory and visual experiences. They add that there is a degree of cultural variation, with up to 90 percent of bereaved spouses reporting sensed presence experiences in some cultures, and that these experiences are also met with a range of different cultural attitudes.

In a survey of all literature published on the topic in English-language peer-reviewed journals, Castelnovo et al. (2015) conclude from the various findings that perception-like experiences of the deceased arise with a frequency of between 30 percent and 60 percent in widows. Nonspecific feelings of presence are most common, followed by visual and then auditory experiences. There appears to be a correlation with level of attachment to the deceased, and there are conflicting findings regarding the relevance of marriage length. Likelihood of occurrence is not associated with depression or social isolation, but is associated with intensity of grief.[4] Duration varies considerably; they can occur over a short period of time or continue indefinitely. Castelnovo et al. (2015, 271) also remark that, despite their frequency, these phenomena are underexplored. Consequently, "the phenomenological nature of these experiences remains elusive." Now, if we already had a good grasp of what seemingly modality-specific hallucinations and less specific perception-like experiences consist of, this would not be so much of a problem. But, unfortunately, "hallucination" refers to a wide range of different phenomena, which are seldom adequately distinguished from one another. So we should be wary of using the term here, at least without further qualification. It can be added that the term "hallucination" also conflicts with many people's self-interpretations (Bennett and Bennett 2000), interpretations that are themselves likely to play some role in shaping, reshaping, and even eliciting the relevant experiences. For these reasons, some of the language adopted by Castelnovo et al. (2015) is problematic. They refer to "abnormal sensory experiences" (266) and to "sensory deceptions" (267). However, given the available data, plus an acknowledgment of the diversity of "hallucinations," it is far from clear whether or in what way the relevant experiences are "sensory," or whether they amount to "deceptions" at all. After all, even in severe psychiatric illness, it would be an oversimplification to regard hallucinations as simple deceptions, given a widespread ability to distinguish them from mundane perceptual experiences. As for "abnormal," the authors do not wish to insist that the experiences in question are in one or another way pathological, and so the intended meaning is unclear.

This area of study thus illustrates the need for careful phenomenological research. Without it, we cannot say with any confidence what the relevant phenomena actually are, or whether all those who report perception-like experiences of the deceased have experiences that are similar in kind. Those studies that do adopt a more discerning approach point to the likelihood of considerable diversity. For instance, Normand, Silverman, and Nickman (1996) interviewed twenty-four bereaved children, all of whom had lost a parent when between the ages of ten and twelve. They describe how these children maintained connections with their deceased parents, how these connections differed, and how they developed over time:

> For some the connection took the form of an interactive relationship with the spirit of the dead; for others, it resembled a chaotic relationship with a ghost. Yet others remained connected to their deceased parents by reviving memories from the past, while for some the connection gained an abstract quality by internalization of the deceased's spirits. (94)

Some of those who initially remained connected through memories went on to develop a "more elaborate representation of the deceased as a spirit with whom they could communicate and therefore with whom they could maintain relationships" (95). In the context of such a relationship, how are we to interpret experiences like that of "being able to hear his father's voice in his mind, answering his questions" (97)? Among other things, it is unclear whether such experiences involve a *sense* of perceiving, a *sense* of imagining, or aspects of both. Furthermore, returning to a theme of section 6.5, localized experiences of whatever kind could be embedded in wider "meaning-provinces" or "sub-universes," such as make-believe realms that may or may not be experienced as unambiguously distinct from consensus reality. There is also the issue of whether and how children's experiences at various ages differ from those of adults, where such differences may reflect subtle developmental changes in the modal structure of intentionality and in how experiences are interpersonally regulated.

Bereavement hallucinations, whatever they might turn out to consist of, are not simply perception-like experiences with specific contents. They arise in the context of dynamic and changing interpersonal relationships, both with the living and with the dead. Grief is not an emotional *state* or *episode* that persists for however long, but an interpersonal process that varies in character and duration (Klass, Silverman, and Nickman 1996; Parkes 1996; Solomon 2004; Goldie 2011, 2012; Ratcliffe 2016).[5] And the view that this process ultimately involves resigning one's attachment to the deceased is, despite its popularity in some cultures, rather misleading. A growing literature on "continuing bonds" suggests instead that grief processes have no clear end point, and that relationships with the deceased are renegotiated and sustained in one or another way rather than abandoned (e.g., Klass, Silverman, and Nickman 1996). These continuing bonds are said to be ubiquitous and mostly healthy, rather than occasional and pathological (e.g., Silverman and Klass 1996, 3). Of course, we should be wary of making generalizations about what experiences of grief consist of, as there is considerable diversity. Differences are attributable to a range of factors, including the circumstances of the death, the nature of the bereavement (e.g., a spouse, sibling, or child), inherited and acquired dispositions and vulnerabilities, the effect on a person's financial situation, and the availability of social support. There are also cultural differences to consider.[6] Even so, I think it is plausible to insist that grief, in general, is a multifaceted process that does not, or at least need not, conclude with *letting go*. For those who have experienced multiple bereavements, relations with the dead can be a salient aspect of daily life, perhaps more salient for some than relations with the living. Perception-like experiences of the deceased arise during the course of these relations. They can persist indefinitely, are often welcomed, and can constitute or contribute to enduring bonds with deceased.

During profound grief, systems of habitual expectation are profoundly disrupted and gradually altered. There is an alternation between retention and loss of habitual ways of experiencing the shared world, something that can involve experiences of both presence (including experiences of relating to and interacting with the deceased) and absence. A grieving process can include many different ways of experiencing and relating to the deceased. It might be as though he were still alive, even present in some way. He might also be experienced as remembered, as imagined, and as somehow present *in* his absence. I will later show how a current, ongoing relationship with the deceased can even involve a consistent sense of his irrevocable absence. There is a fine line between perceptual or quasi-perceptual experiences of presence and other ways in which a person might be experienced or thought of as enduring or even as *here, now*. He might continue to reside in the past, or in some other realm. And, alongside the feeling that *part of me has gone*, there can also be a sense that *he endures as part of me*, in the guise of commitments and values that are adopted, new ways of acting, and associated ways in which things appear salient and significant. So a sense of continuing presence need not involve relating to a localized entity that is experienced as wholly distinct from oneself. There are also experiences, which I will describe shortly, where what we might call a "sense of presence" is inseparable from how the world as a whole is perceived.

In considering the phenomenology of grief, it is again apparent that thinking of "hallucination" as a singular kind of experience, where something that is absent appears to be present, is an oversimplification. Grief involves a range of localized and nonlocalized experiences that do not involve taking someone to be present or absent in a clear-cut way. The sense of presence and absence is often much more equivocal and ambiguous. Consequently, although bereavement hallucinations may well turn out to be quite diverse in nature, it is very likely that most or even all of them do not conform to orthodox definitions of hallucination. Even where an experience of grief does not involve wide-ranging and enduring disturbances of intentionality, it should be acknowledged that the sense of perceptual presence is multifaceted and variable. So, in any given instance, it is far from clear what is meant by experiencing the deceased as present. As I will further argue in chapter 8, the modal structure of intentionality is not to be construed in terms of a few categorically distinct types of intentional states, which are only disrupted in extreme circumstances. The example of grief serves to make explicit something that applies more generally: neither our sense of *presence* nor our sense of *what is the case* is univocal. In addition, grief further illustrates how human experience is riddled with anticipation, in a way that is interpersonally regulated. Chapter 6 emphasized our relations with other people in general. But grief provides a complementary perspective on how the integrity of experience can come to depend on relations with particular individuals.

To illustrate these various points, let us turn to some recurrent themes in autobiographical accounts of grief. The accounts I will consider were all written by professional authors, who may be more inclined than others to express and interpret their experiences through narrative, and to do so in a particular way: "Writing is what I have, and it's how I make sense of experience" (Humphreys 2013, 24). So they may not be representative of grief experiences more generally. Another concern to keep in mind is that it may not be possible to separate an experience of grief from the narratives that convey it, as it is arguable that grieving processes are partly *constituted* by dynamic narratives that shape and regulate experience (Goldie 2011; Higgins 2013). Furthermore, it is often remarked that grief is hard to express in words and hard for others to comprehend. Hence the relevant phenomenology cannot simply be "read off" first-person descriptions; we should interpret them cautiously. I concede that grief is expressed—and most likely experienced—in many different ways. Nevertheless, it is possible to identify a number of core themes that are common to many first-person accounts, themes that complement what I have said about the anticipatory structure of experience and its interpersonal regulation.

Simple descriptions and definitions of grief are easy to come by. For instance, Wilkinson (2000, 290) states that "someone is grieving only if the emotional response to a real or perceived loss (usually, though not necessarily, of another person) involves some degree of distress or suffering." This might suggest that grief *follows* recognition of loss, whereas one could instead maintain (as I will) that grief is partly *constitutive* of that recognition. But, whichever the case, grief looks like an intentional state directed at something specific: one grieves over the death of A, in a way that is analogous to regretting that *p* or feeling happy about *q*. However, grief also involves a nonlocalized shift in how one experiences and relates to the social world, something that is inextricable from the more specific recognition that a particular individual has died. Whybrow (1997, 2) offers the following description:

> When it strikes, the raw intensity of the feeling comes as a surprise. Life is rolled on its head, and we find ourselves off balance. Routine patterns and familiar assumptions are called into question. Social attachments of love and friendship that gave meaning and purpose are fundamentally changed. Inevitably we are confronted with the

challenge of finding for ourselves a new fit with the world, for that which was once a stable and accustomed part of life's routine has been irretrievably lost. The external world has changed and with it the inner world of personal meaning.

Why would the external world appear changed? We can understand this in terms of an effect on projects, pastimes, commitments, habitual activities, and expectations that explicitly or implicitly implicate the deceased in one or another way. Many of the social norms and roles that regulate activity apply to people in general: one walks on the footpath rather than the road, and one pays the cashier in a shop rather than the security guard, regardless of who one is. But what strikes us as practically meaningful and salient, "to be done," "to be avoided," "worth doing," "exciting," or "disappointing," also depends on projects and wider concerns that are, to varying degrees, idiosyncratic. As argued in chapter 6, the ways in which things matter to us, the kinds of significance they have for us, are integral to our experiences of them (regardless of whether or not the significance of something is admitted as a content of more specifically *sensory perceptual* experience). A hammer *looks* different, depending on whether you have been searching for it while immersed in a DIY project or you are being chased by a hammer-wielding attacker. If nothing mattered in quite the same way, the world as a whole would look different.

How things matter to us depends in part on whom we are with, how we relate to them, and whom we share our various projects and wider concerns with. When we act purposively in relation to a goal-directed project, a particular person such as a spouse can be implicated in a range of ways: "I do it because you asked me to"; "I do it for you"; "I am doing it because you care"; "we do it together to achieve something that matters to us both"; "I am helping you to do something"; "you are there to fall back on if I fail." Even when a project does not concern the person in any of these ways, there can remain the appreciation that "I will come home to you when it is finished" and "I will be able to tell you about it." In fact, the telling can be anticipated as an end in itself, and thus motivate one's activities:

> As for doing what I liked: for me, this usually meant doing things with her. Insofar as I liked doing things by myself, it was partly for the pleasure of telling her about them afterwards. (Barnes 2013, 80–81)

Bereavement therefore undermines, to varying degrees, a previously taken-for-granted sense of what matters and how it matters. In so doing, it renders unintelligible a range of integrated practices that contributed to the world's coherence, regulated activity, and shaped anticipation. Joyce Carol Oates (2011, 63) expresses this in terms of coming to inhabit a world of "things," where "these *things* retain but the faintest glimmer of their original identity and meaning as in a dead and desiccated husk of something once organic there might be discerned a glimmer of its original identity and meaning." The world ceases to offer what it once did, and, as what things offer is integral to how they look, the world as a whole is somehow different, lacking. C. S. Lewis (1966, 12) describes the sense of absence as follows: "It is not local at all. ... The act of living is different through and through. Her absence is like the sky, spread over everything." Julian Barnes (2013, 81) similarly writes, "I miss her in every action, and in every inaction."

All or almost all of one's interactions with the social world, and the anticipation-fulfillment patterns they involve, can come to presuppose a relationship with a particular person. Importantly, then, the deceased is not just a person *within* the experienced world but also an intelligibility condition *for* a world that was once taken as given. A singular experience of loss is both specifically focused and at the same time all-enveloping; that person is gone and the world as a whole lacks an elaborate, cohesive system of practical meanings that was previously experienced as integral to it.[7] One feels disconnected from everything, somehow dislodged: "There is a sort of invisible blanket between the world and me" (Lewis 1966, 5). This, I think, is why people sometimes say that part of them has died too. The sense of participating in a meaningful world depends not just on an isolated self and its projects but on relations with particular others:

> Death feels a bit like a vanished city, like wandering through a landscape I used to recognize but that has now been radically altered. It was a mistake to think that life was solid ground under my feet, and that every day I would be able to step back down onto the same earth. To have you gone—you, who went clear to the bottom of my world—has thrown everything off balance, has left me wandering like a ghost in my own life. (Humphreys 2013, 58)

It is not that one comes to believe that a particular person has died, at which point all activities instantaneously lose their meaning. Certain activities may be relatively well insulated from a bereavement. Oates (2011, 172) describes how she was able to retreat into her professional duties and temporarily reimmerse herself in the world through her teaching, an aspect of her life that had always been set apart from her relationship with her husband. And, where activities are not insulated, there is an ongoing alternation between retention and loss of practical meaning. It is commonplace to "know that *p*" in a propositional way while continually "forgetting that *p*" when habitually engaging with the world. For instance, one might reorganize an office, know where everything is, but continue to look for things in their former locations. Something like this happens in grief, but the experience is much more widespread. The interplay between habitual expectations and the episodic realization that there is no longer any prospect of their ever being fulfilled involves repeated experiences of negation, of continually confronting situations from which something is missing.

One form that retention of practical meaning can take is what Joan Didion calls "magical thinking." Although one explicitly assents to the belief that someone has died, one continues to think and act in ways that conflict with it. The loss is conceived of as temporary and reversible, insulating—on some occasions and to some extent—the world from a collapse of practical meaning: "'Bringing him back' had been through those months my hidden focus, a magic trick"; "I realized that since the last morning of 2003, the morning after he died, I had been trying to reverse time, to run the film backward" (Didion 2005, 44, 183–184). So it is an oversimplification to state that one either "believes that A has died" or "believes that A has not died." To fully comprehend that someone has died is not only a matter of explicitly acknowledging the irreversible absence of a particular entity from one's world, given that a sense of that person's being part of the world is also constituted by a wider context of experience, thought, and activity. Where part of a system of practical meanings endures consistently or sporadically, despite its dependence on the deceased, one might be said to *not quite believe it*—it doesn't seem real; the world endures and yet it cannot endure. It would be equally wrong, however, to say that one does not believe it. As Parkes (1996, 65) observes, remarks such as "I can't believe it's true" are commonplace among the bereaved, but disbelief is "seldom complete." Hence, in using the term "belief" to refer to the different degrees and kinds of comprehension at play here, we cannot think of it as a simple propositional attitude of the form "B believes that *p*," where *p* is "A has died."[8]

The effects of bereavement on how the world is experienced are not restricted solely to goal-directed projects and associated practical meanings. Chapter 6 addressed how being with a particular person can shape the wider salience of our surroundings in all sorts of subtle ways. For instance, the experience of seeing something with a particular person can differ substantially from that of seeing it on our own or with someone else. Experience shaping of this kind often involves face-to-face interaction or some other form of interaction. On other occasions, our experiences are influenced by imagining the person's presence or imagining interaction with her. There are also occasions when she is not herself a salient object of experience but continues to be implicitly implicated in how the surrounding world appears. Although she is not present, things are experienced, in some respects at least, as they would be if she were present. A garden, a sunset, a film, a journey, a painting—all can appear in a habitual, prereflective way as they would for us, rather than for me alone. Grief can thus involve habitually experiencing something in a way that presupposes the potential or actual presence of the deceased, something that might then be disrupted by the realization of absence. For example:

> Later, at the motel, I stand in the darkened living room and stare out at the dark ocean—a stretch of beach, pale sand—vapor-clouds and a glimpse of the moon—the conviction comes over me suddenly *Ray can't see this, Ray can't breathe.* … As I've been thinking, in restaurants, staring at menus, forced to choose something to eat. *This is wrong. This is cruel, selfish. If Ray can't eat* … (Oates 2011, 244)

So there is a way in which we might be said to experience the *presence of the deceased* that does not involve the localized, perception-like experience of another person but instead a diffuse way of encountering our surroundings. This can be contrasted with a nonlocalized revelation of absence, where an all-enveloping anticipatory structure is recognized as unfulfillable and the world as a whole appears consequently lacking.

These descriptions of how bereavement affects the structure of experience are compatible with empirical findings, which similarly suggest that relationships with specific individuals shape and regulate experience, thought, and activity in a range of important ways. For instance, Hofer (1984, 184) discusses how bereavement disrupts experience and thought, observing that there are "impairments of concentration, memory, judgment, and decisiveness, including illusions and even hallucinations of the lost person in 12–40% of cases." All of this, he observes, adds up to a "sense of impending loss of control." He mentions several parallels between grief and the effects of separation on infants, which together point to the conclusion that relationships in adult life continue to play important regulatory roles. More specifically, he hypothesizes that some symptoms of grief may be attributable to the "withdrawal of specific sensorimotor regulators"

(188). In support of that view, Sbarra and Hazan (2008) propose that homeostatic processes are not encapsulated within the individual; they also include regulatory interactions with others, which serve above all else to sustain a sense of security:

> When long-term mate relationships end, many adults lose the person who helps them maintain psychological and physiological homeostasis. In human attachments, the core of this homeostatic set point is the experience of felt security, a sense that the world is safe and nonthreatening and that exploratory activities can be pursued without the risk of danger. (2008, 142)[9]

Of course, loss of an "interpersonal regulator" is not specific to grief. For instance, it could apply equally to the breakup of a long-term relationship or to leaving the parental home and moving to a new city. Even so, there are differences. For instance, where a relationship deteriorates before a breakup, there may be a gradual process of adjustment rather than a sudden shock, and there is often the option of returning to a place when feeling homesick. Not all bereavements are sudden and unexpected, and not all geographical moves involve the possibility of return. However, my claim is not that grief should be identified with the collapse of a regulatory process, just that this is an important aspect of grief. And, in certain other respects, experiences of grief are distinguishable from responses to other kinds of event. Most obviously, when grieving, one is confronted with the irrevocable absence of the deceased. Nevertheless, recognition of absence is not unequivocal or consistently maintained. For instance, grief is often associated with searching behavior (Parkes 1996, chap. 4). The bereaved person needs and seeks the deceased, in a way that can again be construed in terms of habitual, practical anticipation more so than propositional attitudes of the form "I desire to see A" and "I believe there is some likelihood of A's appearing":

> I could not count the times during the average day when something would come up that I needed to tell him. This impulse did not end with his death. What ended was the possibility of response. (Didion 2005, 194)

It is likely that not all searching ends unfulfilled. To account for some experiences of sensed presence, as well as more specific experiences in one or more sensory modalities, we can appeal to what Hoffman (2007) calls "social deafferentation." To recap, the idea is that certain hallucinatory experiences involving other people are comparable to phantom limb experiences, and are generated in response to a lack of specifically social stimulation. While Hoffman associates these experiences with schizophrenia, which frequently involves social isolation, his account is perhaps better suited to experiences of grief. A specific individual can be so bound up with one's experiencing, thinking, and acting that one constantly anticipates her presence, at least in some situations. There is a readiness to perceive, arising out of need and habitual expectation. Hence, where a situation is perceptually indeterminate or noisy, one is poised to sense her presence, hear her voice, or glimpse her.

However, it could well be that other experiences, which appear superficially similar, are in fact what I have called "horizonal hallucinations" rather than misinterpretations or overinterpretations of perceptual stimuli. Where the bereaved person is unusually passive, disengaged from activity, and removed from the social world, he will be more susceptible to having experiences of affective anticipation that do not attach to the perceived environment. And, if he has spent a great deal of time anticipating, interacting with, and thinking about a particular individual, he will be especially prone to experiencing possibilities that involve her. To the extent that an experience of possibility approximates a horizonal structure specific to the deceased, the relevant experience might be described in terms of perception in one or another modality, or a less specific sense of presence. There is also a potential role for nonperceptual imagination, in constructing make-believe realms or sub-universes that cultivate perception-like experiences of one or another kind, as well as for vivid memories that prime anticipation. And, as already noted, something of the other person also remains embedded in the world, in the guise of places, situations, or arrangements of possessions that implicate her actual or potential presence in some way. So the scene is already set for her arrival. Furthermore, a bereaved person may actively seek to preserve patterns of anticipation, and to interact with his surroundings so as to maintain and even amplify types of perception-like experience that form part of an enduring relationship with the deceased. This would be consistent with the observation that hallucinations can persist long after someone has apparently adjusted to a loss.

Along with localized and nonlocalized experiences of *presence*, there are also experiences of *absence*. The world as a whole may appear lacking, but such experiences can also be more specific in nature. A system of habitual, practical expectations that implicates person A includes the expectation of encountering A in particular situations and locations, such as when entering a certain room or engaging in an activity that involved

A. When these expectations are negated by the explicit recognition of A's irrevocable absence, the experience is comparable in some respects to Sartre's (1943/1989) well-known description of waiting to meet Pierre in a café when Pierre fails to arrive. Pierre's absence is experienced in a localized way, when someone else enters and is encountered as "not Pierre." And it is also experienced in a slightly more diffuse way. How the café appears is shaped by the expectation of meeting Pierre; it is a background to an absent foreground. And, when that background endures, Pierre's absence is present, akin to seeing a picture frame without a picture. A grieving process likewise includes frequent realizations that "A is not here" and, occasionally, "this is not A." Some of these may be fleeting and others more enduring. In contrast to Sartre's example, they are not restricted to a specific place or a single occasion. The presence of the deceased is anticipated in many different places and in many different kinds of social situation. So incessant experiences of absence become an inescapable aspect of grief.

Although grief involves wide-ranging disturbances of the anticipatory structure of experience, these are not usually pronounced or pervasive enough to induce modally ambiguous experiences of the kinds described in chapters 3 and 4. Loss of a particular person from one's world, however close the relationship may have been, does not automatically amount to an all-enveloping loss of trust, confidence, or certainty, although it can do. How a grieving process unfolds depends in part on the nature of continuing relations with others. Interpersonal relations can help to sustain or restore trust in the world, and to preserve the overall integrity of experience. Among other things, other people participate in the construction and revision of narratives, which themselves aid in regulating experience and, more specifically, in shaping one's changing relationship with the deceased (Higgins 2013). On the other hand, other people can exacerbate a sense of estrangement. For example, Aleksandar Hemon (2013, 203) remarks that "one of the most common platitudes we heard was that 'words failed,'" but adds that "it was not true that there was no way to describe our experience." What failed, he says, were platitudes and clichés that had little bearing on the situation. Whether others understand, fail to understand, listen, pretend to listen, offer what is perceived as genuine support, retain an emotional distance, or withdraw altogether further shapes how one experiences and relates to the world as a whole. Following a bereavement, everything seems different not only because someone has died but because others seem different too; and they do indeed act differently. So there is a fine line between profound grief and the global loss of trust or confidence described in chapter 5. Those who are recently bereaved are often more dependent than ever on others to regulate, sustain, and restore the integrity of experience, thought, and activity, and are therefore more vulnerable to others as well.

Grief thus involves a diverse, dynamic, and socially embedded interplay between experiences of localized and nonlocalized presence and absence. One does not simply come to recognize that a person was present at time 1 and became absent at time 2: "The paradox of grief: if I have survived what is now four years of her absence, it is because I have had four years of her presence" (Barnes 2013, 103). The sense of loss is to be understood in terms of this interplay; it is integral to the grieving process rather than a form of recognition that precedes and elicits grief. However, there are still further dimensions to explore, which again challenge any simple opposition between the experience of someone as present and as absent. It might be assumed that an experience of currently relating to somebody can be sustained only when one continues to experience or think of her as present in some way, and that full acknowledgment of absence implies the impossibility of such a relationship. But some narratives of grief suggest otherwise. For example, in her book, *Time Lived, Without Its Flow*, Denise Riley describes a profound transformation of her world that persisted for three years after the death of her adult son. She focuses on an experience of time as bereft of *flow*. It is not that *time for everyone* stopped flowing. What Riley describes is a sense of having been removed from the time of others, from a place where time still flows: it is a "sensation of having been lifted clean out of habitual time"; the "sensation of living outside time" (2012, 10, 45). This can be interpreted (in part, at least) in terms of something already described: the absence of a particular person from one's world impacts, to varying degrees, on the anticipatory structure of experience, draining things of a significance they previously had. In the extreme case, nothing matters anymore, and significant transitions from one moment to the next are neither anticipated nor experienced; things still change but nothing meaningful happens. Barnes (2013, 84) offers the complementary remark that "grief reconfigures time, its length, its texture, its function: one day means no more than the next, so why have they been picked out and given separate names?"

The experience could be construed as one of recognizing a person to be gone, and, in so doing, recognizing the loss of all those practical meanings that implicated him. But, although this has a role to play, it is not what Riley seeks to convey. She does not say that things ceased to matter due to an inability to relate to her son. Instead, she attributes her detachment from the social world and from shared time to an enduring relationship with him, of a kind that fully acknowledges his no longer being part of the world. This relationship amounts to a disengagement from the world of the living, a kind of participation in death: "I tried always to be there for him, solidly. And I shall continue to be. (The logic of this conviction: in order to be there, I too have died)" (2012, 21). Sustained concern for someone who is still alive can also constitute a sense of dislodgement from the wider world. For example, Hemon describes the experience of driving to the hospital to visit his terminally ill baby daughter:

> It took me about fifteen minutes to get to the hospital, through traffic that existed in an entirely different space-time, where people did not rush crossing the streets and no infant life was in danger, where everything turned away quite leisurely from the disaster. ...
>
> I had an intensely physical sensation of being inside an aquarium: I could see outside, the people outside could see me inside (if they somehow chose to pay attention), but we lived and breathed in entirely different environments. Isabel's illness and our experience had little connection to, and even less impact on, the world outside. (2013, 190, 201–202)

However, what Riley describes includes something further: a sense of relating to someone *as dead*. The connection endures after the death, in a way that does not rely on a sense of continuing presence. Recognition of her son's absence from the consensus world, combined with retention of a second-person connection in the face of it, amounts to a sense of her own separation from the world of the living:

> My new ability to live in the present is a joining-in of that timelessness of being dead. ...
>
> You already share the "timeless time" of the dead child. As if you'd died too, or had lost the greater part of your own life. (2012, 23, 38)

We might go so far as to construe this as a kind of *second-person experience of death*. I am thinking here of Edith Stein's (1917/1989) account of empathy, according to which empathy is a way of *experiencing* the mental lives of others. There is, Stein admits, a substantial difference between first-person and second-person experience, between how I experience my own mental life and how I experience yours. But this is not to admit that the latter is a poor approximation of the former. Instead, they are two qualitatively different ways of accessing experience.[10] To some degree at least, I experience your mental life in your observed behavior. And, when I do so, I also have a more general sense of being in the presence of a locus of experience distinct from myself (Ratcliffe 2015, chap. 8). I suggest, somewhat tentatively, that such an approach can be extended to at least some grief experiences. One not only recognizes the absence of a person from one's world; one also experiences, in a second-person way, the loss of intelligibility of *that person's* world. Indeed, unless we acknowledge something like this, we risk construing grief as more self-absorbed than it often is, as a matter of what is lost from *my* world or *my* losing a certain relationship. What is needed is an account of its other-directedness, of its being concerned with what has happened to *you*, not just what has happened to *me*. Solomon (2004, 90) suggests that grief is not only a matter of *my* having lost someone; it is also a "continuation of love" for that person. The view that grief can involve a continuing second-person relationship with the deceased, one that incorporates recognition of her death, is consistent with this.

Other accounts also convey this aspect of experience, although not quite so explicitly. For instance, Helen Humphreys' *True Story: The Life and Death of My Brother* addresses him in the second-person throughout, sometimes referring to the time "after you died." She relates to him, reaches out to him, while at the same time acknowledging his death. The distinction between retaining a second-person relation and recognizing its impossibility is not always clear. Consider the following passage from Joan Didion's *Blue Nights*:

> I know that I can no longer reach her.
>
> I know that, should I try to reach her—should I take her hand as if she were again sitting next to me in the upstairs cabin on the evening Pan Am from Honolulu to LAX, should I lull her to sleep against my shoulder, should I sing her the song about Daddy gone to get the rabbit skin to wrap his baby bunny in—she will fade from my touch. (2011, 187–188)

Even so, I think this is plausibly interpreted in terms of a kind of relational, second-person experience that recognizes absence (and with it the impossibility of reciprocity), rather than in terms of an absence of second-person experience. Thus, some narratives of grief suggest that an enduring second-person connection with the deceased does not have to involve experiencing or thinking of the other person as still present in one or another way.[11] Riley states that the absence of flow she describes is specific to parental grief, and not unusual among bereaved parents. However, less pronounced or qualitatively different relational experiences of absence may well characterize grief more generally. If that is right, then it is likely that remarks such as "I died with her" and "part of me has died" are not always used in the same way. They can convey importantly different aspects of grief: a second-person experience of death that dislodges one from the world, and a diminishment of one's world due to someone's absence from it.

Once all of these aspects of grief are taken into consideration, it becomes clear that hallucinations and sensed-presence experiences, whatever their precise nature, do not simply involve experiencing something as present when it is actually absent. They are embedded within wider-ranging disturbances of the anticipatory structure of experience, a structure that is largely responsible for our sense of the distinction between presence and absence. They involve complicated interactions between experiences of localized and nonlocalized anticipation, fulfillment, and negation, interactions that are riddled with tensions and ambiguities. Even experiences that do seem to involve a localized sense of presence or to resemble perception in one or another modality most likely come in different forms. Some may occur when systems of anticipation that remain intact misinterpret noisy environmental stimuli, while others are horizonal hallucinations. It is unlikely that any such experiences involve a wholly perception-like experience of unambiguous presence. In fact, some experiences of the *presence* of the deceased may not consist of localized content at all. A sense of personal presence can involve a much more diffuse experience of one's surroundings, which are imbued with a significance they would have if the deceased were there, sharing in the experience. Other experiences involve the presence of absence, in the guise of negated expectation, while others involve enduring relationships with the deceased that fully recognize her irrevocable absence. In many cases, the lines between memory, imagination, expectation, belief, pretense, and/or perception are unclear.

When grief involves progressive loss of trust, social isolation, and, ultimately, the erosion of global certainty, it is consistent with the kinds of experience discussed in chapters 3 to 6. In all cases, though, it further illustrates the need for an approach that recognizes the complex and sometimes conflictual structure of intentionality, how the integrity of experience involves anticipation-fulfillment profiles, and how experience is interpersonally regulated. We might wonder, though, whether some of the observations made with respect to grief also have much wider applicability. In unexceptional situations, do we operate with a singular, unambiguous sense of presence, absence, what is the case, and what is not the case? Or are things messier than that? Focusing on the example of belief, I will conclude by suggesting that my consideration of unusual forms of experience serves to highlight something more widespread, something that is otherwise easily overlooked: how subtly different forms of intentionality are also at work in everyday life and, more specifically, in philosophical inquiry.

8 Metaphilosophical Conclusion

I have argued that various kinds of anomalous experience, including many of those phenomena labeled as "hallucinations" and "delusions," occur due to localized and/or global changes in the structure of intentionality. The sense of being in a given type of intentional state is not merely a matter of characteristic experiential content, and neither is it attributable to a separate attitudinal phenomenology or to a combination of attitude and content. It is multifaceted and centrally involves an anticipation-fulfillment dynamic that can be decoupled, at least to some extent, from characteristic content. So a temporal profile that contributes to the sense of being in one type of intentional state can be associated with content more typical of another. The result is an intrinsically peculiar and sometimes conflictual experience, which lies somewhere between more familiar forms of intentionality. Such experiences usually involve wider-ranging disturbances in the modal structure of intentionality as well. This structure is sustained by a distinctive, overarching style of anticipation, which is integral to practically engaged perceptual experience. The integrity of global anticipatory style depends on ways of anticipating and relating to other people. Hence pronounced and all-enveloping changes in how one experiences other people are, at the same time, disturbances in the overall structure of intentionality and even the most minimal sense of self.

This concluding chapter offers some brief and tentative remarks concerning the implications of this position for philosophy and for clinical practice. First of all, it should be conceded that what I have said is far from complete. I have not sought to provide a comprehensive analysis of the modalities of intentionality and their relationship to the interpersonal world, but instead to open up an area of philosophical inquiry where there is much work to be done. While my discussion has been restricted for the most part to broad categories of intentionality, such as remembering, perceiving, and imagining, we could go on to formulate more specific accounts of how and why certain subtypes of imagining or remembering are associated with a sense of perceiving through one or another sensory modality. There is also more to be said about the various constituents of the sense of being in an intentional state and how they interrelate. For all types of intentional state, we could seek to provide an inventory of characteristics that are individually necessary or jointly sufficient for the ambiguous, unambiguous, conflicted, or nonconflicted sense of being in an intentional state of that kind. Such a project would involve describing, in detail, the characteristic temporal profiles of different intentional state types, and specifying how they implicate and interact with one other. It would also involve further exploring the underlying sense of confidence or certainty that is central to the modal structure of intentionality, describing the many subtly different kinds of change it is susceptible to, and showing precisely how these alterations affect the more specific temporal profiles of intentional states. In addition to all of this, there is the issue of how various different degrees and kinds of alteration in how other people are anticipated and experienced impact on the modal structure of intentionality.

So one philosophical implication of my discussion is that it points to a novel field of philosophical inquiry and interdisciplinary research. However, there are also potential implications for how we conceive of philosophy itself. To be more specific, when we start to reflect on the possibility of subtle differences not just in the *contents* of philosophical beliefs but also in their *form*, we face the metaphilosophical problem of pinning down what it is to endorse one or another philosophical position. It is likely that belief in the truth of a philosophical position is not merely something that comes in differing degrees; philosophers also believe things in quite different *ways*, a point that applies equally to beliefs more generally. I have argued that a range of different factors contribute to a sense of something as present and to a more general sense of something as the case. Changes in the modal structure of intentionality can alter the sense of what it is to be the case, such that the phenomenological distance between belief and other forms of intentionality is lessened. Now, although such alterations are to be contrasted with more mundane forms of experience, this is not to imply that everyday perception involves a singular, unwavering way of experiencing things as present, or that everyday belief involves a similarly consistent way of taking things to be the case.

Most of us are familiar with subtle changes in the sense of presence. For instance, when we are suffering from a minor illness, our surroundings can seem oddly distant, as though things are not quite there. Elsewhere, I have described a wide range of changes in the overall structure of experience in terms of "existential feelings" (Ratcliffe 2005, 2008, 2015). Where more subtle changes are concerned, the integrity of intentionality is preserved. In other words, although perception is altered, it is not altered in such a way and to such an extent that it is no longer experienced as clearly distinct from other kinds of intentionality. Even without wide-ranging shifts in the structure of perception, we do not perceive everything as present in exactly the same way (Noë 2012). The sense of presence is multifaceted and some aspects of it can be more pronounced than others in a given instance. Much the same applies to belief. When we take something to be the case, we can do so in different ways. However, these differences are obscured by artificially tidy philosophical language that identifies a few categorically distinct intentional state types. Thus, discussions of belief are generally insensitive to the range of subtly different attitudes that are accommodated by the term, all of which might be described in terms of taking something to be the case, taking something to be true, or assenting to a proposition.

Of course, I do not mean to imply that philosophers operate with a singular, univocal, and universally accepted conception of belief. Among other things, a philosopher might distinguish between conscious and nonconscious beliefs, and between perceptual and nonperceptual beliefs, as well as engage in debates over whether beliefs are episodes, dispositions, and/or states.[1] For current purposes, I restrict my consideration of belief to situations where a philosopher explicitly and honestly asserts that *p*. This does not just involve putting a tick next to a proposition; sincere expressions of belief also involve a *sense of conviction* with respect to *p*. I do not wish to suggest that an episodic feeling of conviction is sufficient for the belief that *p*, or that beliefs should be conceived of principally as conscious occurrences rather than longer-term dispositions. In fact, my position is compatible with a dispositional account of belief proposed by Schwitzgebel (2002), according to which the various dispositions that together add up to belief include "phenomenal and cognitive dispositions as well as behavioral dispositions"

(249). In any given instance of belief, he argues, contributing dispositions can be present to differing degrees. This allows us to account for a range of in-between cases, where it seems wrong to say that someone believes that *p* but equally wrong to insist that she does not. Belief, for Schwitzgebel, is a "dispositional stereotype," analogous to "being hot-tempered" (251). No single disposition is necessary or sufficient, and beliefs can depart from the stereotype in different ways. Among the relevant dispositions, Schwitzgebel includes a "disposition to feel assent to an internal utterance" (252), and this is what I am concerned with here. Although belief is not to be identified with consciously taking something to the case, it includes either doing so or at least having a disposition to do so. This is illustrated by the simple observation that someone who sincerely and repeatedly insists that not *p* (or who would emphatically insist that not *p* if asked) cannot be ascribed the unproblematic belief that *p*. I want to suggest that the *feeling of believing* associated with sincere assent, the *sense* of something as the case, is itself heterogeneous in nature. This further complicates the nature of belief.

The utterance "*p* is the case" can involve different kinds of attitude, different ways of taking something to be the case, different kinds of conviction. We saw how this applies to delusional "beliefs" that involve double-bookkeeping. We also saw how a loss of trust, confidence, or certainty can lead to the erosion of a more usual sense of habitual, confident conviction: nothing is experienced as present or taken to be the case in quite the way it was. However, pronounced disruptions of intentionality such as these also serve to make explicit something that applies more generally, something subtle that might otherwise pass unnoticed. During the course of everyday life, we take things to be the case in different ways, an observation that also applies more specifically to philosophical beliefs. Our sense of something as the case or otherwise is, like the more general structure of intentionality, multifaceted. There is no singular feeling of conviction, no simple sense of believing. By implication, belief does not have a singular "functional role" either. Depending on the kind of felt conviction involved, a belief content could relate to other intentional state contents and to actual or potential activities in any number of different ways.

Experiences of grief, as described in chapter 7, can involve especially pronounced tensions between different ways of taking something to be the case. A person can utter the proposition "B is dead" and know the proposition to be true, but at the same time not quite believe it. The world does not appear as it would if B were irrevocably absent; it continues to be experienced through a system of habits that are inextricable from her relationship with B. Different utterances of the proposition "I believe that B is dead" can thus involve different kinds of conviction. Even where the truth of the proposition "B is dead" is never in any doubt, a sense of conviction can be incomplete, lacking, in conflict with the habitual anticipation of B's presence. More generally, beliefs can relate in different ways to the practically significant, shared world in which we are for the most part habitually immersed. They are often immediately relevant to goal-directed activities and may have significant practical implications. Take, for instance, the belief that a tram is fast approaching and the associated decision not to cross the road in front of it. Such beliefs are also firmly rooted in a consensus reality. As I wait with others, the tram appears as something *we* experience together; it is *we* who wait for it to pass. Contrast this with the kinds of idiosyncratic superstition that most people—when pressed for a while—will eventually confess to, such as believing that wearing a particular pair of shoes when going out on a Friday night is unlucky, that one needs to conduct a little private ceremony before giving a talk, or that one can influence the course of life events in all manner of other peculiar ways. It would be an oversimplification to say that a person does not believe such things, pure and simple. When pressed, he might well say "of course I know it is not the case that *p*," where *p* is something like "touching the wall before I leave the house will ensure that nothing goes wrong today." And yet someone who does not perform one or another ritual may subsequently feel uncomfortable, anxious that something will indeed go wrong as a result. There is a kind of conviction involved, but one that is removed, to varying degrees, from the consensus world and from all those things that are taken to be the case in another kind of way. Only when the referent of "belief" is identified exclusively with this latter kind of conviction does the person honestly and unequivocally assert the belief that not *p*.

What, then, of philosophical beliefs—could the category "philosophical belief" encompass different kinds of conviction, where those differences generally pass unacknowledged? Plausibly, yes. Consider some remarks by William James, to the effect that the endorsement of broad philosophical doctrines is more a matter of feeling than an outcome of reasoning and argument: "in the metaphysical and religious sphere, articulate reasons are cogent for us only when our inarticulate feelings of reality have already been impressed in favor of the same conclusion" (1902,74). Now, even if this is true, it does not imply that adopting a philosophical position can involve different *ways of believing*. All it suggests is that feelings steer us toward philosophical beliefs with one or another content. But James's view is more complicated than this. He claims that different philosophical *temperaments* amount to different ways of experiencing one's relationship with the world, involving different *senses* of reality. Here is how he contrasts his own philosophical world with that of the rationalist:

> The "through-and-through" universe seems to suffocate me with its infallible impeccable all-pervasiveness. Its necessity, with no possibilities; its relations, with no subjects, make me feel as if I had entered into a contract with no reserved rights, or rather as if I had to live in a large seaside boarding-house with no private bedroom in which I might take refuge from the society of the place. ... It seems too buttoned-up and white-chokered and clean-shaven a thing to speak for the vast slow-breathing unconscious Kosmos with its dread abysses and its unknown tides. (James 1912, 276–278)

The universe in which James lives, and from which his philosophy springs, differs not only in content but also in form from that of the rationalist. This interpretation is consistent with James's earlier account of the different "sub-universes" we inhabit (also mentioned in chapter 6), where he indicates that the worlds of everyday life, of science, of religion, and of madness differ not only in terms of content; they also have different "styles" of existence (James 1889). The rationalist believes certain things in a different *way* to James; her beliefs are decoupled from how she experiences the world, and the flag of truth is instead placed in an abstract, purified realm. So the disagreement, as he diagnoses it, is not merely a matter of different belief contents, toward which the two parties are steered in part by different feelings. It is also a difference in their respective senses of conviction, in *how* something is taken to be the case or otherwise. For James, a certain kind of conviction is not appropriate to the "vast slow-breathing unconscious Kosmos."

The view that philosophical belief encompasses different kinds of intentionality is also complemented by Schutz's (1945) development of James's ideas (introduced in chapter 6). For Schutz, the difference between a set of religious beliefs and a set of scientific beliefs is not just a matter of content, or at least need not be. The belief systems arise, he suggests, in the context of different "provinces of meaning" (referred to by James as sub-universes), each of which has its own distinctive "cognitive style." And what Schutz means by a cognitive style is a way of believing, a kind of intentionality. As he puts it, the worlds of "dreams, of imageries and phantasms, especially the world of art, the world of religious experience, the world of scientific contemplation, the play world of the child, and the world of the insane" all have "a specific accent of reality" (1945, 552–553). These forms of conviction, he adds, are all abstracted to varying degrees and in different ways from what he calls the world of "work," from purposive, practical engagement in a shared, consensus realm. Other meaning provinces are "modifications" of this "paramount reality," all of which involve a selective loss of structure (555). As we saw in chapter 6, imagination involves a departure from the overarching style of anticipation and fulfillment that is integral to perceptual experience. Schutz indicates that the same applies to belief. There are different ways of believing, which depart, in more or less subtle ways, from taking something to be the case or otherwise in the course of our habitual, purposive, practical engagement with the world.

When previously held beliefs are revised or altogether rejected, the process does not always involve simple acknowledgment of falsehood or implausibility. Belief change does not just concern the *contents* of beliefs; it can also involve recognizing that a *type* of conviction previously adopted was somehow inadequate to a given subject matter. We first take ourselves to believe that *p*, and then come to appreciate that we did not really believe that *p*. For example, Susan Brison (2002, x), herself an academic philosopher, describes how she found her philosophical beliefs ineffective, even irrelevant, in the face of traumatic experience inflicted by another person: "When I was confronted with the utterly strange and paradoxical, philosophy was of no use in making me feel at home in the world." Such experiences can present one with a stark contrast between different kinds of conviction. Even if one has always explicitly and honestly endorsed the proposition "the world is unsafe," one might do so with a different kind of conviction after experiencing traumatic events. It was in relation to an abstract realm, a realm somehow removed from everyday life, that the proposition "the world is unsafe" was accepted. In another way, the world was never taken to be unsafe; all experiences and activities were permeated by prereflective, habitual confidence and trust. Traumatic experience can thus make explicit the differences between kinds of conviction, ways of taking things to be the case, which may be adequate to one meaning province but ineffective or irrelevant with respect to another. In the case of trauma, certain kinds of conviction reveal themselves as inadequate to one's "paramount reality."

A particularly striking illustration of contrasting forms of conviction can be found in Jean Améry's book, *At the Mind's Limits*, which recounts his experience of torture and subsequent incarceration in Auschwitz. At one point, he compares the reality of life in the camp to the continuing attempts by some prisoners to pursue intellectual debates:

> To reach out beyond concrete reality with words became before our very eyes a game that was not only worthless and an impermissible luxury but also mocking and evil. ... Nowhere else in the world did reality have as much effective power as in the camp, nowhere else was reality so real. (1999, 19)

Such debates, he maintains, involved a type of conviction that had no bearing on the reality he and they were confronted with. In the case of philosophical utterances, he remarks:

> Where they still meant something they appeared trivial, and where they were not trivial they no longer meant anything. We didn't require any semantic analysis or logical syntax to recognize this. A glance at the watchtowers, a sniff of burnt fat from the crematories sufficed. ... In the camp the intellect in its totality declared itself to be incompetent. (19)

Although the circumstances he describes are quite exceptional, and the contrast especially heightened, explicit recognition of different ways of believing also occurs in a range of other situations. For instance, in his first-person account of grief, C. S. Lewis (1966) describes an associated crisis of religious faith. Among other things, this involved a realization that beliefs he previously held concerning illness, death, isolation, and their compatibility with a benevolent God were decoupled from the realities of these phenomena:

> If my house has collapsed at one blow, that is because it was a house of cards. The faith which "took these things into account" was not faith but imagination. The taking them into account was not real sympathy. If I had really cared, as I thought I did, about the sorrows of the world, I should not have been so overwhelmed when my own sorrow came. It has been an imaginary faith playing with innocuous counters labelled "Illness," "Pain," "Death" and "Loneliness." I thought I trusted the rope until it mattered to me whether it would bear me. Now it matters, and I find I didn't. (1966, 32–33)

What Lewis's grief exposes is a kind of pseudo-conviction. In one sense, his earlier beliefs about illness, death, pain, and loneliness were quite sincere and held with genuine conviction. Yet they were removed from the realities of phenomena and related instead to an imagined world. In this latter world, phenomena are replaced by "counters" or linguistic concepts that move freely of the paramount reality where grief and loneliness are felt. So beliefs of this kind involve a kind of oblivious make-believe, a simulacrum that the person fails to explicitly distinguish from a more fundamental sense of rootedness in an interpersonal world. For Lewis, this style of conviction collapses when the reality of grief turns out to demand something quite different in kind.

Of course, differences between forms of philosophical conviction are not ordinarily so extreme. Nevertheless, they remain a potential source of confusion. Given the limitations of the current philosophical lexicon, it is in fact quite possible to believe that *p* while at the same time believing that not *p*. Indeed, the coexistence of subtly different attitudes of "belief" with conflicting or even contradictory contents may well be ubiquitous. By implication, it is also possible for one philosopher to believe that *p* while another believes that not *p*, without there being any straightforward disagreement between them.[2] The relevant beliefs can involve different attitudes, different ways of taking something to be the case, different meaning-provinces. Hence, when it comes to philosophical debate, disagreements often prove elusive, and it is commonplace for neither party to find the other's arguments compelling. I think this is what James is attempting to describe in the following passage:

> [The philosopher] *trusts* his temperament. Wanting a universe that suits it, he believes in any representation of the universe that does suit it. He feels men of opposite temper to be out of key with the world's character, and in his heart considers them incompetent and "not in it," in the philosophical business, even though they may far excel him in dialectical ability. ... There arises thus a certain insincerity in our philosophic discussions: the potentest of all our premises is never mentioned. (1907/1981, 8–9)

The feeling that someone is "out of key with the world's character" can involve, I suggest, a sense that he has adopted the wrong kind of conviction toward a subject matter, a way of believing that is somehow inappropriate to it. As with some delusions and hallucinations, everyday life and also philosophical thought can involve forms of double-bookkeeping: we believe something in one way while not believing it in another. However, where everyday and philosophical beliefs are concerned, the phenomenon is more subtle. For instance, none of the relevant beliefs are formed in isolation from a wider community, at least not to the same extent.[3] If all of this is right, we are faced with the difficult tasks of specifying the kind of conviction that is appropriate to a given subject matter, what the criteria are for determining appropriateness, what kind of normativity is involved in appropriateness, and whether different kinds of conviction are appropriate to different areas of philosophical enquiry. Such issues will also complicate discussions of rationality. Whether or not a given combination of beliefs is to be deemed rational will depend on whether or not those beliefs are all of the same type. All of this makes doing philosophy more difficult and, I would say, even more interesting.

The argument of this book also has potential implications for neurobiological research and clinical practice. With regard to the former, a detailed phenomenological account of local and global changes in the structure of experience can serve to sharpen up the explananda for scientific study, and to distinguish phenomena that might otherwise be regarded as belonging to the same psychological type, as in the case of VHs (verbal hallucinations). In addition, I have suggested that more emphasis needs to be placed on the interpersonal, the social, and the cultural, thus emphasizing the limitations of approaches that restrict themselves to what is going on inside an individual's brain.

As for psychiatry, my emphasis has not been so much on the legitimacy of one or another established diagnostic category. Instead, I have sought to formulate a wider perspective, a way of thinking that clarifies the relational dimensions of psychiatric illness. Nevertheless, I have also suggested that VHs of one or another type are not reliably associated with specific diagnostic categories. Neither are they to be regarded as isolated symptoms; they involve wide-ranging disturbances in the structure of experience and cannot be adequately understood in isolation from those disturbances. I have not ruled out the possibility of tidying up diagnostic categories, in order to distinguish between causal processes and/or the types of outcome (including kinds of experience) that one or more processes lead to. For instance, in the case of "schizophrenia," it could well be that a subset of schizophrenia diagnoses correspond to a certain type of causal process, a distinctive type of "self disorder," or both. Phenomenological analysis has an ongoing role to play here, in uncovering differences between phenomena that might otherwise be regarded as similar in kind, and in identifying underlying commonalities between phenomena that are superficially different (Minkowski 1970). It can therefore contribute to the revision and fine-tuning of diagnostic categories, so long as those categories remain based, at least in part, on the relevant phenomenology.

That said, I am doubtful that the best way to proceed is by identifying clusters of symptoms and associating them with diagnostic labels. Alterations in an overarching sense of confidence or certainty can involve long-term processes that are inextricable from changing relations with other people. A disturbance in the modal structure of intentionality could result from any combination of prior vulnerabilities, anomalous experiences, traumatic events, other life events, long-term situations involving other people, how a person reacts to his anomalous experiences, how other people react to him, how experiences are interpreted, and so forth. Importantly, in most cases, the trajectory will be shaped by how other people respond at one or another stage. Now, diagnostic categories can be conceived of in a more or less committal way. For instance, one could regard them as objective disease categories or merely as pragmatically motivated idealizations that are useful for at least some purposes. However permissively they might be regarded, the kinds of experience addressed here should at least be construed in a *dynamic* way, in terms of intra- and interpersonal processes of variable duration as opposed to freeze-framed symptom clusters. This is compatible with the retention of diagnostic categories that acknowledge the interpersonal and social dynamics of psychiatric illness. But perhaps they are not needed. Such processes could just as well be conceptualized in terms of idealized life-narratives, which capture individual cases with varying degrees of success by drawing on many different areas of expertise and sources of evidence. When presented with a particular case, a clinician or therapist could use one or more of these exemplars in order to make causal associations, anticipate unfolding patterns, and consider appropriate responses, gradually moving from the general to the particular.

What I am thinking of is similar in some respects to what De Sousa (1987, 182), in addressing the nature of emotion, calls "paradigm scenarios." His suggestion is that we learn to label our various emotional responses and to associate them with types of situation through exposure to and enculturation into shared narratives and performances. A paradigm scenario is a culturally variable exemplar that serves to illustrate how a type of emotion plays out and also to specify when it is appropriate. The development of an emotional repertoire thus depends on education and training, on learning what to feel and when to feel it. The process has no clear end point and people's emotional lives have differing degrees of sophistication:

> We are made familiar with the vocabulary of emotion by association with *paradigm scenarios*. These are drawn first from our daily life as small children and later reinforced by the stories, art, and culture to which we are exposed. Later still, in literate cultures, they are supplemented and refined by literature. Paradigm scenarios involve two aspects: first, a situation type providing the characteristic *objects* of the specific emotion-type ... and second, a set of characteristic or "normal" *responses* to the situation, where normality is first a biological matter and then very quickly becomes a cultural one. (De Sousa 1987, 182)

In an analogous way, idealized narratives can enable clinicians, researchers, and others to recognize salient situation-response patterns, as well as identify potentially appropriate ways of further exploring and intervening in those patterns. Such narratives can also guide interpretation by patients, clinicians, and others, which itself has an important role to play in shaping and regulating the experience and behavior of all parties concerned. Disturbances in the modal structure of intentionality, and the ways in which these disturbances unfold, cannot be separated from interpersonal and social relations. So we are most likely faced with a range of different processes and outcomes, which depend in part on how people relate to and interpret each other within wider social and cultural contexts. For this reason, idealized narratives, along the lines briefly sketched, may well be the most we can realistically hope for, at least where the various predicaments addressed here are concerned. At a given time, an individual case might resemble however many narratives to differing degrees and in different ways. And it is not clear that labeling these narratives and then insisting that the labels amount to rigid "diagnoses" would render them any more enlightening or practically informative.

Of course, some stories are more accurate than others, and some are more effective than others in furthering one or another aim. I have proposed that, to understand the kinds of experience associated with many forms of psychiatric illness and how those experiences arise, we need to acknowledge the following: (a) the modal structure of intentionality and its susceptibility to disruption; (b) the extent to which the integrity of experience depends on relations with others; and (c) the various ways in which erosion of trust, confidence, or certainty can come about. These themes can assist us in understanding a person's current predicament, how it originated, where it is likely to lead, and how its trajectory might be influenced. Disruptions of the structure of intentionality, however they might occur, are always to some extent relational in nature, rather than purely individual phenomena. So intervention of whatever kind involves engaging in a relational and potentially transformative interpersonal process, rather than treating something that unfolds in relative isolation from social conditions. Although there are many kinds of vulnerability, many trajectories, and many subtly different outcomes, I have emphasized throughout that forms of loneliness and social estrangement are central to the worlds of many psychiatric patients. This applies to some philosophical orientations as well.

Notes

1 Introduction

1. For current purposes, "intentional state" is a term of convenience, and does not imply any commitment to experience having a "state-like" character. One could equally refer to "intentional attitudes" or simply "kinds of intentionality."

2. By "content," I mean simply "what is experienced and how it appears," such as "a cup as experienced visually." Hence it is a fairly noncommittal phenomenological notion, rather than something that implies commitment to "mental representation" in one or another guise. Despite philosophical baggage associated with the term "content," I still find it helpful, insofar as it serves to emphasize what is experienced and how it appears, as opposed to other aspects of experience that might be postulated, such as the act of experiencing itself, or constituents of experience that may not fit neatly into either category. One could of course adopt a conception of content according to which phenomenology, or phenomenology alone, does not serve to specify or fully specify content. As with nonphenomenological conceptions of intentionality, I do not want to rule out such an approach, but I restrict my inquiry to what the phenomenology does include.

3. Elsewhere, I have adopted a philosophical method that is more explicitly anchored in the phenomenological tradition. It draws, in particular, on work by Husserl and Heidegger, and centrally involves my own (somewhat liberal) interpretation and endorsement of the "phenomenological reduction" (Ratcliffe 2008; 2015). What I do here is compatible with that approach but does not demand it.

4. See, e.g., Gallagher and Zahavi 2008 for discussion of various accounts of how interaction between phenomenology and cognitive science should proceed.

2 Schizophrenia and Selfhood

1. Because the term "minimal self" refers to an inextricable aspect of experience, rather than an isolable entity or "thing," I tend to write "minimal self" rather than "*the* minimal self."

2. The "minimal self" account of schizophrenia complements a much larger body of literature in phenomenological psychopathology, which has accumulated over the past century. A consistent theme is that schizophrenia involves a global change in the structure of experience, one that is both qualitatively different from and more profound than the kinds of disturbance associated with other psychiatric diagnoses. That view is broadly consistent with the earliest descriptions of dementia praecox/ schizophrenia offered by Emil Kraepelin and Eugen Bleuler. Both identify a family of disease processes, all characterized by a disruption of self-experience involving pervasive changes in perception, emotion, thought, and agency. According to Kraepelin (1919, 3), there is a "peculiar destruction of the internal connections of the psychic personality," while Bleuler (1950, 9) refers to a "splitting of the psychic functions," where "the personality loses its unity." The tradition of phenomenological psychopathology has further emphasized and elaborated on the theme of a profound shift in the sense of self, something that is taken to be inextricable from experience of the surrounding world, other people, one's body, and one's thoughts, perceptions, emotions, and activities. The "minimal self" view is consistent with this wider tradition. For references to complementary themes in earlier phenomenological writings, see, e.g., Sass 2001 and Fuchs 2012.

3. Sass, for instance, acknowledges that self-disorder is not exclusive to schizophrenia, and also occurs in conditions such as depersonalization syndrome. However, he adds that there is something distinctive and more profound about changes in the sense of self that arise in schizophrenia; they involve an "erosion" or "dissolution" of "first-person perspective" to the extent that "self and other can seem fused or confused" (Sass 2014a, 8).

4. Others have offered complementary descriptions of loss of self. For example, "the real 'me' is not here any more. I am disconnected, disintegrated, diminished. Everything I experience is through a dense fog, created by my own mind, yet it also resides outside my mind. I feel that my real self has left me, seeping through the fog toward a separate reality, which engulfs and dissolves this self" (Kean 2009, 1034).

5. The proximity claim does not apply to all cases, and the extent of its applicability depends on what the content of perceptual experience is taken to consist of. If we can correctly be said to *hear something exploding*, then we can perceive some things through audition that are a considerable distance away. Similarly, if it is right to say that we can *see a star*, rather than first seeing something and then conceiving of it in those terms, vision is not a proximity sense either. In the latter case, it can be added that what we perceive need not be present, as the light takes millions of years to

reach us. However, even if that were allowed, we *experience* something or other as present, and it is this experience of perceptual presence that concerns me here.

6. It is questionable whether or how our phenomenology is sensitive to more refined distinctions, such as that between physical, metaphysical, and logical possibility.

7. Although the question is phrased contrastively, the relevant achievement need not take that form. It could be that I take myself to be perceiving, pure and simple. That I am "not remembering" is implied by this, rather than integral to it.

8. See, e.g., Strawson 2004, for an outright dismissal of the view that intentionality can be treated independently of experience. Horgan and Tienson (2002) also argue that the two are inseparable. They go so far as to maintain that there is a kind of intentionality that is constituted entirely by its phenomenology. My view is not so strong. Where we are concerned with organisms that do have experiences *of* things, I agree that a complete separation of intentionality and phenomenology is untenable. In such cases, I take it that the phenomenology is sufficient for being in some type of intentional state, but that it is not always sufficient to determine which type of intentional state one is in.

9. See the essays in Bayne and Montague 2011 for several different positions concerning the existence and nature of cognitive phenomenology. See also Breyer and Gutland 2016 for a collection of essays that bring the cognitive phenomenology debate into dialogue with work in the phenomenological tradition.

10. See also Roessler 2013 for the point that phenomenological approaches have failed to explain how global changes in the structure of experience generate certain more specific symptoms. A similar criticism applies to a whole family of "self-monitoring" accounts, which propose that AVHs arise due to failure of a mechanism that ordinarily monitors and self-ascribes inner speech (e.g., Frith 1992). Such accounts have not explained why the relevant disruption is both sporadic and content specific.

11. For details of the Hearing Voices Network, see http://www.hearing-voices.org/. For Intervoice, see http://www.intervoiceonline.org/. Both sites last accessed on February 23, 2016.

12. The Hearing Voices Movement is critical of terms such as "psychosis," "delusion," and "auditory hallucination," on the basis that they can stigmatize people and exacerbate emotional distress. The terms "hearing voices" and "having unusual beliefs" are suggested as alternatives (Romme and Escher 2012, 1). I continue to use the term "AVH" here, partly because it is established in much of the literature to be addressed, but also because one of my aims is to progressively reveal the inadequacy of this term, at least if it is construed as an informative way of *describing* the range of phenomena to which it refers. To say that something is an AVH tells us very little about what the relevant experience consists of and serves in some cases to mislead.

13. However, I complicate this view in chapters 4 and 7, by suggesting that it is sometimes not possible to separate the experience of something *as* an AVH from associated distress. Furthermore, there may be no fact of the matter as to when a voice has *gone* and when it is *still present but no longer distressing*. The same phenomenological change could be described in either of these ways.

14. Others have defended a similar position. For example, Andrew, Gray, and Snowden (2008) claim that trauma influences beliefs about voices, which in turn cause distress. So the voices cause distress only if the voice-hearer responds to them in a particular way, one that is contingent and malleable.

15. Given the emphasis on interpreting voices in terms of unpleasant life events from which a person has emotionally dissociated herself, this approach shares obvious similarities with earlier conceptions of multiple personality disorder. Indeed, in some of the hearing voices literature, one need only substitute the term "voice" for "personality." Hence it is arguable that similar concerns apply to both approaches. Work on multiple personality disorder fell into disrepute when therapists began unearthing stories of historical abuse that could not possibly have been true (see, e.g., Hacking 1992 for a discussion). We can add to this a further concern: if, as I go on to argue, some of these phenomena involve erosion of the boundaries between intentional state types, some voice-hearers may be particularly vulnerable to confusion between memories and imaginings. This is not to discredit the approach or to dismiss testimonies of abuse, many of which are highly credible. But what it does suggest is that the presumption of abuse on the part of a therapist would be highly problematic, as would uncritical attempts to seek out histories of abuse. With that in mind, I have serious misgivings about how testimonies were obtained by Romme et al. (2009, 321–322). They asked respondents to report only the "benefits" of the "accepting voices approach," thus taking for granted that there are benefits and also steering them away from mentioning any shortcomings or negative effects. More worrying still is the fact that the authors supplied an "example" to help people prepare their own responses. It refers to sexual abuse in the third line and then, in the second paragraph, dismisses orthodox psychiatry as unsympathetic and pharmacologically driven. It would not be uncharitable to view this as an instruction manual, telling people what to say. Sure enough, most of the fifty detailed first-person accounts included in the book refer to similar themes. Even so, many other sources point to a connection between AVHs and histories of interpersonal trauma (see, e.g., the essays collected in Larkin and Morrison 2006). I address this connection further in chapters 5 and 6.

16. See also Ratcliffe 2007, chapters 5 and 6, for a discussion of the nature of second-person experience, in childhood and in adulthood.

17. In suggesting that introspective access to experience is unable to arbitrate here, this approach is consistent with Schwitzgebel (2008), who raises a number of

concerns about the reliability of what he calls "introspective" access to our own mental states.

18. See also Macpherson 2013 for a clear discussion of various philosophical approaches to perception, including forms of disjunctivism.

19. See also Allen 2015, who addresses how a mistaken imaginings account of hallucination might complement a disjunctivist theory of perception.

20. Gerrans (2014) also offers an account of delusions that questions the applicability of a belief–imagination distinction. He suggests that there is no fact of the matter over whether delusions are beliefs or imaginings. Rather than worrying about which category to put them in, we should get on with the task of providing a mechanistic account of the relevant phenomena. Once we have that, the issue of whether to label them as beliefs or imaginings will quite rightly seem unimportant. Gerrans's positive proposal appeals to the "default mode network," a cognitive system that "represents personally relevant information as narrative elements," which are sometimes but not always synthesized into larger narratives (xv). He suggests that delusions occur when the default mode network responds to certain kinds of salient information in a way that is not supervised by "decontextualized processing" (xix). I am sympathetic to Gerrans's insistence that we figure out what is actually going on, rather than worrying about what we should label as a belief. Although he is largely concerned with nonconscious mechanisms while I seek to address the associated phenomenology, our approaches are also potentially complementary in some respects. For instance, it could well be that some or all changes in the modal structure of intentionality are associated with changes in the functionality of the default mode network. However, as I will argue in chapter 6, more emphasis on the interpersonal and the social is also needed in order to understand these phenomena. They cannot be satisfactorily accounted for by appealing exclusively to what happens inside brains.

3 Thought Insertion Clarified

1. But see Noë 2012 for one recent philosophical discussion of perception that emphasizes presence. Noë also acknowledges that experiences of presence can differ qualitatively, as well as quantitatively. We can, he writes, "speak of the *modality* or *quality* of presence, as opposed merely to its intensity or degree" (34).

2. See Dorsch 2010 for a recent attempt to catalog the "reality characteristics" distinctive of perceptual experience, by drawing on the work of Aggernaes et al. See also Farkas 2013 for a recent discussion of Aggernaes's criteria.

3. Elsewhere, Graham (2004, 96) does state more specifically that TI concerns the "phenomenology of thinking." The "activity" of thinking, he suggests, is ascribed to someone else. For two discussions of TI that explicitly distinguish between episodes of thinking and thought contents, see Roessler 2013 and Vosgerau and Voss 2014.

4. Another advantage of this interpretation is that it points to a clear distinction between the kinds of alienation-experience involved in TI and in obsessive-compulsive thoughts. To speculate, in the case of compulsive thoughts, the person cannot stop herself thinking about something and feels alienated from acts of thinking that are to varying degrees estranged from her own agency. Even so, experiencing thought processes as distressing and somehow outside of her control involves continuing to recognize them as thought processes. So this is quite unlike the alienation of TI, which involves a content seeming to emanate from elsewhere because there is *no* experience of thinking it.

5. See also Austin 1962, whose work Sarbin (1967) draws on, for a discussion of problems involved in specifying the meaning of the word "real" in different situations.

6. As Langland-Hassan (2008, 373) remarks, "patients may be using normal modes of expression in a rough-and-ready way, in order to communicate the nature of experiences that do not fall neatly into any preexisting category."

7. The study was conducted as part of the Wellcome Trust–funded project "Hearing the Voice" in 2013, by several members of the project. It received ethical approval from the Durham University Philosophy Department Research Committee. Study design was closely modeled on earlier work addressing the phenomenology of depression (for details, see Ratcliffe 2015). Participants were recruited via a number of advertisements and invited to provide free-text responses to several questions about voices and voice-like experiences. Respondents quoted in this book reported having the following psychiatric diagnoses: schizophrenia (8, 32, 34, 37); schizoaffective disorder (9, 33, 35, 38); borderline personality disorder (1, 3, 4, 6); dissociative identity disorder (2, 5, 36); post-traumatic stress disorder (21, 22); psychosis (unspecified) (7, 10, 12, 15); bipolar disorder (17, 19, 20, 25, 28); major depression (6, 18, 23, 27, 30, 31). Nineteen of these respondents self-identified as female (2, 3, 4, 5, 6, 7, 10, 17, 18, 19, 20, 21, 22, 23, 27, 28, 30, 35, 37), nine as male (1, 8, 9, 12, 25, 31, 32, 33, 34), and three as other (15, 36, 38). There were no restrictions on who could participate in the study, and potential responses thus encompassed anything that a participant might interpret in terms of "hearing voices" or having "voice-like" experiences. Given this breadth, one could not hope to assemble a cohesive account that accommodated all testimonies, and I instead draw on them selectively.

8. See also Ratcliffe (2015, chap. 1) for a detailed discussion of the methodological issues to be kept in mind when interpreting and drawing on testimonies of this kind.

9. Billon (2013, 306) makes the complementary observation that TI is "somehow akin" to being perceptually presented with sentences or images. But he offers an account according to which inserted thoughts, unlike thoughts more generally, are not "phenomenally conscious." TI, he suggests, involves having a conscious experience of something that is not itself part of one's consciousness and thus appears alien to it. While I maintain that TI involves experiencing one's thoughts in a per-

ception-like way, I do not attribute this to a lack of "first-order phenomenology." Rather, it is a matter of taking oneself to be intentional state *x*, rather than *y*. As we will see in chapter 4, this can be accounted for without appealing to a distinction between phenomenally conscious and unconscious thoughts.

10. See also Aleman and Larøi 2008, 48–49, for a discussion of AVHs in deaf people.

11. See also Garrett and Silva 2003, 453, for the suggestion that VHs involve "a new category of experience that blends elements of perception and thought but remains distinct from both." However, they continue to emphasize the sensory qualities of VHs, whereas I do not.

12. See also Sass 2014b for a detailed discussion of double-bookkeeping, which acknowledges that there can be different types of deviation from the sense of reality or presence.

13. The view that TI involves intact ownership in the absence of agency is also challenged by de Haan and de Bruin (2010), who argue that agency and ownership are inseparable and that both are diminished in TI.

14. Here, I am in agreement with Sousa and Swiney (2013, 644), who adopt a similarly deflationary account of ownership. Talk of "ownership," they note, can have all sorts of different connotations. Where TI is concerned, it is another way of saying that one is not the agent of the thought: "The patient is simply emphasizing via the language of thought ownership that she does not have the sense of being the producer ('source') of the thoughts." See Gallagher 2015 for a response to several criticisms of the agency–ownership distinction and for further clarification of his own view. So far as I can see, his various responses and refinements do not pose a challenge to my own concerns about the agency–ownership distinction as applied to TI, even though they may amount to a case for its applicability elsewhere.

15. Recent contributions to the discussion of agency and ownership/subjectivity in TI have further complicated the distinction. For instance, Maiese (2015) distinguishes subjectivity from ownership on the basis that one can have an intact sense of subjectivity in the absence of both agency and ownership, where ownership involves the experience of a thought arising within a wider affective context. Martin and Pacherie (2013) similarly distinguish ownership from subjectivity, while Vosgerau and Voss (2014) distinguish agency from authorship and seek to understand TI in terms of an ownership–authorship distinction. My claim that the original distinction is uninformative in the case of TI applies equally to such refinements, revisions, and elaborations. TI simply concerns the kind of intentional state one takes oneself to be in, not whether one is the agent, subject, author, or owner of that state, regardless of how those terms might be understood. In appealing to one and then another distinction, there is the risk of incessantly describing and redescribing the phenomenon in ways that distract from the task of understanding it.

4 Voices of Anxiety

1. See, e.g., Glas 2003 for a detailed discussion of differing clinical conceptions of anxiety.

2. Hence what I address here is not to be identified with "anxiety" (*Angst*) in the more specific Heideggerian sense of the term. I am not in any way concerned with Heidegger here. For a detailed discussion of Heidegger on anxiety, see Ratcliffe 2013b.

3. It has become something of a commonplace in the VH literature to observe that "voices" do not just occur in psychiatric illness and that many nonclinical, healthy subjects have them too (e.g., Watkins 2008; McCarthy-Jones 2012, chap. 7). However, we should be wary of claims to the effect that VHs in clinical and nonclinical populations are very similar or even phenomenologically indistinguishable. Stanghellini at al. (2012) note that studies are seldom sufficiently attentive to potential phenomenological differences, and argue that detailed first-person descriptions in fact point to quite different kinds of experience. Henriksen, Raballo and Parnas (2015) also discuss various differences between VHs in schizophrenia and in healthy subjects. However, although they insist that certain kinds of VH are *schizophrenia specific*, they do not address, in any detail, the similarities and differences between those VHs associated with schizophrenia and those associated with other psychiatric diagnoses. The kinds of experience described in this chapter are certainly not specific to schizophrenia, but they are associated with profound changes in the structure of experience, as well as considerable distress. So, even when they do occur in the absence of a psychiatric diagnosis, they are not to be regarded as unproblematic, healthy experiences. I allow that other kinds of experience, which might similarly be described in terms of "hearing a voice," are more plausibly benign. Some of these are discussed in chapter 7.

4. Paulik, Badcock, and Maybery (2008) make the weaker claim that anxiety alone does not cause VHs but can exacerbate them, by interfering with an already compromised ability to suppress intrusive cognitions. In chapters 5 and 6, I also appeal to an additional factor: a weakening of the wider-ranging modal structure of intentionality. However, on my account, this is equally a matter of social anxiety and estrangement.

5. For a more detailed discussion of the relevant mechanisms and their roles in motor prediction and control, see, e.g., Frith, Blakemore, and Wolpert 2000. In their words, "whenever a movement is made, a motor command is generated by the CNS and a predictor estimates the sensory consequences of that motor command." They add that a "controller" matches the "desired state" with the "motor command required to achieve that state" (1772). These mechanisms, they suggest, have a range of functions, including compensating for the effects of movements, distinguishing self-generated movements from other movements, and reducing dependence on sensory feedback in action-guidance by relying on anticipatory processes.

6. The signal is often referred to as a "corollary discharge" and/or "efference copy." These terms are sometimes used as synonyms or near synonyms. However, other accounts draw a clear distinction between them. For example, Fletcher and Frith (2009, 50) define the efference copy as "an internal copy of a motor signal that can be used to predict the sensory consequences of the movement," while the corollary discharge is an "estimate of sensory feedback that is derived from the internal copy of the motor signal (the efference copy)." So the efference copy contains the information that a given action is about to occur, and the corollary discharge then predicts the sensory changes that the action will bring about.

7. This objection was first raised by Akins and Dennett (1986), against an account proposed by Hoffman (1986).

8. Gallagher's account also includes a more detailed discussion of temporal experience, which appeals to the work of Edmund Husserl and, more specifically, the concepts of "protention" and "retention" (e.g., Husserl 1991). In chapter 5, I draw on some related themes in Husserl's later writings. Gallagher associates protention with a sense of agency and retention with a sense of ownership. I argued in chapter 3 that the agency-ownership distinction is uninformative here, a view that is consistent with my discussion in this chapter. While Gallagher appeals to a *loss* of protention and thus a loss of experienced agency, I argue that VH/TI involves alteration of the short-term anticipatory (or "protentional") structure of experience, rather than loss.

9. The analogy is made more compelling by the observation that the somatic and affective components of pain are dissociable (Grahek 2007; Radden 2009, chap. 7). The sense of alienation I have described is attributable to the latter. See also Scarry 1985 for a discussion of the "undeniability" of pain.

10. Even so, we should not be too hasty in identifying the contents of VHs with "inner speech." Fernyhough (2004) rightly places the emphasis on "inner dialogue," rather than simply "speech," but it is also important to distinguish inner dialogue with ourselves from imagined dialogue with others. One person I spoke with informally told me how his anomalous experiences sometimes began with imagined interpersonal interactions, and that the imagined parties gradually developed a kind of autonomy, a life of their own. It could well be that some of those experiences labeled as VHs involve imagined interactions with others rather than inner dialogue. Even if it is admitted that inner dialogue also involves imagination, the point still applies: the two different forms of imagination need to be distinguished. See also Ratcliffe 2007, chap. 6, for the point that, when we imagine others, we tend not just to imagine them and what they will do but, rather, our interactions with them.

11. In fact, in his response to commentaries, Hoffman (1986, 542) acknowledges that VHs can cause distress and increase "arousal." He adds that "these increases in arousal could cause further disruptions in discourse planning and VHs. Thus, causality may be circular and difficult to tease apart."

12. My account of an increasingly determinate experience of thought content can be contrasted with assumptions that philosophers sometimes make about the phenomenology of thought. For instance, Tye and Wright (2011, 342) state that thought contents "do not *unfold* over time in the way that an event like a cricket match unfolds. Once one begins to think that claret is delightful, one has already *achieved* the thinking of it." However, they conceive of the unfolding of a thought as akin to the progressive unraveling of a sentence, and this is a mistake. It can instead be construed as a process whereby content becomes more specific and perhaps more coherent. While Tye and Wright conclude that there is a phenomenology of thinking but no phenomenology of thought content, we can instead take one aspect of the phenomenology of thinking to be the progressive resolution of thought content, something that involves a distinctive kind of anticipatory structure.

13. Although the account I have sketched here is a phenomenological one, I am at least open to the possibility that nonconscious anticipation of thought content could also trigger anxiety and contribute to a subsequent experience of that content as alien.

14. Birchwood et al. (2000) suggest that the distress associated with VHs is attributable to one's "relationship" with the voice rather than to the voice per se. I maintain that the two are inextricable. The sense of alienation from one's own thoughts, memories, or imaginings is constituted by a certain kind of anticipatory structure, a way of relating to a thematic content as it arises and while it lasts. Chapter 7 will address cases where a voice is said to persist in the context of a very different kind of relationship, where it is not dreaded but welcomed, and where what it "says" is benevolent or even supportive rather than distressing.

15. The claim that VH contents are anxiously anticipated is consistent with the finding that VHs are associated with heightened "self-focus" (Allen et al. 2005).

16. This account is taken from a response to another questionnaire study, on experiences of depression. The study was conducted in 2011 as part of the AHRC- and DFG-funded project "Emotional Experience in Depression." This respondent reported a diagnosis of severe depression with hypermanic traits. For full details of the study, see Ratcliffe 2015, chap. 1.

17. See also Bortolotti and Broome 2009.

18. Some of the other responses to the questionnaire study introduced in chapter 3 also mention experiencing an echo, but I am not aware of any research addressing this aspect of the experience. An interesting avenue of enquiry would be to explore the prevalence of "echoes" in VH experiences, especially internal VHs of the kind described here, and to see whether all reports of echoes can be understood as follows: one *feels* something before it is manifested in a more determinate, linguistic way.

19. My position is therefore consistent with the view that the difference between external, audition-like VHs and internal, thought-like VHs is a matter of degree, and

that the term "VH" accommodates a spectrum of experiences (Humpston and Broome 2016).

20. Interestingly, Sass (1992, 434, n. 100) does entertain the possibility that schizophrenia may be an "arousal disorder" that involves anxiety, rather than an information-processing disorder. He also speculates on how this might account for the kinds of experience he addresses. In so doing, he refers to the work of Gjerde (1983), who seeks to account for the symptoms of schizophrenia in terms of high levels of arousal that influence attention, impacting on a wide range of cognitive tasks. For Gjerde, there is an underlying, nonspecific "deficit in attentional capacity" (1983, 62).

5 Trauma and Trust

1. Radden (2011, xv) suggests that "delusions" are better regarded as a "heterogeneous assemblage," and that accounts such as Jaspers', which involve a "bulwark of central cases," are therefore problematic. I agree with her view, and at no point do I claim to address all of those phenomena that might be labeled as "delusions." I further suggest, in chapter 6, that what Jaspers calls "delusional atmosphere" is itself heterogeneous in character. The point applies equally to hallucinations and their wider phenomenological context.

2. See also Henriksen 2013 for a recent discussion of incomprehensibility in schizophrenia.

3. Here, I am in complete agreement with Sass (e.g., 2014b) in maintaining that delusional atmosphere is not phenomenologically intractable. See also Ratcliffe 2013a; 2015, chap. 10.

4. Definitions of torture are contested. According to the Istanbul Protocol, it involves inflicting mental or physical suffering in order to punish, intimidate, obtain information, or extract a confession, and a public official must be implicated. It may involve punishment for something the victim or someone else has done, where the aim is to punish the victim and/or punish somebody else who cares about the victim. Others reject the "public official" condition as too restrictive. For instance, Kenny (2010) instead emphasizes the "instrumentality" of torture: suffering is intentionally caused in order to elicit a behavioral response, in a situation where the torturer has control over the victim. See Peters 1996 for several different definitions of torture.

5. As suggested by ICD-10, in such cases it is "unnecessary to consider personal vulnerabilities in order to explain its profound effect on the personality" (World Health Organization 1992, 209).

6. Hence we can distinguish, among other things, between individual and shared trauma—between those traumatic events that are endured alone and those that are suffered alongside others, sometimes by whole communities or cultures. There may

also be significant cultural differences in the experiences themselves and how they are narrated (see, e.g., Kirmayer 1996). I focus primarily on the case of individual trauma, where suffering is inflicted on a specific individual, although much of what I will say about loss of trust, security, and confidence applies more widely as well.

7. Exactly how this happens is debatable, and the aim here is to describe the resulting experience rather than to offer a precise account of the mechanisms via which it occurs. The victim might well form explicit judgments to the effect that "the interpersonal world is not as I took it to be," which in turn influence her overall style of anticipation. However, it is unlikely that the change in anticipatory style occurs solely via this route. In other situations, conflicts between explicit evaluative judgments and anticipatory style are commonplace. For example, someone who is bitten by a dog may then experience dogs as menacing and unpredictable, despite knowing full well that the incident was anomalous. The point applies equally to the more profound and pervasive effects of interpersonal trauma.

8. For example, Jones (2004, 6) offers the following analysis of three-place trust: "Trust is accepted vulnerability to another person's power over something that one cares about, where (1) the truster forgoes searching (at the time) for ways to reduce such vulnerability, and (2) the truster maintains normative expectations of the one-trusted that they do not use that power to harm what is entrusted."

9. See also Baier 1986, Stolorow 2007, 2011, and Bernstein 2011 for complementary descriptions of what I have called "one-place trust."

10. Experiences of depression are often described in these terms too. See Ratcliffe 2015 for a detailed discussion.

11. Alternatively, belief could be distinguished from an affective, practical responsiveness that usually accompanies it. For example, Gendler (2008) distinguishes "belief" from what she calls "alief." Those who accept such a distinction can say that B believes that *p* and that, following the traumatic event, B also comes to alieve that *p*.

12. As Corbí (2012, 55) observes, a "certain kind of awareness of some facts, deeper than mere knowledge of them, seems to be required to account for the conditions under which our confidence in the world may be lost."

13. Husserl refers to actions in the service of perception as "kinaestheses": "We call these movements, which belong to the essence of perception and serve to bring the object of perception to givenness from all sides insofar as possible, kinaestheses" (1948/1973, §19, p. 84).

14. This perceptual process is often referred to in terms of Merleau-Ponty's theory of "maximal grip," and Husserl is seldom acknowledged (see, e.g., Dreyfus 2002).

15. See Ratcliffe 2015, chaps. 2 and 3, for a more detailed discussion and defense of this point.

16. Noë (2012, 45) uses the term "style" in a similar way, in suggesting that perception and thought are distinctive "*styles* of access to what there is." However, he does not identify a *global style*, which the styles of the various intentional state types presuppose and depend on for their integrity and distinctness. Neither does he provide a detailed account of what the characteristic styles of different intentional state types consist in. He emphasizes only that perception and thought involve different kinds of skillful, practical access. This does not suffice to account for an experience such as VH/TI, which involves a quasi-perceptual experience of thought content, of a kind that does not involve skillful, exploratory activity resembling that associated with one or another sensory modality. Hence a more nuanced account of perceptual presence is needed.

17. See also Morley 2003 for an interesting discussion of Merleau-Ponty on the overall style of experience or "perceptual faith." Morley also relates disturbances of this aspect of experience to the phenomenology of psychiatric illness.

18. See also Scarry 1985 for a sustained argument to the effect that the aim of torture is not to interrogate but to destroy a person. For a comprehensive and convincing critique of the view that torture is an effective means of interrogation, see Costanzo and Gerrity 2009.

19. Extended periods of solitary confinement can similarly involve subversion of a habitual anticipatory style. The person is deliberately starved of kinds of interpersonal relation that were previously taken for granted, and the only kind of social relation that remains is one of powerlessness in the face of an individual or collective that deliberately inflicts harm (Guenther 2013).

20. This testimony is taken from a questionnaire study, which was conducted as part of AHRC- and DFG-funded project "Emotional Experience in Depression." The respondent had diagnoses of depression and PTSD. See Ratcliffe 2015, chap. 1, for further details of the study.

21. This is not to suggest that all Husserl's writings are consistent in this respect or that everything he says corresponds to the view advocated here.

6 Intentionality and Interpersonal Experience

1. Maclaren (2008, 79) describes the effect as follows: "When perceiving another, the other's intentionality sweeps us up and turns us away from the person herself, and towards that which she intends. To see her is to see *through her* towards the thing with which she is engaged. Her intentionality is, in other words, not itself an object of perception so much as a self-effacing directive."

2. We might speculate on the repercussions of this for a family of approaches to VH/TI discussed in chapter 4, according to which the experience arises due to a breakdown of nonconscious anticipation. On a strong reading of the claim that

one's own actions and those of others share a common functional architecture, a predictive mechanism would in fact be unable to distinguish self from nonself even when functioning properly, and so its breakdown could not account for misattribution of source. However, the problem can be avoided by maintaining that a mechanism for anticipating and compensating for the effects of action is common to both, but that a separate "I am initiating an action" signal is specific to the first-person case. This is consistent with Frith (2012), who suggests that delusions and hallucinations are specifically attributable to failure of a "predictive" component, rather than to a component that matches predicted with actual effects.

3. When one person experiences a situation as *ours*, rather than just *mine*, this does not imply that the two parties do in fact experience it in much the same way. The point is that they shape each other's experience of the surrounding environment and that some aspects of it are *experienced as shared*, as significant to *us* in one or another way.

4. These observations (and also my discussion of grief in chapter 7) complement the view that human experience can involve a form of "*plural pre-reflective self-awareness*" (Schmid 2014, 7). Things are first encountered as salient *to us* in one or another way, rather than to me and/or you.

5. Interpersonal experience in schizophrenia has been described in these terms. In some cases, others appear exclusively in the guise of a threat to the self, something that prohibits purposive engagement with shared situations and leaves a person feeling passive, helpless (see, e.g., Laing 1960). Lysaker, Johannesen, and Lysaker (2005) associate the theme of intersubjectivity as threat to an inability to maintain the integrity of "internal dialogue." Although the details differ, my account of VH/TI in chapter 4 is consistent with the suggestion that a change in the structure of interpersonal experience plays a role in disrupting inner dialogue: anxious anticipation of one's own thoughts, which constitutes a sense of alienation from them, corresponds to one's relationship with the social world as a whole.

6. This is consistent with Gerrans' (2014) suggestion that delusions arise when the products of "default thinking" are accepted without intervention from decontextualized cognitive processing. However, I would construe this "processing" in social rather than exclusively individual terms. When isolated from certain kinds of relation with other people, one is also isolated from certain kinds of critical process and from an appreciation of when these processes are appropriate. So estrangement from other people is partly responsible for a disposition toward uncritical acceptance.

7. William James (1897, 24) offers the following insightful remarks: "A social organism of any sort whatever, large or small, is what it is because each member proceeds to his own duty with a trust that the other members will simultaneously do theirs. Wherever a desired result is achieved by the co-operation of many independent persons, its existence as a fact is a pure consequence of the precursive faith in one another of those immediately concerned. A government, an army, a commercial

system, a ship, a college, an athletic team, all exist on this condition, without which not only is nothing achieved, but nothing is even attempted."

8. Colombetti and Krueger (2015) base their discussion on Sterelny's (2010) more general account of how cognition is "scaffolded" by environmental resources that are reliably configured so as to support the development and maintenance of certain abilities.

9. Although my discussion focuses on psychiatric illness, the effects of prolonged solitary confinement are also consistent with what I have said here. There is a difference between being forcibly denied a certain kind of interpersonal relation and experiencing the world as bereft of the possibility of that kind of relation. Nevertheless, the former could lead to the latter, to a progressive change in a person's sense of the kinds of interpersonal relation offered by the world. Guenther (2013) thus maintains that solitary confinement threatens "the most basic sense of identity" (xi). Other people, she says, more usually "support our capacity to make sense of the world, to distinguish between reality and illusion, to follow a train of thought or a causal sequence, and even to tell where our own bodily existence begins and ends" (146). In solitary confinement, a person's sense of the distinction between her body and her surroundings can break down, and she may have difficulty distinguishing waking from dreaming. However, there is a methodological difficulty here, as it is hard to tease apart the effects of interpersonal privation and more general sensory deprivation.

10. This passage was first inserted into the fourth edition, published in German in 1946.

11. This observation complements Sass's analysis, according to which delusional utterances sometimes originate in forms of experience that involve loss of a public reality and thus a quasi-solipsistic predicament (e.g., Sass 1994).

12. References to Wittgenstein refer to the text rather than to the year of publication (*On Certainty*: OC; *Philosophical Investigations*: PI) and to passage numbers rather than page numbers.

13. Hamilton (2014), in contrast, warns that we should not "exaggerate the role of 'non-propositional' certainty" in Wittgenstein's text (100). Nevertheless, he endorses, and attributes to Wittgenstein, a very permissive conception of "proposition." So the extent of substantive disagreement between his claim that hinges are "still somehow propositions" (118) and a refusal to ascribe them propositional status is not so clear.

14. This account of traumatic experience and, more specifically, traumatic memory is compatible with descriptions that emphasize changes in the structure of temporal experience, in the sense of what it is for something to be past, present, or future. For example: "Experiences of emotional trauma become freeze-framed into an eternal present in which one remains forever trapped, or to which one is condemned to be

perpetually returned. ... In the region of trauma, all duration or stretching along collapses; past becomes present, and future loses all meaning other than endless repetition" (Stolorow 2011, 55).

15. See Kirmayer 1996 for a wider-ranging discussion of trauma, dissociation, and narrative, which describes various relationships between traumatic events, memory, narrative, and culture.

16. See also Gallagher 2009b for an interesting application of James and Schutz on multiple realities to the topic of delusional reality. He writes: "It seems quite possible that one can enter into a delusional reality just as one can enter into a dream reality, or a fictional reality, or a virtual reality. Like other multiple realities, some delusional realities are ones that are *more or less* cut off from one's everyday reality" (255). He also notes that the delusional person may have trouble withdrawing from these realities. We can add that there is a distinction to be drawn between the contents of these realities and the kinds of intentionality involved. One does not simply take something to be the case in the context of a delusional reality. The reality itself involves taking things to be the case in a distinctive way.

17. For instance, symptoms of war trauma can be mitigated or exacerbated by the attitudes, narratives, and interpretive resources of a person's community (Hunt 2010).

18. See also Whitfield et al. 2005 and Kelleher et al. 2013 for discussion of the link between childhood trauma and hallucination.

19. Morgan and Gayer-Anderson (2016) raise a number of methodological concerns about some of the studies claiming to demonstrate a connection between childhood adversity and psychosis in later life. Even so, they concede that the balance of evidence points to a link between adversities, especially "multiple adversities involving hostility and threat," and "psychotic disorder" (93).

20. Drawing on Merleau-Ponty, Morley (2003) develops the view that psychiatric illness and, more specifically, hallucination can involve an inability to accept or "surrender to" a degree of indeterminacy that is integral to perceptual experience, something that involves a loss of trust or confidence.

21. What I have said is also in keeping with responses to traumatic experience that emphasize the need to start by re-establishing interpersonal trust. For instance, Herman (1997) describes three broad stages of recovery: a localized sense of safety is first nurtured, after which the person can attempt to construct a narrative around what has happened, and finally there is reengagement with communal life. In a similar vein, Fonagy and Allison (2014, 372) state that effective therapy involves nurturing a trusting relationship that allows the client to "relinquish the rigidity that characterizes individuals with enduring personality pathology" and thus the "relearning of flexibility." See also Janoff-Bulman 1992 for an emphasis on the substantial role that social support has to play and for distinctions between various complementary forms of social support.

22. See also Stanghellini 2004 for a discussion of the phenomenology of schizophrenia that emphasizes loss of common sense.

23. An experience along these lines would be consistent with recent formulations of the dopamine hypothesis of schizophrenia, which emphasize wide-ranging salience dysregulation (e.g., Kapur 2003; Kapur, Mizrahi, and Li 2005). But see also Kendler 2015 for a critique of the hypothesis in its various guises. What I have suggested also complements a phenomenological account offered by Wiggins and Schwartz (2007), according to which a breakdown of Husserlian passive synthesis generates instability and unpredictability.

24. Borda and Sass (2015) and Sass and Borda (2015) provide a detailed, nuanced account of the heterogeneity of schizophrenia and the potential roles played by multiple interacting causes. They make a complementary distinction between "primary" and "secondary" contributing factors, suggesting that one or the other can play a more prominent role in a given case. Cases where onset is early and negative symptoms predominate owe more to primary factors, while secondary factors play a more substantial role in acute, later-onset cases where positive symptoms are more prominent. Further discussion is needed of how the distinction between primary and secondary factors relates to the distinction between impersonal and interpersonal causes, given that both kinds of cause are operative in early and in later life, and are likely to have different effects at different life stages.

25. See also Rooney et al. 1996 for a study of short- and long-term reactions to voluntary and involuntary hospital admission. They note that a patient's response to involuntary detention is not always negative, and that initially negative views may become more positive over time. Even so, there was often a "significant reduction" of self-esteem, and 57 percent of involuntary patients reported initial feelings of anger, frustration, fear, and bewilderment.

26. Watson et al. (2006) also discuss how conceptions of illness can shape and exacerbate symptoms. They remark that "negative illness perceptions in psychosis are clearly related to depression, anxiety and self-esteem. These in turn have been linked to symptom maintenance and recurrence" (761).

27. See, e.g., Sass 1992, chap. 2).

28. The point also applies more generally. For example, de Haan and Fuchs (2010) present two case studies of patients who they take to have impairments of minimal self. Both patients have a history of interpersonal problems. In one case, the parents divorced when the patient was eight years old. He lived with his abusive father and started drinking, then lost contact with his father at the age of eighteen, having already lost contact with his mother, and smoked pot. The other patient was living in social isolation at the time in question. He was born in Iran, moved to Germany with his family at sixteen, and lived in a hostel for asylum seekers in conditions that he regarded as degrading. He had trouble relating to other children at school and

made no friends. While de Haan and Fuchs state that the "basic self" is "first and foremost a bodily and social or 'intercorporeal' self" (328), they do not attempt to relate the patients' self-disturbances to their biographies. Doing so, I suggest, can provide us with a richer understanding of what the relevant phenomenological disturbances consist of and how they come about.

29. For a detailed philosophical treatment of predictive coding, see also Hohwy 2013.

30. See Seth, Suzuki, and Critchley 2012 for an attempt to account for the sense of perceptual presence in terms of predictive processing and prediction error. They also relate heightened interoceptive prediction error to anxiety.

7 Varieties of Hallucination

1. See also Romdenh-Romluc 2007, Morley 2003, and Giorgi 2003 for discussions of Merleau-Ponty on hallucination.

2. See McCarthy-Jones 2012, chap. 6, for a detailed discussion of cross-cultural factors, as well as the religious contexts in which some voices arise and are interpreted. Watkins (2008) also provides a wide-ranging discussion of historically and culturally diverse "voices."

3. Hoffman et al. (2008) offer the complementary suggestion that some people seldom think in words and describe their thoughts in terms of a voice when they do. Experiencing a "voice" in this sense is quite different from experiencing a voice-content as alien due to anxious anticipation.

4. The issue of whether and how experiences of "typical" grief are to be distinguished from depression is a difficult one, and a number of conflicting positions have been proposed. See Ratcliffe in press for an attempt to draw a very general, phenomenologically based distinction.

5. One might therefore wonder how we are to distinguish grief from mourning. The distinction is no doubt an untidy one. In the case of mourning, there is greater emphasis on rituals and on other culturally established public displays. However, once grief is construed as a socially regulated process, rather than an episodic emotion, I am doubtful that the distinction can be sustained. At most, it serves to emphasize different aspects of a singular process.

6. See, e.g., Parkes, Laungani, and Young, 1997, for discussions of cultural differences in expressions and experiences of grief.

7. Carse (1981, 5) thus describes acute grief as a "cosmic crisis," which involves living "in a universe that makes no sense."

8. Goldie (2011, 131) suggests that grief has a narrative structure that resembles free indirect speech, a literary device exploiting the difference between internal and

external perspectives on a situation: "In grief, you might well remember the last time you saw the person you loved, not knowing, as you do now, that it was to be the last time. And this knowledge will infect the way you remember it." The external perspective thus serves to reshape the internal perspective. Slipping in and out of a world that presupposes the deceased can be construed in terms of a gradual process of revision and reconciliation of perspectives. This need not culminate in a world that is no longer shaped by one's relationship with the deceased. Things may continue to be experienced as mattering in the ways they do in light of how one once related to her and, indeed, how one continues to think about and relate to her (Klass, Silverman, and Nickman 1996).

9. See also Hazan and Shaver 1987 for the claim that romantic love is an attachment process, comparable in many respects to infant attachment and involving analogous forms of dependence on another person.

10. See, e.g., Zahavi 2007 and Ratcliffe 2012 for recent discussions of empathy that develop the kind of approach advocated by Stein.

11. An interesting issue for further inquiry is that of whether and to what extent explicit beliefs about life after death serve to insulate a person from or otherwise shape such experiences.

8 Metaphilosophical Conclusion

1. See Braithwaite 1932–1933, 132, for a classic statement of the view that beliefs are dispositions. The view that beliefs are occurrences is associated with Hume (1740/1978). Armstrong (1973) argues that belief is a nonconscious state, as opposed to a disposition, and that occurrent belief is a manifestation of that state rather than a belief in its own right. The term "occurrent belief" is usually associated with awareness, but it is also arguable that there are nonconscious occurrent beliefs, where a disposition is manifested in current behavior but without awareness.

2. Kusch (2011) takes Wittgenstein to be advocating a similar position in his "Lectures on Religious Belief," according to which religious convictions can involve "extraordinary" belief, a type of attitude that differs from "ordinary" belief. As the belief that *p* and the belief that not *p* can involve these different types of conviction, there is the possibility of what Kusch calls "non-standard faultless disagreement" between the two. It is likely, I suggest, that belief encompasses many subtly different kinds of attitude, rather than just an *ordinary* attitude that can be contrasted with an *extraordinary* one.

3. See also Reimar 2010 for a discussion of several similarities between delusions and some philosophical beliefs, such as the lack of a clear relationship between belief and action, other than where an action takes the form of asserting or defending the belief in question.

References

Aggernaes, A. 1972. The experienced reality of hallucinations and other psychological phenomena: An empirical analysis. *Acta Psychiatrica Scandinavica* 48:220–238.

Akins, K. A., and D. C. Dennett. 1986. Who may I say is calling? *Behavioral and Brain Sciences* 9:517–518.

Aleman, A., and F. Larøi. 2008. *Hallucinations: The Science of Idiosyncratic Perception*. Washington, DC: American Psychological Association.

Allen, K. 2015. Hallucination and imagination. *Australasian Journal of Philosophy* 193:287–302.

Allen, J. G., L. Coyne, and D. A. Console. 1997. Dissociative detachment relates to psychotic symptoms and personality decompensation. *Comprehensive Psychiatry* 38:327–334.

Allen, P., D. Freeman, P. McGuire, P. Garety, E. Kuipers, D. Fowler, P. Bebbington, C. Green, G. Dunn, and K. Ray. 2005. The prediction of hallucinatory predisposition in non-clinical individuals: Examining the contribution of emotion and reasoning. *British Journal of Clinical Psychology* 44:127–132.

American Psychiatric Association. 2000. *Diagnostic and Statistical Manual of Mental Disorders*. 4th ed. Text Revision Arlington, VA: American Psychiatric Association.

American Psychiatric Association. 2013. *Diagnostic and Statistical Manual of Mental Disorders*. 5th ed. Arlington, VA: American Psychiatric Association.

Améry, J. 1999. *At the Mind's Limits: Contemplations by a Survivor on Auschwitz and Its Realities*. Trans. S. Rosenfeld and S. P. Rosenfeld. London: Granta Books.

Amnesty International. 1986. *Voices for Freedom*. London: Amnesty International Publications.

Andrew, E. M., N. S. Gray, and R. J. Snowden. 2008. The relationship between trauma and beliefs about hearing voices: A study of psychiatric and non-psychiatric voice hearers. *Psychological Medicine* 38:1409–1417.

Armstrong, D. M. 1973. *Belief, Truth and Knowledge*. Cambridge: Cambridge University Press.

Atkinson, J. R. 2006. The perceptual characteristics of voice-hallucinations in deaf people: Insights into the nature of subvocal thought and sensory feedback loops. *Schizophrenia Bulletin* 32:701–708.

Austin, J. L. 1962. *Sense and Sensibilia*. Oxford: Clarendon Press.

Baier, A. 1986. Trust and antitrust. *Ethics* 96:231–260.

Barnes, J. 2013. *Levels of Life*. London: Jonathan Cape.

Bayliss, A. P., A. Frischen, M. J. Fenske, and S. P. Tipper. 2007. Affective evaluations of objects are influenced by observed gaze direction and emotional expression. *Cognition* 104:644–653.

Bayne, T., and M. Montague, eds. 2011. *Cognitive Phenomenology*. Oxford: Oxford University Press.

Beavan, V., J. Read, and C. Cartwright. 2011. The prevalence of voice-hearers in the general population: A literature review. *Journal of Mental Health* 20:281–292.

Becchio, C., C. Bertone, and U. Castiello. 2008. How the gaze of others influences object processing. *Trends in Cognitive Sciences* 12:254–258.

Bell, V. 2013. A community of one: Social cognition and auditory verbal hallucinations. *PLoS Biology* 11 (12): 1–4.

Bennett, G., and K. M. Bennett. 2000. The presence of the dead: An empirical study. *Mortality* 5:139–157.

Benson, O., S. Gibson, and S. Brand. 2013. The experience of agency in the feeling of being suicidal. *Journal of Consciousness Studies* 20 (7–8): 56–79.

Bentall, R. P. 1990. The illusion of reality: A review and integration of psychological research on hallucinations. *Psychological Bulletin* 107:82–95.

Bentall, R. P. 2003. *Madness Explained: Psychosis and Human Nature*. London: Penguin Books.

Bentall, R. P. 2009. *Doctoring the Mind: Why Psychiatric Treatments Fail*. London: Allen Lane.

Bentall, R. P., and C. Fernyhough. 2008. Social predictors of psychotic experiences: Specificity and psychological mechanisms. *Schizophrenia Bulletin* 34:1012–1020.

Bentall, R. P., and F. Varese. 2013. Psychotic hallucinations. In *Hallucination: Philosophy and Psychology*, ed. F. Macpherson and D. Platchias, 65–86. Cambridge, MA: MIT Press.

Bernstein, J. 2011. Trust: On the real but almost always unnoticed, ever-changing foundation of ethical life. *Metaphilosophy* 42:395–416.

Berrios, G. E., and T. R. Dening. 1996. Pseudohallucinations: A conceptual history. *Psychological Medicine* 26:753–763.

Beveridge, A. 1998. Psychology of compulsory detention. *Psychiatric Bulletin* 22: 115–117.

Billon, A. 2013. Does consciousness entail subjectivity? The puzzle of thought insertion. *Philosophical Psychology* 26:291–314.

Birchwood, M., A. Meaden, P. Trower, P. Gilbert, and J. Plaistow. 2000. The power and omnipotence of voices: Subordination and entrapment by voices and significant others. *Psychological Medicine* 30:337–344.

Birchwood, M., P. Trower, K. Brunet, P. Gilbert, Z. Iqbal, and C. Jackson. 2006. Social anxiety and the shame of psychosis: A study in first episode psychosis. *Behaviour Research and Therapy* 45:1025–1037.

Blakemore, S. J., D. Wolpert, and C. Frith. 2000. Why can't you tickle yourself? *Neuroreport* 11 (11): R11–R16.

Blankenburg, W. 1969/2001. First steps towards a psychopathology of "common sense." Trans. A. L. Mishara. *Philosophy, Psychiatry, & Psychology* 8:303–315.

Blankenburg, W. 1971/2012. *Der Verlust der natürlichen Selbstverständlichkeit: Ein Bertrag zur Psychopathologie symptomarmer Schizophrenien*. Berlin: Parodos Verlag.

Bleuler, E. 1950. *Dementia Praecox or the Group of Schizophrenias*. Trans. J. Zinkin. New York: International Universities Press.

Borda, J. P., and L. A. Sass. 2015. Phenomenology and neurobiology of self disorder in schizophrenia: Primary factors. *Schizophrenia Research* 169:464–473.

Bortolotti, L., and M. Broome. 2009. A role for ownership and authorship in the analysis of thought insertion. *Phenomenology and the Cognitive Sciences* 8:205–224.

Bortolotti, L., and M. Broome. 2012. Affective dimensions of the phenomenon of double bookkeeping in delusions. *Emotion Review* 4:187–191.

Braithwaite, R. B. 1932–1933. The nature of believing. *Proceedings of the Aristotelian Society* 33:129–146.

Breyer, T., and C. Gutland, eds. 2016. *Phenomenology of Thinking: Philosophical Investigations into the Character of Cognitive Experiences*. London: Routledge.

Brison, S. J. 2002. *Aftermath: Violence and the Remaking of a Self*. Princeton, NJ: Princeton University Press.

Broome, M. R., J. B. Woolley, P. Tabraham, L. C. Johns, E. Bramon, G. K. Murray, C. Pariante, P. K. McGuire, and R. M. Murray. 2005. What causes the onset of psychosis? *Schizophrenia Research* 79:23–34.

Cahill, C., and C. Frith. 1996. False perceptions or false beliefs? Hallucinations and delusions in schizophrenia. In *Method in Madness: Case Studies in Cognitive Neuropsychiatry*, ed. P. W. Halligan and J. C. Marshall, 267–291. Hove: Psychology Press.

Campbell, J. 1999. Schizophrenia, the space of reasons, and thinking as a motor process. *Monist* 82:609–625.

Campbell, J. 2001. Rationality, meaning, and the analysis of delusion. *Philosophy, Psychiatry, & Psychology* 8:89–100.

Campbell, S. 1997. *Interpreting the Personal: Expression and the Formation of Feelings*. Ithaca: Cornell University Press.

Carel, H. 2013. Bodily doubt. *Journal of Consciousness Studies* 20 (7–8): 178–197.

Carse, J. P. 1981. Grief as a cosmic crisis. In *Acute Grief: Counseling the Bereaved*, ed. O. S. Margolis, H. C. Raether, A. H. Kutscher, J. B. Powers, I. B. Seeland, R. DeBillis and D. J. Cherico, 3–8. New York: Columbia University Press.

Castelnovo, A., S. Cavalloti, O. Gambini, and A. D'Agostino. 2015. Post-bereavement hallucinatory experiences: A critical overview of population and clinical studies. *Journal of Affective Disorders* 186:266–274.

Cermolacce, M., J. Naudin, and J. Parnas. 2007. The "minimal self" in psychopathology: Re-examining the self-disorders in the schizophrenia spectrum. *Consciousness and Cognition* 16:703–714.

Chadwick, P., and M. Birchwood. 1994. The omnipotence of voices: A cognitive approach to auditory hallucinations. *British Journal of Psychiatry* 164:190–201.

Clark, A. 2013. Whatever next? Predictive brains, situated agents, and the future of cognitive science. *Behavioral and Brain Sciences* 36:181–204.

Clark, A. 2016. *Surfing Uncertainty; Prediction, Action, and the Embodied Mind*. New York: Oxford University Press.

Colombetti, G. 2009. What language does to feelings. *Journal of Consciousness Studies* 16:4–26.

Colombetti, G., and J. Krueger. 2015. Scaffoldings of the affective mind. *Philosophical Psychology* 28:1157–1176.

Colombetti, G., and S. Torrance. 2009. Emotion and ethics: An inter(en)active approach. *Phenomenology and the Cognitive Sciences* 8:505–526.

Conrad, K. 2012. Beginning schizophrenia: Attempt for a Gestalt-analysis of delusion. Trans. A. Mishara. In *The Maudsley Reader in Phenomenological Psychiatry*, ed. M.

R. Broome, R. Harland, G. S. Owen and A. Stringaris, 176–193. Cambridge: Cambridge University Press.

Copolov, D. L., A. Mackinnon, and T. Trauer. 2004. Correlates of the affective impact of auditory hallucinations in psychotic disorders. *Schizophrenia Bulletin* 30:163–171.

Corbí, J. E. 2012. *Morality, Self-Knowledge, and Human Suffering: An Essay on the Loss of Confidence in the World.* London: Routledge.

Corlett, P. R., J. H. Krystal, J. R. Taylor, and P. C. Fletcher. 2009. Why do delusions persist? *Frontiers in Human Neuroscience* 3/12:1–9.

Corlett, P. R., J. R. Taylor, X.-J. Wang, P. C. Fletcher, and J. H. Krystal. 2010. Toward a neurobiology of delusions. *Progress in Neurobiology* 92:345–369.

Corstens, D., E. Longden, and R. May. 2012. Talking with voices: Exploring what is expressed by the voices people hear. *Psychosis* 4:95–104.

Costanzo, M. A., and E. Gerrity. 2009. The effects and effectiveness of using torture as an interrogation device: Using research to inform the policy debate. *Social Issues and Policy Review* 3:179–210.

Csibra, G., and G. Gergely. 2009. Natural pedagogy. *Trends in Cognitive Sciences* 13: 148–153.

Currie, G. 2000. Imagination, delusion, and hallucinations. In *Pathologies of Belief*, ed. M. Coltheart and M. Davies, 167–182. Oxford: Blackwell.

Currie, G., and J. Jureidini. 2001. Delusion, rationality, empathy: Commentary on Davies et al. *Philosophy, Psychiatry, & Psychology* 8:159–162.

Currie, G., and J. Jureidini. 2004. Narrative and coherence. *Mind & Language* 19: 409–427.

Currie, G., and I. Ravenscroft. 2002. *Recreative Minds*. Oxford: Oxford University Press.

David, A. S. 1994. The neuropsychological origin of auditory hallucinations. In *The Neuropsychology of Schizophrenia*, ed. A. S. David and J. C. Cutting, 269–313. Hove: Psychology Press.

de Haan, S., and L. de Bruin. 2010. Reconstructing the minimal self, or How to make sense of agency and ownership. *Phenomenology and the Cognitive Sciences* 9:373–396.

de Haan, S., and T. Fuchs. 2010. The ghost in the machine: Disembodiment in schizophrenia—two case studies. *Psychopathology* 43:327–333.

De Jaegher, H., and E. Di Paolo. 2007. Participatory sense-making: An enactive approach to social cognition. *Phenomenology and the Cognitive Sciences* 6:485–507.

Delespaul, P., M. de Vries, and J. van Os. 2002. Determinants of occurrence and recovery from hallucinations in daily life. *Social Psychiatry and Psychiatric Epidemiology* 37:97–104.

De Sousa, R. 1987. *The Rationality of Emotion*. Cambridge, MA: MIT Press.

Diamond, L. M., and L. G. Aspinwall. 2003. Emotion regulation across the life span: An integrative perspective emphasizing self-regulation, positive affect, and dyadic processes. *Motivation and Emotion* 27:125–156.

Didion, J. 2005. *The Year of Magical Thinking*. London: Harper Perennial.

Didion, J. 2011. *Blue Nights*. London: Fourth Estate.

Dodgson, G., and S. Gordon. 2009. Avoiding false negatives: Are some auditory hallucinations an evolved design flaw? *Behavioural and Cognitive Psychotherapy* 37:325–334.

Dorsch, F. 2010. The unity of hallucinations. *Phenomenology and the Cognitive Sciences* 9:71–191.

Dreyfus, H. L. 2002. Intelligence without representation—Merleau-Ponty's critique of mental representation. *Phenomenology and the Cognitive Sciences* 1:367–383.

Earnshaw, O. 2011. Recovering the voice of insanity: A phenomenology of delusions. Doctoral thesis, Durham University. http://etheses.dur.ac.uk/3225/.

Egan, A. 2009. Imagination, delusion, and self-deception. In *Delusion and Self-Deception*, ed. T. Byne and J. Fernández, 263–280. London: Psychology Press.

Farkas, K. 2013. A sense of reality. In *Hallucination: Philosophy and Psychology*, ed. F. Macpherson and D. Platchias, 399–415. Cambridge, MA: MIT Press.

Fernyhough, C. 2004. Alien voices and inner dialogue: Towards a developmental account of auditory verbal hallucinations. *New Ideas in Psychology* 22:49–68.

Fernyhough, C., and S. McCarthy-Jones. 2013. Thinking aloud about mental voices. In *Hallucination: Philosophy and Psychology*, ed. F. Macpherson and D. Platchias, 87–104. Cambridge, MA: MIT Press.

Fletcher, P. C., and C. D. Frith. 2009. Perceiving is believing: A Bayesian approach to explaining the positive symptoms of schizophrenia. *Nature Reviews: Neuroscience* 10:48–58.

Fonagy, P., and E. Allison. 2014. The role of mentalizing and epistemic trust in the therapeutic relationship. *Psychotherapy* 51:372–380.

Ford, J. R. 1999. Disorders of extreme stress following warzone military trauma: Associated features of post-traumatic stress disorder (PTSD) or comorbid but distinct syndromes? *Journal of Consulting and Clinical Psychology* 67:3–12.

Freeman, D., and A. Garety. 2003. Connecting neurosis and psychosis: The direct influence of emotion on delusions and hallucinations. *Behaviour Research and Therapy* 41:923–947.

Freeman, M. 2000. When the story's over: Narrative foreclosure and the possibility of self-renewal. In *Lines of Narrative: Psychosocial Perspectives*, ed. M. Andrews, S. D. Sclater, C. Squire and A. Treacher, 81–91. London: Routledge.

Frith, C. 1992. *The Cognitive Neuropsychology of Schizophrenia*. Hove: Psychology Press.

Frith, C. 2012. Explaining delusions of control: The comparator model 20 years on. *Consciousness and Cognition* 21:52–54.

Frith, C. D., S.-J. Blakemore, and D. M. Wolpert. 2000. Abnormalities in the awareness and control of action. *Philosophical Transactions of the Royal Society of London, Series B* 355:1771–1788.

Froese, T., and T. Fuchs. 2012. The extended body: A case study in the neurophenomenology of social interaction. *Phenomenology and the Cognitive Sciences* 11: 205–235.

Fuchs, T. 2012. Selbst und Schizophrenie. *Deutsche Zeitschrift fur Philosophie* 60:887–901.

Fuchs, T. 2013. The self in schizophrenia: Jaspers, Schneider and beyond. In *One Century of Karl Jaspers' General Psychopathology*, ed. G. Stanghellini and T. Fuchs, 245–257. Oxford: Oxford University Press.

Fuchs, T. 2015. Pathologies of intersubjectivity in autism and schizophrenia. *Journal of Consciousness Studies* 22 (1–2): 191–214.

Fuchs, T., and H. De Jaegher. 2009. Enactive intersubjectivity: Participatory sense-making and mutual incorporation. *Phenomenology and the Cognitive Sciences* 8: 465–486.

Gallagher, S. 2005. *How the Body Shapes the Mind*. Oxford: Oxford University Press.

Gallagher, S. 2009a. Two problems of intersubjectivity. *Journal of Consciousness Studies* 16 (6–8): 289–308.

Gallagher, S. 2009b. Delusional realities. In *Psychiatry as Cognitive Neuroscience: Philosophical Perspectives*, ed. M. Broome and L. Bortolotti, 245–266. Oxford: Oxford University Press.

Gallagher, S. 2015. Relations between agency and ownership in the case of schizophrenic thought insertion and delusions of control. *Review of Philosophy and Psychology* 6:865–879.

Gallagher, S., and D. Zahavi. 2008. *The Phenomenological Mind*. London: Routledge.

Garrett, M., and R. Silva. 2003. Auditory hallucinations, source monitoring, and the belief that "voices" are real. *Schizophrenia Bulletin* 29:445–457.

Gendler, T. S. 2008. Alief and belief. *Journal of Philosophy* 105:634–663.

Gendlin, E. T. 1978/2003. *Focusing: How to Gain Direct Access to Your Body's Knowledge*. London: Rider Books.

Gerrans, P. 2014. *The Measure of Madness: Philosophy of Mind, Cognitive Neuroscience, and Delusional Thought*. Cambridge, MA: MIT Press.

Giorgi, A. 2003. A phenomenological approach to research on hallucinations. In *Imagination and Its Pathologies*, ed. J. Phillips and J. Morley, 209–224. Cambridge, MA: MIT Press.

Gjerde, P. F. 1983. Attention capacity dysfunction and arousal in schizophrenia. *Psychological Bulletin* 93:57–72.

Glas, G. 2003. A conceptual history of anxiety and depression. In *Handbook of Depression and Anxiety*, 2nd ed., ed. S. Kasper, J. A. de Boer and A. Sitsen, 1–48. New York: Marcel Dekker.

Goldman, A. 2006. *Simulating Minds: The Philosophy, Psychology, and Neuroscience of Mindreading*. Oxford: Oxford University Press.

Goldie, P. 2000. *The Emotions: A Philosophical Exploration*. Oxford: Clarendon Press.

Goldie, P. 2011. Grief: A narrative account. *Ratio* 24:119–137.

Goldie, P. 2012. *The Mess Inside: Narrative, Emotion, and the Mind*. Oxford: Oxford University Press.

Graham, G. 2004. Self-ascription: Thought insertion. In *The Philosophy of Psychiatry: A Companion*, ed. J. Radden, 89–105. Oxford: Oxford University Press.

Grahek, N. 2007. *Feeling Pain and Being in Pain*. 2nd ed. Cambridge, MA: MIT Press.

Greening, T. 1990. PTSD from the perspective of existential-humanistic psychology. *Journal of Traumatic Stress* 3:323–326.

Griffiths, P., and A. Scarantino. 2009. Emotions in the wild: The situated perspective on emotion. In *The Cambridge Handbook of Situated Cognition*, ed. P. Robbins and M. Aydede, 437–453. Cambridge: Cambridge University Press.

Gross, J. J. 1999. Emotion regulation: Past, present, future. *Cognition and Emotion* 13:551–573.

Gross, J. J. 2001. Emotion regulation in adulthood: Timing is everything. *Current Directions in Psychological Science* 10:214–219.

Guenther, L. 2013. *Solitary Confinement: Social Death and Its Afterlives*. Minneapolis: University of Minnesota Press.

Hacking, I. 1992. Multiple personality disorder and its hosts. *History of the Human Sciences* 5 (2): 3–31.

Halligan, P. W., and J. C. Marshall. 1996. The wise prophet makes sure of the event first: Hallucinations, amnesia and delusions. In *Method in Madness: Case Studies in Cognitive Neuropsychiatry*, ed. P. W. Halligan and J. C. Marshall, 237–266. Hove: Psychology Press.

Hamilton, A. 2014. *Routledge Philosophy Guidebook to Wittgenstein and "On Certainty."* London: Routledge.

Havens, L. 1986. *Making Contact: Uses of Language in Psychotherapy*. Cambridge, MA: Harvard University Press.

Hayward, M., K. Berry, and A. Ashton. 2011. Applying interpersonal theories to the understanding of and therapy for auditory hallucinations: A review of the literature and directions for further research. *Clinical Psychology Review* 31:1313–1323.

Hazan, C., and P. Shaver. 1987. Romantic love conceptualized as an attachment process. *Journal of Personality and Social Psychology* 52:511–524.

Heidegger, M. 1927/1962. *Being and Time*. Trans. J. Macquarrie and E. Robinson. Oxford: Blackwell.

Hemon, A. 2013. *The Book of My Lives*. London: Picador.

Henriksen, M. G. 2013. On incomprehensibility in schizophrenia. *Phenomenology and the Cognitive Sciences* 12:105–129.

Henriksen, M. G., A. Raballo, and J. Parnas. 2015. The pathogenesis of auditory verbal hallucinations in schizophrenia: A clinical-phenomenological account. *Philosophy, Psychiatry, & Psychology* 22:165–181.

Herman, J. 1997. *Trauma and Recovery*. 2nd ed. New York: Basic Books.

Hersch, E. L. 2003. Imagination: Looking in the right place (and in the right way). In *Imagination and Its Pathologies*, ed. J. Phillips and J. Morley, 21–36. Cambridge, MA: MIT Press.

Higgins, K. M. 2013. Love and death. In *On Emotions: Philosophical Essays*, ed. J. Deigh, 159–178. Oxford: Oxford University Press.

Hinton, D. E., and L. J. Kirmayer. 2013. Local responses to trauma: Symptom, affect, and healing. *Transcultural Psychiatry* 50:607–621.

Hobson, P. 1993. *Autism and the Development of Mind*. Hove: Erlbaum.

Hobson, P. 2002. *The Cradle of Thought*. London: Macmillan.

Hoerl, C. 2001. On thought insertion. *Philosophy, Psychiatry, & Psychology* 8:189–200.

Hofer, M. A. 1984. Relationships as regulators: A psychobiologic perspective on bereavement. *Psychosomatic Medicine* 46:183–197.

Hoffman, R. E. 1986. Verbal hallucinations and language production processes in schizophrenia. *Behavioral and Brain Sciences* 9:503–548.

Hoffman, R. E. 2007. A social deafferentation hypothesis for induction of active schizophrenia. *Schizophrenia Bulletin* 33:1066–1070.

Hoffman, R. E., and J. Rapaport. 1994. A psycholinguistic study of auditory/verbal hallucinations: Preliminary findings. In *The Neuropsychology of Schizophrenia*, ed. A. S. David and J. C. Cutting, 255–267. Hove: Psychology Press.

Hoffman, R. E., M. Varanko, J. Gilmore, and A. L. Mishara. 2008. Experiential features used by patients with schizophrenia to differentiate "voices" from ordinary verbal thought. *Psychological Medicine* 38:1167–1176.

Hohwy, J. 2013. *The Predictive Mind*. Oxford: Oxford University Press.

Horgan, T., and J. Tienson. 2002. The intentionality of phenomenology and the phenomenology of intentionality. In *Philosophy of Mind: Classical and Contemporary Readings*, ed. D. J. Chalmers, 520–533. Oxford: Oxford University Press.

Hume, D. 1740/1978. *A Treatise of Human Nature*. Ed. L. A. Selby-Bigge, with text revised by P. H. Nidditch. Oxford: Clarendon Press.

Humphreys, H. 2013. *True Story: The Life and Death of My Brother*. London: Serpent's Tail.

Humpston, C. S., and M. R. Broome. 2016. The spectra of soundless voices and audible thoughts: Towards an integrative model of auditory verbal hallucinations and thought insertion. *Review of Philosophy and Psychology* 7:611–629.

Hunt, N. C. 2010. *Memory, War and Trauma*. Cambridge: Cambridge University Press.

Husserl, E. 1948/1973. *Experience and Judgment: Investigations in a Genealogy of Logic*. Trans. J. S. Churchill and K. Ameriks. London: Routledge.

Husserl, E. 1952/1989. *Ideas Pertaining to a Pure Phenomenology and to a Phenomenological Philosophy: Second Book*. Trans. R. Rojcewicz and A. Schuwer. Dordrecht: Kluwer.

Husserl, E. 1991. *On the Phenomenology of the Consciousness of Internal Time (1893–1917)*. Trans. J. B. Brough. Dordrecht: Kluwer.

Husserl, E. 2001. *Analyses Concerning Passive and Active Synthesis: Lectures on Transcendental Logic*. Trans. A. J. Steinbock. Dordrecht: Kluwer.

Ichikawa, J. 2009. Dreaming and imagination. *Mind & Language* 24:103–121.

Istanbul Protocol. 1999. *Manual on the Effective Investigation and Documentation of Torture and Other Cruel, Inhuman or Degrading Treatment or Punishment.* Geneva: United Nations.

James, W. 1889. The psychology of belief. *Mind* 14:321–352.

James, W. 1897. *The Will to Believe and Other Essays in Popular Philosophy*. New York: Longmans, Green.

James, W. 1902. *The Varieties of Religious Experience*. New York: Longmans, Green.

James, W. 1907/1981. *Pragmatism*. Indianapolis: Hackett.

James, W. 1912. *Absolutism and Empiricism*. In his *Essays in Radical Empiricism*, 266–279. New York: Longmans, Green.

Janoff-Bulman, R. 1992. *Shattered Assumptions: Towards a New Psychology of Trauma*. New York: The Free Press.

Jaspers, K. 1963. *General Psychopathology*. Trans. from the 7th German ed. (1959) by J. Hoenig and M. W. Hamilton. Manchester: University Press.

Johns, L., K. Kompus, M. Connell, C. Humpston, T. Lincoln, E. Longden, A. Preti, et al. 2014. Auditory verbal hallucinations in persons with and without need for care. *Schizophrenia Bulletin* 40 (suppl. 4): S255–S264.

Jones, K. 2004. Trust and terror. In *Moral Psychology: Feminist Ethics and Social Theory*, ed. P. Des Autels and M. U. Walker, 3–18. Lanham, MD: Rowman & Littlefield.

Jones, S. R. 2010. Do we need multiple models of auditory verbal hallucinations? Examining the phenomenological fit of cognitive and neurological models. *Schizophrenia Bulletin* 36:566–575.

Kapur, S. 2003. Psychosis as a state of aberrant salience: A framework linking biology, phenomenology, and pharmacology in schizophrenia. *American Journal of Psychiatry* 160:13–23.

Kapur, S., R. Mizrahi, and M. Li. 2005. From dopamine to salience to psychosis—linking biology, pharmacology and phenomenology of psychosis. *Schizophrenia Research* 79:59–68.

Karlsson, L.-B. 2008. "More real than reality": A study of voice hearing. *International Journal of Social Welfare* 17:365–373.

Kean, C. 2009. Silencing the self: Schizophrenia as a self-disturbance. *Schizophrenia Bulletin* 35:1034–1036.

Keen, C., C. Murray, and S. Payne. 2013. Sensing the presence of the deceased: A narrative review. *Mental Health, Religion, & Culture* 16:384–402.

Kelleher, I., H. Keeley, P. Corcoran, H. Ramsay, C. Wasserman, V. Carli, M. Sarchiapone, C. Hoven, D. Wasserman, and M. Cannon. 2013. Childhood trauma and psychosis in a prospective cohort study: Cause, effect, and directionality. *American Journal of Psychiatry* 170:734–741.

Kendler, K. S. 2015. The dopamine hypothesis of schizophrenia: An updated perspective. In *Philosophical Issues in Psychiatry III: The Nature and Sources of Historical Change,* ed. K. S. Kendler and J. Parnas, 283–294. Oxford: Oxford University Press.

Kenny, P. D. 2010. The meaning of torture. *Polity* 42:131–155.

Kilcommons, A. M., and A. P. Morrison. 2005. Relationships between trauma and psychosis: An exploration of cognitive and dissociative factors. *Acta Psychiatrica Scandinavica* 112:351–359.

Kirmayer, L. J. 1996. Landscapes of memory: Trauma, narrative, and dissociation. In *Tense Past: Cultural Essays on Memory and Trauma,* ed. P. Antze and M. Lambek, 173–198. London: Routledge.

Klass, D., P. R. Silverman, and S. L. Nickman, eds. 1996. *Continuing Bonds: New Understandings of Grief.* London: Routledge.

Kraepelin, E. 1919. *Dementia Praecox and Paraphrenia.* Trans. R. M. Barclay. Edinburgh: E. & S. Livingstone.

Kraus, A. 2007. Schizophrenic delusion and hallucination as the expression and consequence of an alteration of the existential a prioris. In *Reconceiving Schizophrenia,* ed. M. C. Chung, K. W. M. Fulford and G. Graham, 97–111. Oxford: Oxford University Press.

Kuipers, E., P. Garety, D. Fowler, D. Freeman, G. Dunn, and P. Bebbington. 2006. Cognitive, emotional, and social processes in psychosis: Refining cognitive behavioral therapy for persistent positive symptoms. *Schizophrenia Bulletin* 32 (S1): 24–31.

Kusch, M. 2011. Disagreement and picture in Wittgenstein's "Lectures on Religious Belief." In *Image and Imaging in Philosophy, Science and the Arts,* vol. 1, ed. R. Heinrich, E. Nemeth, W. Pichler, and D. Wagner, 35–38. Publications of the Austrian Ludwig Wittgenstein Society, New Series, vol. 16. Frankfurt: Ontos Verlag.

Kusch, M. Forthcoming. Analysing holocaust survivor testimony: Certainties, scepticism, relativism.

Laing, R. D. 1960. *The Divided Self: A Study of Sanity and Madness.* London: Tavistock Publications.

Lamb, K., R. Pies, and S. Zisook. 2010. The bereavement exclusion for the diagnosis of major depression: To be, or not to be. *Psychiatry* 7 (7): 19–25.

Landis, C. 1964. *Varieties of Psychopathological Experience.* New York: Holt, Rinehart & Winston.

Langland-Hassan, P. 2008. Fractured phenomenologies: Thought insertion, inner speech, and the puzzle of extraneity. *Mind & Language* 23:369–401.

Larkin, W., and A. P. Morrison, eds. 2006. *Trauma and Psychosis: New Directions for Theory and Therapy*. London: Routledge.

Larkin, W., and J. Read. 2012. Childhood trauma and psychosis: Revisiting the evidence. In *Psychosis as a Personal Crisis: An Experience-Based Approach*, ed. M. Romme and S. Escher, 61–73. London: Routledge.

Larøi, F. 2006. The phenomenological diversity of hallucinations: Some theoretical and clinical implications. *Psychologica Belgica* 46:163–183.

Larøi, F., S. de Haan, S. Jones, and A. Raballo. 2010. Auditory verbal hallucinations: Dialoguing between the cognitive sciences and phenomenology. *Phenomenology and the Cognitive Sciences* 9:225–240.

Laub, D. 2001. Introduction to the English-Language edition. In *At the Side of Torture Survivors: Treating a Terrible Assault on Human Dignity*, ed. S. Graessner, G. Norbert, and C. Pross, trans. J. M. Riemer. Baltimore: The John Hopkins University Press.

Lear, J. 2006. *Radical Hope: Ethics in the Face of Cultural Devastation*. Cambridge, MA: Harvard University Press.

Leudar, I., P. Thomas, D. McNally, and A. Glinski. 1997. What voices can do with words: Pragmatics of verbal hallucinations. *Psychological Medicine* 27:885–898.

Lewis, C. S. 1966. *A Grief Observed*. London: Faber & Faber.

Løgstrup, K. E. 1956/1997. *The Ethical Demand*. Notre Dame: University of Notre Dame Press.

Longden, E., A. Madill, and M. G. Waterman. 2012. Dissociation, trauma, and the role of lived experience: Toward a new conceptualization of voice hearing. *Psychological Bulletin* 138:28–76.

Luhrmann, T. M., R. Padmavati, H. Tharoor, and A. Osei. 2015. Hearing voices in different cultures: A social kindling hypothesis. *Topics in Cognitive Science* 7:646–663.

Lysaker, P. H., J. K. Johannesen, and J. T. Lysaker. 2005. Schizophrenia and the experience of intersubjectivity as threat. *Phenomenology and the Cognitive Sciences* 4:335–352.

Maclaren, K. 2008. Embodied perceptions of others as a condition of selfhood? Empirical and phenomenological considerations. *Journal of Consciousness Studies* 15 (8): 63–93.

Macpherson, F. 2013. The philosophy and psychology of hallucination: An introduction. In *Hallucination: Philosophy and Psychology*, ed. F. Macpherson and D. Platchias, 1–38. Cambridge, MA: MIT Press.

Madary, M. 2012. How would the world look if it looked as if it were encoded as an intertwined set of probability density distributions? *Frontiers in Psychology* 3 (art. 419):1–2.

Madary, M. 2013. Anticipation and variation in visual content. *Philosophical Studies* 165:335–347.

Maiese, M. 2015. Thought insertion as a disownership symptom. *Phenomenology and the Cognitive Sciences* 14:911–927.

Martin, J.-R., and E. Pacherie. 2013. Out of nowhere: Thought insertion, ownership, and context-integration. *Consciousness and Cognition* 22:111–122.

Martin, M. G. F. 2002. The transparency of experience. *Mind & Language* 17:376–425.

Martin, M. G. F. 2004. The limits of self-awareness. *Philosophical Studies* 120:37–89.

McCarthy-Jones, S. 2012. *Hearing Voices: The Histories, Causes, and Meanings of Auditory Verbal Hallucinations*. Cambridge: Cambridge University Press.

McCarthy-Jones, S., T. Trauer, A. Mackinnon, E. Sims, N. Thomas, and D. L. Copolov. 2014. A new phenomenological survey of auditory hallucinations: Evidence for subtypes and implications for theory and practice. *Schizophrenia Bulletin* 40:231–235.

McGann, M., and H. De Jaegher. 2009. Self-other contingencies: Enacting social perception. *Phenomenology and the Cognitive Sciences* 8:417–437.

Mellor, C. H. 1970. First rank symptoms of schizophrenia. *British Journal of Psychiatry* 117:15–23.

Merleau-Ponty, M. 1945/2012. *Phenomenology of Perception*. Trans. D. Landes. London: Routledge.

Merleau-Ponty, M. 1964. *The Primacy of Perception*. Ed. J. M. Edie. Evanston: Northwestern University Press.

Merleau-Ponty, M. 1968. *The Visible and the Invisible*. Trans. A. Lingis. Evanston: Northwestern University Press.

Michie, P. T., J. C. Badcock, F. A. V. Waters, and M. T. Maybery. 2005. Auditory hallucinations: Failure to inhibit irrelevant memories. *Cognitive Neuropsychiatry* 10:125–136.

Minkowski, E. 1970. *Lived Time: Phenomenological and Psychopathological Studies*. Trans. N. Metzel. Evanston: Northwestern University Press.

Morgan, C., and C. Gayer-Anderson. 2016. Childhood adversities and psychosis: Evidence, challenges, implications. *World Psychiatry* 15:93–102.

Moritz, S., and F. Larøi. 2008. Differences and similarities in the sensory and cognitive signatures of voice-hearing, intrusions, and thoughts. *Schizophrenia Research* 102:96–107.

Morley, J. 2003. The texture of the real: Merleau-Ponty on imagination and psychopathology. In *Imagination and Its Pathologies*, ed. J. Phillips and J. Morley, 93–108. Cambridge, MA: MIT Press.

Morrison, A. P., L. Frame, and W. Larkin. 2003. Relationships between trauma and psychosis: A review and integration. *British Journal of Clinical Psychology* 42:331–353.

Moyal-Sharrock, D. 2005. *Understanding Wittgenstein's "On Certainty."* Basingstoke: Palgrave Macmillan.

Mueser, K. T., S. D. Rosenberg, L. A. Goodman, and S. L. Trumbetta. 2002. Trauma, PTSD, and the course of severe mental illness: An interactive model. *Schizophrenia Research* 53:123–143.

Myin-Germeys, I., and J. van Os. 2007. Stress-reactivity in psychosis: Evidence for an affective pathway to psychosis. *Clinical Psychology Review* 27:409–424.

Nayani, T. H., and A. S. David. 1996. The auditory hallucination: A phenomenological survey. *Psychological Medicine* 26:177–189.

Noë, A. 2004. *Action in Perception*. Cambridge, MA: MIT Press.

Noë, A. 2012. *Varieties of Presence*. Cambridge, MA: Harvard University Press.

Normand, C. L., P. R. Silverman, and S. L. Nickman. 1996. Bereaved children's changing relationships with the deceased. In *Continuing Bonds: New Understandings of Grief*, ed. D. Klass, P. R. Silverman and S. L. Nickman, 87–111. London: Routledge.

Oates, J. C. 2011. *A Widow's Story*. London: Fourth Estate.

Parkes, C. M. 1996. *Bereavement: Studies of Grief in Adult Life*. 3rd ed. London: Penguin Books.

Parkes, C. M., P. Laungani, and B. Young, eds. 1997. *Death and Bereavement across Cultures*. London: Routledge.

Parnas, J. 2013. On psychosis: Karl Jaspers and beyond. In *One Century of Karl Jaspers' General Psychopathology*, ed. G.Stanghellini and T. Fuchs, 208–228. Oxford: Oxford University Press.

Parnas, J., P. Møller, T. Kircher, J. Thalbitzer, L. Jansson, P. Handest, and D. Zahavi. 2005. EASE: Examination of anomalous self-experience. *Psychopathology* 38:236–258.

Parnas, J., and L. A. Sass. 2001. Self, solipsism, and schizophrenic delusions. *Philosophy, Psychiatry, & Psychology* 8:101–120.

Paulik, G., J. C. Badcock, and M. Y. Maybery. 2006. The multifactorial structure of the predisposition to hallucinate and associations with anxiety, depression, and stress. *Personality and Individual Differences* 41:1067–1076.

Paulik, G., J. C. Badcock, and M. Y. Maybery. 2008. Dissociating the components of inhibitory control involved in predisposition to hallucinations. *Cognitive Neuropsychiatry* 13:33–46.

Peters, E. 1996. *Torture*. Expanded ed. Philadelphia: University of Pennsylvania Press.

Pleasants, N. 2008. Wittgenstein, ethics and basic moral certainty. *Inquiry* 51: 241–267.

Pleasants, N. 2009. Wittgenstein and basic moral certainty. *Philosophia* 37:669–679.

Prinz, J. 2004. *Gut Reactions: A Perceptual Theory of Emotion*. Oxford: Oxford University Press.

Raballo, A., and F. Larøi. 2011. Murmurs of thought: Phenomenology of hallucinatory consciousness in impending psychosis. *Psychosis* 3:163–166.

Raballo, A., and J. Parnas. 2011. The silent side of the spectrum: Schizotypy and the schizotaxic self. *Schizophrenia Bulletin* 37:1017–1026.

Raballo, A., D. Sæbye, and J. Parnas. 2009. Looking at the schizophrenia spectrum through the prism of self-disorders: An empirical study. *Schizophrenia Bulletin* 37:344–351.

Radden, J. 2009. *Moody Minds Distempered: Essays on Melancholy and Depression*. Oxford: Oxford University Press.

Radden, J. 2011. *On Delusion*. London: Routledge.

Ratcliffe, M. 2005. The feeling of being. *Journal of Consciousness Studies* 12 (8–10): 43–60.

Ratcliffe, M. 2007. *Rethinking Commonsense Psychology: A Critique of Folk Psychology, Theory of Mind and Simulation*. Basingstoke: Palgrave Macmillan.

Ratcliffe, M. 2008. *Feelings of Being: Phenomenology, Psychiatry and the Sense of Reality*. Oxford: Oxford University Press.

Ratcliffe, M. 2012. Phenomenology as a form of empathy. *Inquiry* 55:473–495.

Ratcliffe, M. 2013a. Delusional atmosphere and the sense of unreality. In *One Century of Karl Jaspers' General Psychopathology*, ed. G. Stanghellini and T. Fuchs, 229–244. Oxford: Oxford University Press.

Ratcliffe, M. 2013b. Why mood matters. In *Cambridge Companion to "Being and Time,"* ed. M. Wrathall, 157–176. Cambridge: Cambridge University Press.

Ratcliffe, M. 2015. *Experiences of Depression: A Study in Phenomenology*. Oxford: Oxford University Press.

Ratcliffe, M. 2016. Relating to the dead: Social cognition and the phenomenology of grief. In *The Phenomenology of Sociality: Discovering the "We,"* ed. T. Szanto and D. Moran, 202–215. London: Routledge.

Ratcliffe, M. In press. The phenomenological clarification of grief and its relevance for psychiatry. In *Oxford Handbook of Phenomenological Psychopathology*, ed. G. Stanghellini et al. Oxford: Oxford University Press.

Read, J., K. Agar, N. Argyle, and V. Aderhold. 2003. Sexual and physical abuse during childhood and adulthood as predictors of hallucinations, delusions and thought disorder. *Psychology and Psychotherapy: Theory, Research and Practice* 76:1–22.

Read, J., J. van Os, A. P. Morrison, and C. A. Ross. 2005. Childhood trauma, psychosis and schizophrenia: A literature review with theoretical and clinical implications. *Acta Psychiatrica Scandinavica* 112:330–350.

Reddy, V. 2008. *How Infants Know Minds*. Cambridge, MA: Harvard University Press.

Rees, W. D. 1971. The hallucinations of widowhood. *British Medical Journal* 4:37–41.

Reimar, M. 2010. Only a philosopher or a madman: Impractical delusions in philosophy and psychiatry. *Philosophy, Psychiatry, & Psychology* 17:315–328.

Rhodes, J., and R. G. T. Gipps. 2008. Delusions, certainty and the background. *Philosophy, Psychiatry, & Psychology* 15:295–310.

Riley, D. 2012. *Time Lived, Without Its Flow*. London: Capsule Editions.

Roessler, J. 2013. Thought insertion, self-awareness, and rationality. In *The Oxford Handbook of Philosophy and Psychiatry*, ed. K. W. M. Fulford, M. Davies, R. G. T. Gipps, G. Graham, J. Z. Sadler, G. Stanghellini, and T. Thornton, 658–672. Oxford: Oxford University Press.

Romdenh-Romluc, K. 2007. Merleau-Ponty's account of hallucination. *European Journal of Philosophy* 17:76–90.

Romme, M., and S. Escher, eds. 2012. *Psychosis as a Personal Crisis: An Experience-Based Approach*. London: Routledge.

Romme, M., S. Escher, J. Dillon, D. Corstens, and M. Morris. 2009. *Living with Voices: 50 Stories of Recovery*. Ross-on-Wye: PCCS Books.

Rooney, S., K. C. Murphy, F. Mulvaney, E. O'Callaghan, and C. Larkin. 1996. A comparison of voluntary and involuntary patients admitted to hospital. *Irish Journal of Psychological Medicine* 13:132–138.

Sacks, O. 2012. *Hallucinations*. London: Picador.

Saks, E. R. 2007. *The Centre Cannot Hold: A Memoir of My Schizophrenia*. London: Virago.

Sarbin, T. R. 1967. The concept of hallucination. *Journal of Personality* 35:359–380.

Sartre, J. P. 1943/1989. *Being and Nothingness*. Trans. H. E. Barnes. London: Routledge.

Sass, L. A. 1992. *Madness and Modernism: Insanity in the Light of Modern Art, Literature, and Thought*. New York: Basic Books.

Sass, L. A. 1994. *The Paradoxes of Delusion: Wittgenstein, Schreber, and the Schizophrenic Mind*. Ithaca: Cornell University Press.

Sass, L. A. 2001. Self and world in schizophrenia: Three classic approaches. *Philosophy, Psychiatry, & Psychology* 8:251–270.

Sass, L. A. 2003. "Negative symptoms," schizophrenia, and the self. *International Journal of Psychology & Psychological Therapy* 3:153–180.

Sass, L. A. 2007. Contradictions of emotion in schizophrenia. *Cognition and Emotion* 21:351–390.

Sass, L. A. 2014a. Self-disturbance and schizophrenia: Structure, specificity, pathogenesis. *Schizophrenia Research* 152:5–11.

Sass, L. A. 2014b. Delusion and double bookkeeping. In *Karl Jaspers' Philosophy and Psychopathology*, ed. T. Fuchs, T. Breyer, and C. Mundt, 125–147. New York: Springer.

Sass, L. A., and J. P. Borda. 2015. Phenomenology and neurobiology of self disorder in schizophrenia: Secondary factors. *Schizophrenia Research* 169:474–482.

Sass, L. A., and G. Byrom. 2015. Phenomenological and neurocognitive perspectives on delusions: A critical overview. *World Psychiatry* 14:164–173.

Sass, L. A., and J. Parnas. 2007. Explaining schizophrenia: The relevance of phenomenology. In *Reconceiving Schizophrenia*, ed. M. C. Chung, K. W. M. Fulford and G. Graham, 63–95. Oxford: Oxford University Press.

Sbarra, D. A., and C. Hazan. 2008. Coregulation, dysregulation, self-regulation: An integrative analysis and empirical agenda for understanding adult attachment, separation, loss, and recovery. *Personality and Social Psychology Review* 12:141–167.

Scarry, E. 1985. *The Body in Pain: The Making and Unmaking of the World*. Oxford: Oxford University Press.

Schmid, H. B. 2014. Plural self-awareness. *Phenomenology and the Cognitive Sciences* 13:7–24.

Schutz, A. 1945. On multiple realities. *Philosophy and Phenomenological Research* 5:533–576.

Schwitzgebel, E. 2002. A phenomenal, dispositional account of belief. *Noûs* 36:249–275.

Schwitzgebel, E. 2008. The unreliability of naïve introspection. *Philosophical Review* 117:245–273.

Sebanz, N., H. Bekkering, and G. Knoblich. 2006. Joint action: Bodies and minds moving together. *Trends in Cognitive Sciences* 10:70–76.

Sebanz, N., and G. Knoblich. 2009. Prediction in joint action: What, when, and where. *Topics in Cognitive Science* 1:353–367.

Sechehaye, M. 1970. *Autobiography of a Schizophrenic Girl*. New York: Signet.

Seth, A. K., K. Suzuki, and H. D. Critchley. 2012. An interoceptive predictive coding model of conscious presence. *Frontiers in Psychology* 2/395:1–16.

Silverman, P., and D. Klass. 1996. Introduction: What's the problem? In *Continuing Bonds: New Understandings of Grief*, ed. D. Klass, P. R. Silverman and S. L. Nickman, 3–27. London: Routledge.

Slaby, J. 2014. Emotions and the extended mind. In *Collective Emotions*, ed. C. von Scheve and M. Salmela, 32–46. Oxford: Oxford University Press.

Solomon, R. C. 2004. *In Defense of Sentimentality*. Oxford: Oxford University Press.

Sousa, P., and L. Swiney. 2013. Thought insertion: Abnormal sense of thought agency or thought endorsement? *Phenomenology and the Cognitive Sciences* 12:637–654.

Stanghellini, G. 2004. *Disembodied Spirits and Deanimated Bodies: The Psychopathology of Common Sense*. Oxford: Oxford University Press.

Stanghellini, G., A. I. Langer, A. Ambrosini, and A. J. Cangas. 2012. Quality of hallucinatory experiences: Differences between a clinical and a non-clinical sample. *World Psychiatry* 11:110–113.

Stein, E. 1917/1989. *On the Problem of Empathy*. Trans. W. Stein. Washington, DC: ICS Publications.

Stephens, G. L., and G. Graham. 2000. *When Self-Consciousness Breaks: Alien Voices and Inserted Thoughts*. Cambridge, MA: MIT Press.

Sterelny, K. 2010. Minds: Extended or scaffolded? *Phenomenology and the Cognitive Sciences* 9:465–481.

Stern, D. 1993. The role of feelings for an interpersonal self. In *The Perceived Self: Ecological and Interpersonal Sources of Self-Knowledge*, ed. U. Neisser, 205–215. Cambridge: Cambridge University Press.

Stolorow, R. D. 2007. *Trauma and Human Existence: Autobiographical, Psychoanalytic and Philosophical Reflections*. Hove: Analytic Press.

Stolorow, R. D. 2011. *World, Affectivity, Trauma: Heidegger and Post-Cartesian Psychoanalysis*. London: Routledge.

Straus, E. W. 1958. Aesthesiology and hallucinations. In *Existence*, ed. R. May, E. Angel and H. F. Ellenberger, 139–169. New York: Simon & Schuster.

Strawson, G. 2004. Real intentionality. *Phenomenology and the Cognitive Sciences* 3:287–313.

Strawson, P. F. 1974. Imagination and perception. In P. F. Strawson, *Freedom and Resentment and Other Essays*, 50–72. London: Methuen.

Trevarthen, C. 1993. The self born in intersubjectivity: The psychology of an infant communicating. In *The Perceived Self: Ecological and Interpersonal Sources of Self-Knowledge*, ed. U. Neisser, 121–173. Cambridge: Cambridge University Press.

Tronick, E. Z., N. Bruschweiler-Stern, A. M. Harrison, K. Lyons-Ruth, A. C. Morgan, J. P. Nahum, L. Sander, and D. N. Stern. 1998. Dyadically expanded states of consciousness and the process of therapeutic change. *Infant Mental Health Journal* 19:290–299.

Tye, M. 2002. Representationalism and the transparency of experience. *Noûs* 36: 137–151.

Tye, M., and B. Wright. 2011. Is there a phenomenology of thought? In *Cognitive Phenomenology*, ed. T. Bayne and M. Montague, 326–344. Oxford: Oxford University Press.

Upthegrove, R., M. R. Broome, K. Caldwell, J. Ives, F. Oyebode, and S. J. Wood. 2016. Understanding auditory verbal hallucinations: A systematic review of current evidence. *Acta Psychiatrica Scandinavica* 133:352–367.

van den Berg, J. H. 1966. *The Psychology of the Sickbed*. Pittsburgh: Duquesne University Press.

van den Berg, J. H. 1972. *A Different Existence*. Pittsburgh: Duquesne University Press.

van den Berg, J. H. 1982. On hallucinating: Critical-historical overview and guidelines for further study. In *Phenomenology and Psychiatry*, ed. A. J. J. de Koning and F. A. Jenner, 97–110. London: Academic Press.

Varese, F., E. Barkus, and R. P. Bentall. 2012. Dissociation mediates the relationship between childhood trauma and hallucination-proneness. *Psychological Medicine* 42:1025–1036.

Varese, F., F. Smeets, M. Drukker, R. Lieverse, T. Lataster, W. Viechtbauer, J. Read, J. van Os, and R. P. Bentall. 2012. Childhood adversities increase the risk of psychosis: A meta-analysis of patient-control, prospective, and cross-sectional cohort studies. *Schizophrenia Bulletin* 38:661–671.

Vosgerau, G., and M. Voss. 2014. Authorship and control over thoughts. *Mind & Language* 29:534–565.

Wakefield, J. C., and M. B. First. 2012. Validity of the bereavement exclusion to major depression: Does the empirical evidence support the proposal to eliminate the exclusion in DSM-5? *World Psychiatry* 11:3–10.

Watkins, J. 2008. *Hearing Voices: A Common Human Experience*. South Yarra, Australia: Michelle Anderson.

Watson, P. W. B., P. A. Garety, J. Weinman, G. Dunn, P. E. Bebbington, D. Fowler, D. Freeman, and E. Kuipers. 2006. Emotional dysfunction in schizophrenia spectrum psychosis: The role of illness perceptions. *Psychological Medicine* 36:761–770.

Whitfield, C. L., S. R. Dube, V. J. Felitti, and R. F. Anda. 2005. Adverse childhood experiences and hallucinations. *Child Abuse and Neglect* 29:797–810.

Whybrow, P. 1997. *A Mood Apart*. London: Picador.

Wiggins, O. P., and M. A. Schwartz. 2007. Schizophrenia: A phenomenological-anthropological approach. In *Reconceiving Schizophrenia*, ed. M. C. Chung, K. W. M. Fulford and G. Graham, 113–127. Oxford: Oxford University Press.

Wilkinson, S. 2000. Is "normal grief" a mental disorder? *Philosophical Quarterly* 50:289–304.

Wittgenstein, L. 1953. *Philosophical Investigations*. Trans. G. E. M. Anscombe. Oxford: Blackwell.

Wittgenstein, L. 1975. *On Certainty*. Trans. D. Paul and G. E. M. Anscombe. Oxford: Blackwell.

World Health Organization. 1992. *The ICD-10 Classification of Mental and Behavioural Disorders: Clinical Descriptions and Diagnostic Guidelines*. Geneva: World Health Organization.

Wu, W. 2012. Explaining schizophrenia: Auditory verbal hallucination and self-monitoring. *Mind & Language* 27:86–107.

Zahavi, D. 2007. Expression and empathy. In *Folk Psychology Re-assessed*, ed. D. D. Hutto and M. Ratcliffe, 25–40. Dordrecht: Springer.

Zahavi, D. 2014. *Self and Other: Exploring Subjectivity, Empathy, and Shame*. Oxford: Oxford University Press.

Zahavi, D. 2017. Thin, thinner, thinnest. In *Embodiment, Enaction, and Culture: Investigating the Constitution of the Shared World*, ed. C. Durt, T. Fuchs, and C. Tewes, 193–199. Cambridge, MA: MIT Press.

Zeedyk, M. S. 2006. From intersubjectivity to subjectivity: The transformative roles of emotional intimacy and imitation. *Infant and Child Development* 15:321–344.

Index